A CLASSROOM OF ONE

OTHER BOOKS BY GENE I. MAEROFF

The Learning Connection (2001), editor,
with Patrick M. Callan and Michael D. Usdan

Imaging Education (1998), editor

Altered Destinies (1998)

Scholarship Assessed (1997), with Charles E. Glassick
and Mary Taylor Huber

Team Building for School Change (1993)

Sources of Inspiration (1992), editor

The School Smart Parent (1989)

The Empowerment of Teachers (1988)

School and College (1983)

Don't Blame the Kids (1981)

The Guide to Suburban Public Schools (1975),
with Leonard Buder

A CLASSROOM OF ONE

How Online Learning Is Changing Our Schools and Colleges

Gene I. Maeroff

palgrave
macmillan

First published in hardcover in 2003 by Palgrave Macmillan
First PALGRAVE MACMILLAN™ paperback edition: May 2004
175 Fifth Avenue, New York, N.Y. 10010 and
Houndmills, Basingstoke, Hampshire, England RG21 6XS.
Companies and representatives throughout the world.

PALGRAVE MACMILLAN is the global academic imprint of the
Palgrave Macmillan division of St. Martin's Press, LLC and of Palgrave
Macmillan Ltd. Macmillan® is a registered trademark in the United
States, United Kingdom and other countries. Palgrave is a registered
trademark in the European Union and other countries.

ISBN 1-4039-6537-4

Library of Congress Cataloging-in-Publication Data

Maeroff, Gene I.
    A classroom of one : how online learning is changing our schools and
colleges / Gene I. Maeroff.
        p.   cm.
    Includes bibliographical references and index.
    ISBN 1-4039-6537-4
    1. Distance education—Computer-assisted instruction.
2. Individual instruction.   I. Title.
LC5803.C65 M34   2003
371.3'5—dc 21

                                                            2002041042

A catalogue record for this book is available from the British Library.

Design by Letra Libre.

First PALGRAVE MACMILLAN paperback edition: May 2004

10 9 8 7 6 5 4 3 2 1

Printed in the United States of America.

for my grandchildren—
Romy, Max, Harrison, Chloe, and Dalia—
For whom the virtual world will be very real

CONTENTS

PREFACE

I wasn't planning to start a new book, certainly not one about online courses, but curiosity got the better of me. I kept reading and hearing about the topic, and my interest was piqued. I wondered how the process worked. I wanted to know more about online learning in general. I began to think about the implications for classroom-based education. After all, how often does a new way of delivering knowledge come along? The more I found out about online learning, the more appealing the idea of writing such a book grew.

I knew from the outset that I didn't want to trash online courses. Others have already done this, repeatedly. It is too obvious a slant to take. Almost everyone harbors suspicions at the very mention of online learning, so that is nothing new. Online learning is the proverbial fish in the barrel. How can any criticism of online courses miss the mark? Teachers and students don't see each other—a situation ripe for exploit. The work can be insubstantial, the credentials at the end amounting to little more than a sham. It all seems so secret and suspicious—seemingly no one to check up on anyone else. And, while online chat rooms and threaded discussions may advance knowledge, they also may degenerate into computerized versions of talk radio, trite and banal, hardly what one calls educational. To give critics their due, online learning is replete with unsettling features.

There was another way to approach the subject, I decided. Describe it. Discuss the relationship to classroom-based courses. Raise policy implications. I thought the book would be most effective by staking out a point of view. I settled on presenting a somewhat sympathetic portrayal of this phenomenon, recognizing that to do so would court controversy and censure. Online courses threaten established interests. Some providers view such courses as vehicles to (dare I write the word?) *profits*, though most online learning is not-for-profit, like the rest of education. This book, admittedly, gives online learning the benefit of the doubt. Does this mean that I see no flaws in online courses? Of course not. Only a fool could fail to recognize the difficulties that arise in delivering learning from afar. I point out shortcomings as I go along, trying to avoid the obvious.

On the other hand, as I mention several times in the book, one should not presume that teaching and learning in classrooms have achieved nirvana. I have chosen an irreverent path in my exploration of e-learning. I cite the downside of traditional classroom learning—not because I think that online courses are necessarily better but to emphasize that education must be open to new ways of doing what, on close examination, has sometimes been less than a rousing success. There is room for an additional approach, another way of doing things, possibly an improvement under some circumstances, if done well. More importantly, students and education itself can benefit from efforts to overcome strictures of time and place.

I have chronicled events in teaching and learning since 1965. The classroom has been the cockpit of action in education all that time, as it was for previous generations. My investigation for this book has assured me that the classroom will retain its centrality, but online courses almost certainly will find a place for themselves. Such courses logically succeed those offered by correspondence, which also permitted students to overcome the obstacles of place and time.

Online learning differs, though, in its immediacy and in its ability to lend new vitality to text and image. E-learning's major impact will be in classroom-based courses, the vast majority of which will almost certainly take on facets of the technology that makes online courses possible. Hybrid courses, combining elements of the classroom and online features, will become the rule in higher education. Furthermore, many students will enroll simultaneously in classroom-based and online courses. In fact, resident undergraduate students on many campuses are already including an online course or two in their schedules.

Secondary education and, to a lesser extent, elementary schools are also headed in this direction, but more slowly and with less commitment. Online learning at this level is more problematic than in higher education. Home schooling, for better or for worse, will benefit most at the precollegiate level. There may also be a place for e-learning in conjunction with the move toward smaller secondary schools, which will have to find new ways to create a critical mass of enrollment for some of the more specialized courses.

My previous books were mostly products of field visits, during which I gleaned information through observations and interviews at various sites. I went about my research differently for this book. There were the usual hours in the library to pore over books and journals with pertinent articles. The field visits, though, were far less frequent. How do you watch students at widely scattered sites pursue their learning individually, often without a spoken word passing among them? How do you observe teachers, sitting at keyboards, who do not resort to lectures or classroom discussions to instill knowledge in their students? I conducted some face-to-face interviews and I visited some offices, lined with computer terminals, from where providers fashioned courses.

I gathered most of my information, though, via the same Internet that was the subject of my book. I went to web sites. I read what was posted. I obtained access for online visits to courses, chat rooms, and threaded discussions. I exchanged a multitude of e-messages with people I interviewed without speaking to them. Telephone conversations figured prominently in my work, too. I also went to some conferences to hear speakers in person and to mix with attendees and listen to their discussions. By and large, though, this book is the product of the same sort of activity carried out from a distance as the courses that it describes.

Quotes from many of the interviews appear throughout the book. The interviews were conducted during 2001 and 2002, and, for the most part, all of the quotations that appear without citation come from those interviews.

Online learning is dynamic, changing even as you read these words. That is why the book is written mostly in the past tense. My challenge was to take a snapshot of a cyclone. I have tried to adhere to the big picture, using examples and anecdotes to explain and illustrate details of online programs. These courses will flourish only to the extent that they serve the desires of students. Online learning, as nothing more than an option, must demonstrate that it is friendly to consumers. One hopes that this will mean more than simply filling the need that some students feel to accumulate quick and easy academic credits. There are already more than enough opportunities to do that in classrooms. Online courses, in the right hands, can contribute to the totality of education without reducing academic rigor. Will they fulfill this potential? Who knows!

Ultimately, I suspect, these courses will work best and prove most attractive when directed at mature adult learners, particularly at the certificate and postbaccalaureate levels. Courses of this sort will orient themselves largely to career and occupational interests. Online courses in the liberal arts and the humanities are not apt to fare as well. This is not because it is impossible to fashion online courses of quality in the liberal arts and the humanities, but, for now, because most students who turn to web-based instruction want to learn about application, not theory.

Higher education will transform itself most, but precollegiate education, especially secondary schools, will change, too. The genie is out of the computer and it has already grown too large to shove back in. While the for-profit sector of education first generated the greatest activity on behalf of online learning, mounting pressure will force traditional institutions to respond to students who increasingly will demand the right to determine the time and place of their learning.

The ascendancy of online courses was swift during the last decade of the twentieth century, but the fiscal disasters of the early 2000s crimped the expansion and sent some of the lofty ambitions crashing to the ground, along with many of the dot-coms. Nonetheless, as the 1980s drew to a close almost no one expected that online learning would blossom to the extent that it has. Even the *Chronicle of Higher Education*, the weekly newspaper of record in higher education, had barely taken notice of online courses as a dimension of distance education as recently as 1989.

Some educationists regard online learning as a device apart, an alternate pursuit forever marginalized at the fringes of institutions. They are mistaken. Online courses will edge closer to the mainstream with each passing year, so much so that eventually few distinctions will be made between courses taken online, courses taken in the classroom, and courses that incorporate attributes of both settings. Much remains to be settled so far as policies regarding online courses are concerned, however. Institutions and regulators must resolve issues involving the financing of these programs, the eligibility of students in online courses for financial aid, the equivalency of work done in classrooms and online, and expectations for faculty who assume online responsibilities.

I try in this book to provide a comprehensive look at a large and unfolding phenomenon. The first chapter sets a context for thinking about online courses in both K through 12 education and higher education; it also provides a global perspective for considering the role that this new delivery system might play. Chapter 2 details some of the history of distance learning and begins a discussion of the main elements of online courses—content, design, and instruction. Chapters 3 and 4 describe the electronic interaction between and among students and teachers that is at the heart of e-learning, as well as some of the specifics of how courses operate. The adaptations required of those involved in online courses are the topic of chapter 5, and chapter 6 deals with the responsibilities that students and instructors must take on for online learning to be successful.

These courses are part of a new, business-oriented landscape that is taking shape in education, as pointed out in chapter 7. Chapter 8 deals with the career focus already prevalent in so many online courses, and chapter 9 considers the legitimacy of this new way of learning. This sets the stage, in chapter 10, for looking at the roles of accreditors and regulators who oversee all forms of education. Chapter 11 focuses on the impact of online education on the time and place of learning, on learning outcomes, and on costs. Chapter 12 weighs the prospects for using e-learning to reach those who have been served least well by the traditional system. The possibilities for redefining the meaning and shape of educational institutions through online learning are examined in chapter 13, and the discussion continues into chapter 14 with a further look at the courses themselves. Finally, chapter 15 discusses how online learning may conform with or conflict with the traditional goals and purposes of education.

Perhaps initial expectations for online learning were too high. The phenomenon arrived simultaneously with the glory days of the Internet. The most optimistic boosters of the Internet thought that classroom-based education, along with face-to-face commerce, would fall victim to the convenience of purchasing goods and services online. Venture capitalists poured billions of dollars into what in retrospect were flights of fancy. Some of this wealth found its way to educational start-ups that used the Internet.

Some supporters unrealistically expected online courses to capture a broad new market for education and to take over part of the old market as well. However, many disappointments of the kind that proliferated through other Internet activities after the fatal spring of 2000 also affected online education. Now, in a more sober climate, Americans can view e-learning through the lens of reality. What they ought to see is that the classroom will not be rendered obsolete, but it should be apparent, too, that online courses are here to stay.

—Gene I. Maeroff
Teachers College, Columbia University
New York City
November 2002

CHAPTER 1

AN INVITATION TO A REVOLUTION

Mark Hopkins, first a memorable teacher and then a president of Williams College during the nineteenth century, inspired a vision of perfect education based on his reputation for instructional prowess—a log with Hopkins, the exemplary teacher, sitting on one end and a student sitting on the other. This ideal, a classroom of one, seems to be an icon for the technological age, except for one aspect. It places teacher and student in face-to-face proximity, eyeballs to eyeballs, a not wholly apt symbol for a time when hundreds, if not thousands, of miles may separate teacher and student, their contact mediated by a pair of keyboards and monitor screens.

Yet, with the aid of technology, wide-range one-on-one education may be closer at hand than ever before. An encounter between student and teacher via the Internet is very different from the exchanges in formal classrooms that have until now characterized education. This fulfillment of the classroom of one embodies an intimacy all its own. Such a shift does not signify an end to education as it has existed but the coming of a paradigm in which a course offered to a classroom full of students may be less compelling than it has been. The question is not whether formal learning will continue—of course it will—but what forms it will take among a multiplicity of possibilities. E-learning has come on the scene to augment and sometimes supplant the traditional classroom.

Technology's potential for strengthening instruction in the traditional classroom remains enormous. This is not a book about using computers in classrooms, though. Instead, it examines a revolution that gives signs of driving a portion of education out of schools and colleges. It considers the implications for the classroom when technology delivers education from a distance, creating settings in which individual students sometimes learn on their own, not sitting amid classmates, not in the presence of teachers. By 2001, more than 1,000 colleges and universities in the United States offered at least some virtual courses; one-third of those institutions were community colleges.[1] Moreover, a growing number of classroom-based courses included online portions that personalized education in new ways.

The swiftness with which online learning gained significance in higher education during the last decade of the twentieth century can be seen in a review of the news coverage at the turn of 1990. E-learning was scarcely mentioned in an article about distance learning in the *Chronicle of Higher Education,* the field's paper of record, on September 27, 1989.[2] The piece described mostly courses offered by correspondence and public television, with some mention of independent study, tutorial software, and audiotapes. It barely referred to computer links. It spoke of faculty members not wanting to teach such courses as they could not see if students were absorbing the material. The article nonetheless contained praise for the motivation and persistence of distance education students. There was no hint of the avalanche that was about to rumble.

Developments in online learning in just a little more than ten years force one to conclude that this is a sea change, not a fad. By the end of the twenty-first century's first decade, e-learning will be an embedded feature of education, widely available and no longer an object of controversy. Whether it will be a source of financial gain, as some for-profit providers hope, remains to be seen. Nonetheless, online courses will proliferate at traditional not-for-profit institutions, and students will have far more opportunity to choose between studying in a classroom with other students or in a virtual classroom in which they work alone.

Almost certainly, most courses—including the vast majority in classrooms—at most institutions of higher education and to a lesser extent in secondary schools will have online components as essential features. Instructors who in coming years ignore the potential of web-based embellishments will be as remiss as their peers of past years who did not expect students to enrich their learning by consulting sources beyond their books.

Some see as most important in these developments the emergence of technology as a prime tool of learning. This, in the final analysis, will be incidental. Technology's role will be an enabling one, as printing presses have been to the production of books. Online education is here to stay and the technology will fade into the background for most students, essential but not of great concern to them, a kind of catalyst to a learning revolution. We fly without worrying about what keeps airplanes aloft. We reap the benefits of magnetic imaging without knowing how radiologists can peer into our bodies without cutting them open. We watch television with no comprehension of how the pictures get onto the screens in our living rooms. And, increasingly, we will take online courses for granted, as if they have always existed, and pay little heed to what makes a classroom of one possible.

Much that is happening in the delivery of learning threatens the hegemony of the traditional approach. Higher education will transform itself most, but secondary schools too will change and, to a lesser extent, even elementary education. The Internet ranks among the most formidable foes ever to confront the intransigence of traditional education. Despite an inclination to think of online learning in terms of profits for providers, there is no reason why the nonprofit sector, which provides most of the formal education in this country, cannot expand its offerings in distance education. Such a shift will require the vision of educators in public school systems and at nonprofit colleges and universities who recognize that education can be education regardless of its form of delivery.

Traditional educational institutions are apt to dominate online learning. They have the infrastructure and the reputations upon which to install a new delivery system for a product that has been their stock in trade: education. Online courses will simply be one more way to provide learning. The future of online learning, both for-profit and not-for-profit, is taking shape along these lines:

1. virtual schools and colleges that exist wholly online, operating without campuses;
2. brick-and-mortar educational institutions that offer a growing number of courses entirely online but at which most classes continue to meet in person;
3. brick-and-mortar educational institutions that offer few courses entirely online but with web-based features in an increasing number of campus-based courses.

What has developed, courtesy of the Internet, is the possibility of offering learning on a scale more far-reaching than previously imagined. Building on distance education that once comprised correspondence, audio, and video, online learning adds such twists as web pages, e-messages, and discussion boards to let students pursue certificates and even degrees from computers in their homes and offices. The push to breach classroom walls has accelerated and will continue unabated during the remaining years of the opening decade of the twenty-first century. These programs, with their ability to transcend state lines and even national borders, circumvent geographic barriers that were often used in the past to protect campus-based education from competition.

EDUCATIONAL CHOICE

The development of online learning fits comfortably within the philosophy of those who preach that education should move toward a free-market approach. The more that choice is injected into the system, advocates reason, the richer the offerings and the greater the benefits to consumers (students and their families). It is the familiar let-them-vote-with-their-feet argument. Choice is the order of the day, especially in elementary and secondary education.

Charter schools began operating at the start of the 1990s and spread through the country by the end of the decade. In just a decade, 2,372 charter schools were established to serve elementary and secondary students in 34 states.[3] These schools, funded by tax dollars, have leeway to innovate and to break with the status quo. This autonomy liberates them from many district and state regulations on the assumption that, unfettered, they can provide children with an education superior to that available in other public schools. Critics charge that the result is merely a loss of public oversight for schools that have not proved themselves to be any better than other public schools.

The idea of choice has now been joined to the possibilities of the Internet. Proponents of choice took advantage of charter school laws to establish cyber schools in Ohio and Pennsylvania, for instance. Online learning injects fresh possibilities into the most extreme version of choice, school vouchers, raising the possibility of awarding vouchers to be spent for online education, including education of a private and sectarian nature that can be carried out at home.

Benefits at the Elementary and Secondary Levels

Online learning may turn out to be the greatest bonus ever for home schooling. It eases the way for parents who want to educate their children at home. Policymakers do not ordinarily regard home schooling as a form of public school choice, but that is exactly what it could become with the aid of online programs. More and more, e-learning and home schooling—sometimes religiously inspired—combine forces under the banner of choice as officials designate virtual schools as charters. This twist lets parents who school their children at home turn to cyber schools to secure public funds for their endeavor. The number of children involved in home schooling is large and expanding rapidly. A survey released in 2001 by the National Center for Education Statistics estimated that 850,000 children were schooled at home.

Julie E. Young, executive director of the Florida Virtual School, saw her institution as "an absolute boon to home schooling" and said she saw no reason why the state should not help families who opt to pull their children out of the public schools and educate them at home. "From a citizen's perspective, not speaking as an educator," she said, "the state should do all it can to embrace home schooling and to make sure that these children get the same quality of education as in a school."

Cyber schools sprouted throughout Pennsylvania at the start of this century, and home schoolers apparently constituted a substantial portion of the enrollment. A survey by the Pennsylvania School Boards Association found that almost half the students enrolled in one of the state's biggest cyber charter schools were home schoolers. There were seven such schools in the state by 2002 and others preparing to open. All of these schools operated under Pennsylvania's charter school act, which enabled individual public school districts and intermediate regional school units to grant charters.

The Western Pennsylvania Cyber Charter School in Midland, a town near the intersection of Pennsylvania, Ohio, and West Virginia, had 529 students its first year and doubled its enrollment to about 1,100 by its second year. The town of Midland's entire population was 3,300, so the only way that the school could grow so large was to enroll students from throughout the state, taking youngsters from 105 school systems in 23 counties. The state school boards association said that only 11 of Western Pennsylvania Cyber Charter School's students lived in the chartering district. Students, ranging from kindergarten to twelfth grade, chose courses from nine different curriculums. Home schoolers in Pennsylvania's cyber schools, just as students in all of the state's public schools, had to have 900 hours annually of instruction at the elementary level and 990 hours at the secondary level. Furthermore, the cyber schools, along with brick-and-mortar charter schools, had to meet state regulations that included annual reporting on educational and financial matters. The instructional methods at Western Pennsylvania Cyber Charter School, depending on the courses, took four main forms:

1. real-time, online, synchronous instruction, in which students communicated with teachers from their computers as the teachers taught the lessons;
2. asynchronous instruction in which students worked on their own and later received messages on their computers from the teachers;

3. web-based, packaged programs consisting of a pretest, a tutorial, a practice, and a post-test that the student submitted electronically, without contact with teachers;

4. traditional book-based courses in which students, working online at a pace that they set for themselves, got assignments, turned them in, and received responses from teachers.

State-supported home schooling as provided through e-learning will probably benefit from the favorable ruling in 2002 by the U.S. Supreme Court on vouchers, which represent one of the great polarizing issues in American elementary and secondary education. Cyber schooling could be a route to public funding to enable children at home—not in a school building—to get the education of their choice, even if what they study in the privacy of their homes has a religious slant. Most families throughout the country will almost certainly maintain their allegiance to brick-and-mortar schools but, nonetheless, online learning could make inroads among the 53 million children who study at the elementary and secondary levels. Such fears invoked bitter opposition to cyber charter schools in such states as Ohio and Pennsylvania, where the legality of the schools was challenged in lawsuits.

Restrictions in Higher Education Choice

At first blush it appears that higher education is already replete with choice and that a free market flourishes among postsecondary institutions. The United States boasts a panoply of 9,619 postsecondary institutions, 4,182 of them traditional, degree-granting, two-year and four-year colleges and universities under both public and private auspices, according to the National Center for Education Statistics. The remaining 5,437 are post–high school vocational and technical institutes, more than 90 percent of them operated for profit. Despite this array of institutions, choice in higher education has been restricted largely to a mode of delivery that requires students to attend courses in person. In addition, until recently, as was formerly true of the nation's banking system, degree-granting institutions operated mostly within certain geographic locales and had to turn somersaults to offer courses away from their principal campuses. This was especially the case when they sought to cross state lines.

Less than a generation ago, the institution now known as Nova Southeastern University was treated as a pariah in some places when it tried to offer nontraditional programs outside its home state of Florida. Nova hoped to compete for students who wanted graduate degrees in education by establishing learning centers in several states. Students could attend these centers perhaps one weekend a month and a few weeks during the summer while writing theses that drew on their experiences in the full-time jobs in schools in which they continued to work. Nova carried out contentious but ultimately successful campaigns to win approval in several states, but New Jersey balked. New Jersey's recalcitrance meant that educators from that state had to drive to Pennsylvania or Delaware to join one of the official study clusters through which the university offered its peripatetic course work. However, some New Jerseyans, like clandestine revolutionaries, stubbornly met at locations within the state to pursue the Nova program, defying officials. New Jersey's Department of Education, outraged by the obstinate educators, sent a cease and desist letter to Nova in 1974 that contained the delicious phrase "under no circumstances shall any learning take place in the State of New Jersey."[4]

Echoes of this attitude were heard in China in the 1990s, when the government exiled Wang Dan, a leader of the Tiananmen Square protest. A pretext for his banishment was his enrollment in a correspondence course offered by a school in California, behavior that was characterized by the government as evidence that he was plotting to overthrow the government.[5] Some opponents of online learning in the United States see as no less conspiratorial the conduct of institutions that want to offer online courses to students scattered over wide areas. Perhaps this practice is subversive in that it seeks to overthrow a system that until now has been as unresponsive to the needs of learners as it chooses to be.

No longer will traditionalists so easily block competition when an institution can deliver courses by the Internet, silently and possibly without need to seek approval, though some states continue to try to regulate online learning transmitted from other states to their residents. Such attitudes smack of trying to keep people from tuning their radio dials to out-of-state stations, something like the policies of totalitarian countries that electronically jammed the broadcasts of Radio Free Europe. Change is in the air, though, and opposition to online learning shows signs of yielding.

So pronounced was the shift in climate that by 2001 legislation was introduced in Congress to smooth the way for students in distance education courses at traditional colleges and universities to qualify for federal student aid. They had been ineligible for assistance under a 1992 law that was adopted ostensibly to guard against transferring tax monies to diploma mills and fraudulent correspondence courses. "Congress and the administration may have ultimately imposed a straightjacket on all of higher education where handcuffs on a few bad actors would have sufficed," said U.S. Rep. Howard P. McKeon, a California Republican.[6]

GLOBALIZATION AND THE IMPLICATIONS FOR ONLINE EDUCATION

The need for new ways to deliver education is seen in its starkest terms outside the United States. The limits on education internationally illustrate why traditional approaches are insufficient. More than 125 million children around the world have no elementary and secondary schools to attend, according to the United Nations Educational, Scientific, and Cultural Organization (UNESCO). Some 160 countries rallied for universal schooling at the World Education Forum in Senegal in 2000, repeating a call that they had made in 1990. Economic exigencies in Turkey were emblematic of the barriers. Though a more advanced country than many others, Turkey had an insufficient number of schools for even young children in some of the country's far-flung villages. The educational challenge remains monumental in many parts of the world. The college-going rate in Asia, Africa, and Latin American is infinitesimal. UNESCO said that only about 3 percent of young people in sub-Saharan Africa and 7 percent in Asia attend a postsecondary institution.

Online Learning around the World

The expense of building classrooms is enough in itself to restrict educational opportunities and to leave less-developed countries with only the most fragmentary physical infrastructure for education. Furthermore, even if structures were built, money for books, laboratories, supplies, and teachers would be scarce. On top of fiscal obstacles, geographic constraints in societies that are still mostly rural make it impossible to gather a critical mass of students in many places. The problems feed upon themselves. The lack of graduates of high school and postsecondary education institutions curtails the supply of teachers and professors for brick-and-mortar facilities in many parts of the world. Adding to the problem is the spread of AIDS, which on the African continent alone, according to the World Bank, kills teachers faster than countries can train replacements.

Political instability, too, haunts the classrooms that do exist in underdeveloped countries. And, in some locales, cultural and religious biases keep much of the female half of the population away from classrooms, consigning girls and women to the lowest stations in life. The situation in Afghanistan in which the Taliban banished females from schools was merely one of the more egregious examples. In addition to these obstacles, ethnic minorities and disabled children need not even try to enter classrooms in certain countries where discrimination is rife. Communist oppression in Eastern Europe forced learning underground, where so-called flying universities kept shifting the sites of their classes to thwart totalitarian regimes. Online learning could play this kind of role today in such countries as, say, Iran, where religious hardliners obstruct the freedoms of university students and professors.

Events in several parts of the world at the beginning of this century underscored the growing possibilities for e-learning. Tunisia announced that it would establish a national virtual university, saying that it hoped to offer distance learning to those for whom it was relatively unavailable in the many countries of Africa. Japan's education ministry decided to let universities grant credit for online courses that had previously been regarded with suspicion. Britain seemed poised to spread higher education in the English language through a worldwide electronic university project to which the Higher Education Funding Council of England had allocated some $88 million for development. The University of Virginia began laying plans to collaborate with several universities in southern Africa to create joint online courses to tap expertise on both continents. The University of Maryland in 2001 sent representatives to confer with officials in Uzbekistan about setting up a virtual university that would first depend on videotape and CD-ROM, and later, after the country develops more technological infrastructure, on the Internet. Thus, countries throughout the world recognize the potential of distance learning to expand educational opportunity.

The United States Army provided a glimpse of the possibilities of education that stretches around the globe. Army University Access Online began offering courses in 2001. Located on the world wide web at eArmyU.com, the institution gave Army enlisted personnel the chance to earn certificates and associate's, bachelor's, and master's degrees. Soldiers selected a home institution from among the 23 American colleges and universities participating in the program and could take online courses toward their certificate or degree from any of the institutions. The Army created the university to help soldiers circumvent the interruptions that occurred in their education each time they were reassigned to another base. Soldiers were suddenly able to take the university with them, a portability that the Army assisted by giving each enrollee a laptop, printer, Internet access, e-mail account, 24-hour technical support, books, and a waiver of all tuition and fees. Soldiers were eligible to participate upon enlistment, at reenlistment, or if they had at least three years of duty remaining.

However much it might cost to develop online courses and to bolster such other forms of distance education as correspondence courses, which already have a toehold in some locales around the world, the expense would almost certainly be less than building new campuses in underserved countries. Yet, the challenges are formidable. Few people own computers or even have access to them in many countries. Some more remote locales lack any infrastructure whatsoever to carry the Internet, though wireless telecommunications could possibly figure in these situations eventually.

The events of September 11, 2001, provided a new reason for students throughout the world to look to online learning. Lawmakers and policy advisors in the United States urged in the wake of the disaster at the World Trade Center that America protect itself by limiting visas for foreigners who want to study in the United States, which 425,000 did each year until then. The City University of New York weighed in by assessing out-of-state tuition rates on undocumented aliens—slightly more than 1 percent of its 200,000 students—who previously paid in-state rates if they had attended high schools in New York state. Moreover, the Bush administration moved in the months following the attack not only to limit visas for foreign students, but to ban their enrollment in programs bearing on the development and use of weapons of mass destruction. This proposal alarmed higher education institutions, which rely heavily on students from abroad to fill out graduate enrollments in science, technology, and engineering programs.

The student visa question will fester as long as Americans fear further acts of terrorism. As a result, online learning could loom more important for students abroad if it turns out to be the main way—or at least an unrestricted way—to pursue courses that carry the faith and credit of American colleges and universities. Enrolling in online courses would not put foreign students in seats in American classrooms, but it might suffice for otherwise limited access to campuses in the United States. This approach could at least open a virtual door to education for students around the world, starting in English and, then, perhaps adding other languages as well.

Controversy over the Globalization of Learning

This is not to say that everyone abroad rejoices at the prospect of Americans using technology to extend their dominion over education. Exporting education in this way can represent a new sort of manifest destiny to people in other countries. The specter of the globalization of higher education may arouse critics who think that colleges and universities peddling courses under their "brand names" smacks of imperialism, akin to selling the products of Coca-Cola or McDonalds. E-learning sponsored by institutions in the United States, for all its ostensible advantages, could appear to critics as just one more form of American cultural and economic hegemony. But that doesn't mean it won't happen.

It is unlikely that online courses would be the subject of protests on the order of those aimed at the World Bank, the International Monetary Fund, and other titans of the global economy, but e-learning could get tangled in controversies of its own. As it is, the World Trade Organization in 2001 flirted with the idea of regulating higher education, just as the WTO does with other commodities, because it crosses borders. Such a measure could remove some of the decision making about online courses from academic officials and treat education much like trade in steel or bananas.

Trade regulation is not the only threat to worldwide cyber learning. Those who want to control the globalization of education through the Internet have other weapons in their arsenal, making it possible for them to use technology to trump technology. They can, for instance, identify users whose computers receive online courses from distant providers. In light of such threats to privacy, the International Broadcasting Bureau, the U.S. government agency that oversees the Voice of America, embarked on a project in 2001 to develop servers to help disguise the web sites that computer users view. Filtering technology that allows governments to block access to web sites is another potential impediment. Software companies in 2001, for example, competed for a contract to help Saudi Arabia blackout sites carrying pornography and material sensitive for political and religious reasons.[7] One could imagine similar incentives to block an online course dealing with the writings of Salman Rushdie or some other controversial author. The attraction of filtering can be seen in its use by schools and libraries in the United States to obstruct students' access to sites offering pornography.

The deliberations of the Council of Europe, a body representing 43 countries, illustrated the extent that machinations might accompany an expansion of international online learning. The group weighed action in 2001 to ban from the Internet sites that promote hate and racism. At about the same time, a court in France ordered Yahoo, an American-based search engine that, of course, can be accessed in France, to halt the sale of Nazi paraphernalia on its web site. A lower court in the United States held that the verdict could not be enforced, and this decision was under appeal in 2002 in a San Francisco Court of Appeals. More such litigation remains possible in the wake of the hate that fueled the September 11 disaster. Such suits could take a slightly different tack, as well. Who is to say that a university in, say, Italy, might not eventually persuade a court that the availability of online courses from an American university undermines the viability of Italian education and culture? Then a country might take protective action against online learning in the national interest, not unlike the imposition of tariffs to protect indigenous industries.

Finally, there is the matter of ensuring that the quality of the online version of an American education offered overseas equals what students get on campus. Would courses available on a global basis require some kind of policing to keep institutions from embarrassing the United States by dispensing a substandard online product? Until the advent of the Internet, each country could pretty well regulate higher education within its borders. Imagine the specter of international diploma mills that use online learning to dupe naïve students around the globe.

INFLUENCE ON POLICY

A problem with the proliferation of online learning, even that aimed largely at Americans and free of the potential disputes engendered by globalization, has been the laissez-faire aspect of its growth. This is the nineteenth century all over again. Like the rivers and streams of antebellum California, the tributaries of the Internet seduce educational entrepreneurs who pan for a new kind of gold. It is as if those who lead universities were blinded by the glitter of the dot-com mania. Temple University, for example, seeing a possible golden goose to seize and squeeze, spun off a for-profit, online operation in 1999 that it shut down just a year and a half later, calling it unfeasible. Institutions of higher education, school districts, states, and other government-related units rushed to stake claims on online learning with scant regard for the implications. Profit-seeking entities elbowed their way into the fray, throwing fear into the hearts of educationists who thought that the words schooling and profits did not fit together unless one spoke of learning how to cut hair or how to fix computers. The policy issues that these new approaches engender have gotten all too little public airing.

"[I]t has emerged on campuses with little broad discussion of its larger educational implications, and even less of its relationship to the fundamental purposes of colleges and universities," Stanley N. Katz of Princeton University wrote of online learning, calling its development piecemeal and unsystematic. "Indeed, educational goals have generally been secondary to organizational and financial concerns."[8] The public and even educators have not focused sufficiently on questions of who originates the courses, how they compare with classroom-based courses, and whether all aspects of this approach are in the public interest. More importantly, it is time to recognize that students of all ages and all circumstances pursue cyber learning and that they want some assurance that, by going online, they can achieve their educational goals at a reasonable cost and with some sort of stamp of endorsement.

Mainstreaming Online Learning

Some educationists mistakenly regard online learning as a device apart, an alternate pursuit, an activity to be pushed to the fringes of the institution. They are mistaken. Why should traditional schools and colleges not embrace e-learning and draw it into the mainstream, making it their own, and adapting their policies and practices to do so? Online courses need not be abandoned to those who seek profit from them, though they have a right to do so. Such courses need not be ceded to those who would do a less than excellent job with them. Even some traditional not-for-profit institutions have tended to overlook the most important aspect of online learning: what it can do to enhance the delivery system. Students who want a high-quality education should be able to obtain elements of it as readily online as in a classroom. That, mainly, should be the concern of the traditional providers—adapting their expertise to a more convenient method of education for those who want it and doing so in a manner that does not dilute the quality in which they take pride.

Pennsylvania State University's creation of the World Campus represented one of the better examples of an institution deciding that e-learning belonged in the academic mainstream, not as a separate, for-profit entity. Officials at Penn State determined early on—planning began in 1996 and World Campus offered its first courses in 1998—that they wanted an entity to give regular faculty members experiences with technology that they could then apply in their classroom courses. Penn State reasoned that if online learning were a for-profit enterprise, it would have to be walled off from regular programs and that the regular programs could then not as readily reap the pedagogical benefits of instructional technology. Thus, online efforts were not separated from the university's main concerns.

Penn State set up World Campus with no faculty of its own and used only those who already taught in Penn State classrooms. These faculty increasingly taught online courses as part of their normal teaching load rather than as add-ons, the goal being to replicate on-campus courses. Toward this end, essentially every World Campus course had been offered in person before going online, according to school officials. The notable exceptions were the courses in the web master's program, not available in classrooms, and a master's of business administration degree program that the World Campus created expressly for online learners.

Making Other Adjustments

Policies regarding the implementation of online learning will have to take greater cognizance of the impact on teaching. The prospect of online learning unsettles some teachers and stirs fear among them for the future. They worry about the security of their profession. Those who are most alarmed characterize e-learning as inhuman and inhumane, a mechanistic, robotlike approach to education that cannot possibly be the equal of a teacher in a classroom with a group of students. They call it a scheme to demean and diminish teachers. Like colleagues in other places, faculty members in the State of Washington closed ranks to fight a proposal in that state to use online learning as a way to reduce the need for building new classrooms for higher education. In Ohio, a teachers' organization was party to a suit to kill cyber learning. "It's sad because traditional education is not working for some kids and educators should be forward looking," said Tom Baker, the superintendent responsible for a public cyber school in Ohio. Faculty members also worry that profit-making ventures will undermine the academic culture. And so, for example, the idea of e-learning created an uproar over intellectual property rights and other issues among professors in the spring of 2000 at Cornell University, when details about a new venture started leaking out.

Schools, colleges, and universities should recognize as they move toward an online presence that success depends on acting in ways that encourage and assist faculty to alter habits and attitudes that have sustained them for their entire careers. Faculty, as much as students, must change their ways markedly to make online courses successful. Rushing headlong into cyber learning leaves too many questions of policy unanswered. Teaching online calls for a thoughtful interweaving of the old and the new, making a course more than simply a collection of lecture notes delivered by computer. Lectures or some cybernetic variation of them will always play a role in education, but those in education must develop the capacity to take full advantage of new technologies that enable them to enhance the learning of their students.

As the dust settles in the wake of the early scramble by some educational institutions to get online as quickly as possible, the implications of this vast transformation merit attention. The capacity for delivering formal learning has been ineluctably expanded. There is no end to the policy considerations brought to the fore by online learning. The whole idea of different tuitions for in-state and out-of-state students at public universities is challenged by the ability of students to sit in their homes, wherever they may live, and take the same course. According to the Association of Governing Boards of Universities and Colleges, "a few states are adopting an 'e-rate' tuition that is independent of geography, while many others are adopting a permissive stance and allowing institutions to change pricing policy."[9] This is just one of many policy considerations.

At the elementary and secondary levels, other issues have come to the fore as online learning has spread. Questions of oversight and funding figure prominently. E-learning in some states seems to have less supervision and accountability than education in classrooms. Methods of financing online courses range from putting most of the responsibility on the student's family to the state paying entirely for the courses. Also, there are varying degrees of allowing online learning to serve the interests of home schooling. In such states as Colorado, students cannot enroll in online courses unless they attended a public school the previous year. In other states, there is no such restriction and home schoolers use online programs to reap public support for what they were already doing privately.

Exactly two-thirds of the respondents to a 2001 Phi Delta Kappa/ Gallup Poll[10] disapproved of cyber learning, though parents of students were more accepting of cyber learning than those with no children in school. Of those who approved of high school students earning credits online, respondents were divided, roughly 50–50, over allowing a child of theirs to take most courses online at home instead of going to school. Supporters of online courses at the precollegiate level ought to find reassurance in this poll. The results are fairly favorable, considering the newness of the innovation and the likelihood that many people, before being asked in the survey, probably never thought about the prospect of high school students earning credits online.

It would be unwise, though, to regard online learning as the salvation of education, the panacea for the ills of a system that has often been inflexible and reluctant to change. The realization that progress will be incremental, not exponential, tempers the exuberance that greeted the advent of online learning in the 1990s. The heady forecasts of huge enrollments and limitless revenues have been pricked along with the dotcom balloon. The authors of *Teaching and Learning at a Distance,* a 2000 book that was generally supportive and encouraging of online education, nonetheless took the position that students prefer not to learn at a distance, that they do not learn any more or any less in distance education, and that distance education should not be touted "as the next great technological solution to education's problems."[11]

Hype, not solid information, fueled the early enthusiasm for online learning, as was true in the '90s of so much of the hullabaloo surrounding the Internet generally. Yet, in spite of the P. T. Barnums who orchestrated some of the ill-fated start-ups, online courses are here to stay. They are revolutionary because they represent a fundamentally different delivery system that breaks the monopoly of the classroom, forcing an examination of habits of teaching and learning that for too long have defied scrutiny. Online learning will not banish the many problems of teaching and learning, but it offers one more tool for trying to deal with them.

CHAPTER 2

DELIVERING THE GOODS

Students pursuing the master of science degree through the LEEP option at the University of Illinois at Urbana-Champaign took 40 semester hours of the usual courses, including "Libraries, Information, and Society" and "Information Organization and Access." Much of the content of their education in the Graduate School of Library and Information Science (GSLIS) would be familiar to those who know the discipline. What would be surprising, though, was that the students mostly remained in their hometowns throughout Illinois, in other states, and in several countries around the world. LEEP, originally called Library Education Experimental Program but later known only by its acronym, was one of the few online programs of its kind and its on-campus requirements were minimal. GSLIS officials felt that with only 49 accredited master's programs in library science in the country they could serve the many candidates who did not live close to an institution with a program.

When it began in 1996, LEEP was the first online degree program at the University of Illinois at Urbana-Champaign. The library school insisted that all requirements and standards would be the same as for on-campus students. Almost all online students, though, attended part time, typically taking two courses in each of the two semesters during the academic year and one course over the summer, which enabled many to complete the degree in as few as two calendar years. An attraction of e-learning for librarians was that it enabled them to pursue their education using much of the same technology that would be critical to performing their jobs. So attractive was this proposition that many on-campus students also took some of their courses through LEEP on a space-available basis.

Formal education relies on some form of two-way communication to produce learning and, as in LEEP, it need not involve a teacher and students gathering in a classroom. The ability to learn depends, as always, primarily on the learner, regardless of the setting. The notion of a class of one therefore is neither new nor radical. People have read books and learned on their own for centuries. What Gutenberg wrought in the fifteenth century provided a foundation for education that has been augmented by successive waves of technology. Gutenberg, with his invention of movable type, made it possible to print books, assuring that mass-produced content itself could function as instructor. People reading about John Adams in David McCullough's Pulitzer Prize–winning book, for example, can learn for the first time about incidents in the life of the second president or, if already familiar with those incidents, readers may reappraise their attitudes toward Adams as a result of McCullough's interpretation. Interaction with an instructor and even with other students can help promote learning, but it is clearly not essential.

Nevertheless, attendance in a classroom remains the standard by which most people define "going to school," and they will do so for the foreseeable future. Using a computer as the main vehicle for formal education remains alien to most Americans. When Columbia University put its noncredit Fathom program online, the institution thought it was constructing a virtual field of dreams—build it and they will come. Columbia was quickly disabused of this idea and recognized that, like the Apostle Paul, Fathom would have to start evangelizing, focusing the gospel in this case on the older elite audience that it sought. So free online seminars were offered at Fathom's site to help acclimate users to this new way of learning. Later, Columbia made further changes in Fathom in its pursuit of users.

While opponents resist online learning as something inauthentic, the technology has penetrated other spheres in ways that demonstrate its worth and reliability. The frontiers of medicine, for instance, push ever outward as a result of a willingness to use technology. Consultations occur online; physicians in one place view and interpret medical images made elsewhere; and doctors even perform surgery on patients in operating rooms hundreds of miles away. They can transmit high-speed signals to robotic surgical tools. The time has arrived to encourage learning that breaks free of the classroom if it can serve the needs of students without short-changing them.

DISTANCE EDUCATION HISTORY

Educational institutions delivered knowledge to students beyond classroom walls long before the computer was invented, the Internet was developed, or the first online course appeared. Correspondence courses have been available since at least the mid-nineteenth century. They were the original distance education. Isaac Pitman began teaching shorthand by mail in England in 1840. The decision by the University of London in 1858 to allow people to sit for examinations without taking courses set the stage for the creation of private correspondence courses to prepare candidates for exams.[1] William Rainey Harper developed correspondence courses at the Chautauqua College in the 1880s and, using what he had learned, instituted correspondence programs at the University of Chicago after he became its founding president in 1892.

Growing numbers of universities across the country adopted education by correspondence throughout the late nineteenth century and into the early twentieth century. An impetus was the outreach mission, through so-called extension courses, that was vested in the many land-grant institutions established by states during the second half of the nineteenth century. Outreach by correspondence courses continues into the cyber age. The University of Missouri's online high school stemmed from a correspondence program, and for some students distance education is still a combination of correspondence and online courses.

Penn State's World Campus, its online division, evolved from a distance education program rooted in the correspondence study that the university began in 1892 for farmers throughout the state. Penn State took advantage of the availability of the post office's Rural Free Delivery to send and receive course materials relating to new developments in agriculture and home economics, part of its mission as a land-grant university. A resident of Vermont who learned how to make ice cream in the 1970s through one of these Penn State correspondence courses was Ben Cohen, and he had a friend named Jerry Greenfield. The rest is history. World Campus remained under Penn State's Department of Distance Education, which included continuing education, cooperative extension, and public broadcasting.

Each advance in technology during the twentieth century added its imprint to distance education. Film in the first two decades, radio in the 1920s and 1930s, and television in the 1950s were incorporated into distance learning. In the early 1960s, before cable or satellites were readily available, corporate support enabled Purdue University to send an airplane flying figure-eights over several midwestern states to transmit exemplary instructional programs—a so-called Flying Classroom—to elementary and secondary pupils. Audiotapes, videotapes, and eventually CD-ROMs built on these advances. Sunrise Semester was one of television's first contributions to formal education, and to this day the Public Broadcasting System (PBS) still offers its Adult Learning Service through colleges and universities. These taped telecourses in a wide range of disciplines try to make full use of television's most sophisticated production techniques to come up with segments that are more than simply a series of talking heads. But despite the freedom that the PBS approach provides to earn academic credits without going to a campus, potential students have never regarded the courses with anything near the enthusiasm that quickly enveloped online learning.

Common to various modes of distance education—even prior to the advent of e-learning—was the philosophy that a lone learner in his virtual classroom of one should be able to pursue education without having to enter a formal classroom. This notion has prevailed whether the student followed the Great Books program organized in 1946 by Mortimer J. Adler and Robert Maynard Hutchins or bought audio and video recordings from the Teaching Company that more than a decade ago started to sell lectures by distinguished professors. And, in a way, the nontraditional colleges founded a generation ago—New York's Empire

State and New Jersey's Thomas A. Edison, for example—were progen-
itors of online learning. Whether one called the approach independent
study or open learning or lifelong learning or credit for life experience,
the idea was to give students greater control over the circumstances of
their education, much as online learning seeks to do.

Therefore, the newness of online learning is not the use of distance
education or the idea that students might pursue knowledge largely on
their own, but the fact that it harnesses digital technology for this purpose. Self-education preceded the organization of formal schooling and
has persisted as an alternative to the classrooms that formal schooling
produced. Children were taught in their homes by their parents long before the burgeoning of the first one-room schoolhouses, and some people, such as Abraham Lincoln, were autodidacts. In some ways, online
learning is a return—courtesy of technology—to what formerly existed.

The experience that the University of Maryland University College
(UMUC) gained through operating a far-flung program in classrooms
in Europe and Asia for the U.S. military laid the foundation for an extensive program of e-learning. Online courses were a natural outgrowth
for the institution in the university system of Maryland that was
charged with serving adult, part-time students. Distance education offerings that began in the mid-1990s evolved into an endeavor serving
thousands of undergraduates and graduate students by 2002 with complete online degree programs. "When the Internet came," said Gerald
A. Heeger, president of UMUC, "it found a sympathetic organization
in us, an organization with faculty and students around the world."

REALITIES OF THE TRADITIONAL CLASSROOM

Presumably, education in a regular classroom enhances learning beyond
what one can accomplish on one's own—with, say, a book or an online
course. The give and take of a well run classroom does, in fact, heighten
learning. Students learn from each other as questions and dialogue
punctuate the air. These exchanges provide answers when you cannot
find them yourself. Classmates challenge your conclusions. They add insights during discussions. Classmates model good learning behavior.

They pose hypotheses that did not occur to you. There are wonderful classrooms like these at all levels of education in which masterful teachers weave everyone's comments into a fine fabric that forms a beautiful tapestry of learning. There are also small seminars, especially at the graduate level, in which students thrive as interaction among classmates and with the teacher builds a foundation for deep understanding.

But do classrooms always operate in this fashion? "Because the classroom allows for 'genuine interpersonal interaction' does not mean that it actually occurs," said Rory McGreal, executive director of TeleEducation NB TeleEducation in New Brunswick, Canada. "The reason that students can remember the few 'teachers who changed their lives' is because genuine interactions between teachers and students are so rare."[2] First of all, students at many large research universities and even sometimes in oversized high schools attend classes with dozens, if not hundreds, of students. Universities in the Big Ten conference, for example, are notorious for courses that meet in sprawling lecture halls and auditoriums, especially at the freshman level. Each class session typically features a lecture and offers students no chance for questions or discussion. These courses may include periodic discussion sections in which class members break into smaller groups led by graduate students of limited teaching experience. This is the so-called humanizing feature of a course that often may as well be taught on television.

Then, even in some courses in which the size of the class is manageable, a host of factors may thwart interaction and retard the growth of knowledge. Some teachers simply do not like students to interrupt their lectures to ask questions. Others manage classroom discussion poorly, lacking the skills to make these interchanges as worthwhile as they might be. Still other teachers focus on just a few members of the class, responding mainly to their questions, largely ignoring other students. The tendency for some teachers, in this regard, to lavish attention on male members of the class is documented and helps explain why dozens of all-female colleges continue to exist. Some observers maintain that there are many reasons to argue that traditional classroom teaching is not the best option for all students. They cite the price that students pay—tuition, housing, travel, and opportunity costs arising from forgoing other employment—for the privilege of being on campus. "On-campus, real-time, face-to-face teaching relations are experienced by some prospective students as high-pressure, uncomfortable, even exclusionary circumstances," said education professors Nicholas C. Burbules and Thomas A. Callister.[3]

Students find it stultifying to sit through courses in which classmates offer little to each other. People who would rather be somewhere else tune in and out of what transpires. They seldom raise their hands and some of their questions may hardly rise above the level of "Will that be on the test?" Teachers drone on, oblivious to the stupor that they induce, seeming to care little about whether they have engaged the students. "If your classes do little more than parrot what is in the textbook, why should students give you their respect?" asked Don Duggan-Haas, an assistant professor of science education at Cornell University. "The vast majority of individuals learn little from someone's simply telling them something, but this is precisely what continues to happen in a tremendous number of classrooms across the country."[4]

The academy signals its lack of appreciation for good teaching in many ways. The best teachers in colleges and universities get plaques and commendations, but their teaching skills alone seldom win them promotion or tenure. The book *Scholarship Assessed: Evaluation of the Professoriate* sought to make the case that higher education should begin to right an imbalance by valuing teaching as much as it does research: "Institutions seeking a national reputation gained it primarily through the research accomplishments of their faculty, and young professors seeking status and mobility found it more rewarding—in a quite literal sense—to deliver papers at national meetings than to teach undergraduates."[5] Little that occurs in the professional preparation of college and university professors is aimed at honing their teaching prowess. Once on the job, only the most egregious behavior might—*might*—draw attention to someone whose teaching skills need bolstering. And only in recent years have institutions of higher education taken steps to begin assisting faculty members to improve their instructional methods.

The most familiar mode of learning for most Americans is a straightforward lecture, sometimes delivered in the manner of an automaton by someone who might pause periodically to ask for questions or to respond to some uninvited questions. This so-called lecture method of teaching has attracted much criticism during the last generation. Detractors deplore the lecture method as uninspired, nonparticipatory, unengaging, and nonproductive of learning. Teachers at the precollegiate level receive more preparation in pedagogy than their counterparts in higher education, but they, too, may not rise above mundane lecturing, especially in secondary schools. The condemnation has not always been fair. Lecturing remains a valuable way to present information. Not the only way, mind you, but a helpful way. Perhaps lecturing has fallen on hard times mostly because the entertainment media have raised up a generation without patience and with the attention span of a flea.

Teachers who have mastered lectures have a place in education. But there is no good reason why an institution should compel students to sit through a succession of such lectures in the company of others. All that is needed for a lecture is a classroom of one and modern technology has made this possible. Pop the tape in the audio player or in the VCR. Plop the disc in a CD-ROM player. Turn on the radio or the television at the assigned time. Download the lecture from the web and print it out or read it on your computer screen, perhaps with links that direct you toward additional information to embellish the presentation. Lectures are by no means the sum and substance of online learning, nor should they be, but so long as instructors lecture they may as well do so at a time and place convenient to students, which online education permits.

ONLINE LEARNING AS AN ALTERNATIVE

Educational institutions have diverse reasons for deciding to offer online courses. Some observers dismiss all such initiatives as a crass attempt to make money, but that is simplistic and does not take other motives into account. The University of Central Florida (UCF), for example, had a president in the mid-1990s who was a board director of EDUCOM, an early forum for those seeking to make room for technology in higher education. His interest in the topic spurred him to create a high-ranking post in the university hierarchy for a vice provost for information technology. Central Florida offered its first fully online course—for aspiring vocational education teachers—in 1996, and eventually that course was followed by UCF's first fully online degree program, aimed especially at community college graduates who wanted to obtain bachelor's degrees.

A neighboring community college, a principal feeder institution to UCF, wanted the university to establish a distance education program for its graduates whose jobs and family responsibilities made it difficult for them to pursue the bachelor's degree in classrooms. Thus, the University of Central Florida established an online baccalaureate in liberal studies for such students. Another of UCF's earliest online endeavors came at the request of this same community college that wanted a graduate certificate program for its faculty and administrators. This was an outgrowth of a classroom-based doctoral program that already existed in the university's college of education.

These online ventures served another purpose as well. UCF was crowded and growing, a trend that continued during the late 1990s and into the new century. Enrollment reached 37,000 by 2002. Allocations from the state for construction were becoming more difficult to obtain, and the university was running out of space to put new buildings anyway. UCF spent $2 million a year to rent office and classroom facilities off campus. The many commuting students cruised in vain, on and off campus, for parking spaces. In retrospect, some wags contend that the University of Central Florida was pushed into online education because it ran out of space in its parking lots.

Another institution, San Diego State University, moved gingerly into online education, carefully addressing faculty anxieties and trying to craft policies to satisfy the needs of both students and faculty members. For instance, the university's faculty senate approved a 12-point statement pertaining to distance learning courses that included the following provisions:

- Each program shall provide the opportunity for substantial, personal, and timely interactions between faculty and students and among students.

- The proportion of tenured and probationary faculty teaching shall approximate that of the campus-based program.
- Admissions criteria shall be comparable for students on and off campus.
- Students shall have adequate access to library and student services.
- The university shall offer appropriate training and support services to faculty.
- Nothing in this policy shall imply that distance education is a preferred or required mode of instruction.[6]

As will become clear throughout this book, the faculty senate of San Diego State University recognized many of the issues that ended up assuming prominence in online learning as it spread across campuses and throughout the country. They saw that interaction was an essential part of the learning in such courses. They tried to keep a strong faculty hand on the tiller. They didn't want online courses to become a backdoor entry into the university for students who couldn't meet the regular admissions criteria. They saw the need for explicit arrangements to ensure that these students who might never come to the campus still had the underpinning of the library and student services. They recognized that faculty, taking on an unfamiliar role, would need professional preparation to do the job properly. And they guarded the status quo by stressing that distance education generally and online learning specifically was neither preferred nor required.

The Alfred P. Sloan Foundation provided a boost for online learning in the early 1990s by funding what it referred to as Asynchronous Learning Networks (ALN) at colleges and universities around the United States. Ralph E. Gomory, the foundation's president, felt that the emerging technology offered new possibilities for distance education. He saw the price of technology falling, making it more affordable, and was intrigued by the idea that this kind of distance education—unlike previous forms—presented an opportunity for the learner to connect in substantial ways with the material, the instructor, and fellow students. A. Frank Mayadas joined Sloan at the end of 1992, charged with trying to convince faculty members at various institutions to give ALN a chance. He used the foundation's grants to breach a wall of skepticism. Eventually, Sloan gave money to 60 traditional institutions of higher education and they provided fertile ground in which to sow the seeds of online learning. Forty other colleges and universities later joined the Sloan consortium and, like the original 60, resolved to have regular faculty members use content of the quality that they used in classrooms to teach online courses.

The virtual classroom is no less a legitimate place for learning than the actual classroom. It simply calls for a different mode of delivery. This has implications for course content, course design, and methods of instruction. Nothing inherent in the technology precludes an online course from containing the same content as a course taught in a classroom. The design of the course to make it accessible from a distance is perhaps the most distinctive aspect of online learning. The role of the instructor can vary greatly from online course to online course. Some courses may have no instructor per se and others may have instructors who are as much of a presence as classroom teachers, except that students cannot see them. Electronic interaction crucially enhances an online course. In good online education, it is not merely a way to keep in touch but a prime component of the learning.

Yet, hopes and realities do not always mesh in e-learning. The methods by which some providers have put courses online have been haphazard. Caveat emptor. In some cases, even at established educational institutions, a course amounts to no more than a collection of a professor's lecture notes dumped on the Internet. When courses have been specifically developed for online use, costs have ranged from a few hundred dollars to hundreds of thousands of dollars for a single course, indicating the variability of the effort. When the Wisconsin Technical College system created its online web portal, etechcollege.com, one goal was not only to make course taking easier for prospective students but to improve the quality of the offerings. Though the 16 individual colleges in the system were to continue to originate the courses, some officials saw the unified portal as a vehicle to whittle down duplicative offerings and preserve the better ones. Faculty members were to receive allocations to collaborate with colleagues at some of the other colleges in the system to develop new courses. Furthermore, there was a plan for the portal to offer its own course to help the system's faculty members with the design and pedagogy of e-learning.

In online learning, outside contractors may train faculty members in course design and in the techniques of online instruction as well. In other instances, institutions pay their information technology students to serve as technical staff to help faculty design courses for online learning. A variation on this approach was used by Rio Salado College in Arizona, where the English department consisted of two full-time faculty members and dozens of adjuncts. The small full-time faculty with the aid of course technicians developed the content of online courses, and the adjuncts served as the instructors. There was little room for the instructors to make modifications, according to Keith Anderson, one of the two regular faculty members. This was in keeping with the approach of Rio Salado to almost all of its courses, online and classroom-based, which were standardized and largely taught by adjuncts.

E-learning elicits anew familiar questions about pedagogical practices. How long should students take to submit work? How quickly should e-messages receive responses? What should instructors do about students who fail to contribute to collaborative assignments or do not sign into courses regularly? How may one monitor cheating and plagiarism when students work out of sight? Are there occasions to ask students, if possible, to gather in person? Which tasks are best done synchronously and which asynchronously? What instructional responsibilities can instructors rightfully delegate to assistants? These are questions that institutions answer, tacitly or explicitly, by the ways in which they approach matters involving content, course design, and instructional responsibilities.

Delivering Content

Some people unfamiliar with online learning tend to assume that the content is delivered entirely over the Internet. This is not the case. In addition to downloading some of the less voluminous content, students have books that they may order by mail or buy in bookstores. Many, if not most, online courses use textbooks and other printed materials, just as classroom courses do. For one thing, it would take too long to read books while seated at a computer monitor, and downloading them would tax the capabilities of a printer. There is nothing contrary to on-line learning about using books in conjunction with a course. The main goal of e-learning is convenience for the learner, rendering it unneces-sary to appear at a certain place at a certain time. This doesn't mean that a course must eschew material that is not best conveyed online.

On the other hand, with some of the content and related discussions online, institutions want online students to gain some facility with the computer. The Graduate School of Library and Information Science at the University of Illinois, for instance, expected students in its LEEP program to have rudimentary knowledge of a microcomputer operating system, information retrieval skills, e-mail and electronic bulletin board skills, and knowledge of basic html coding for putting information on the world wide web. Students also needed access at home or at work to the necessary hardware—either UNIX, IBM-compatible, or Macintosh personal computers with sound capacity, software, and network connec-tivity. Students spent up to two hours per week in "live" Internet inter-action at regularly scheduled times for each course. Much of the remainder of the course work was offered asynchronously at times con-venient to the students, who had access to the course materials from web pages.

Students began the program each academic year with a nine-day summer sojourn on the excruciatingly flat Urbana-Champaign campus. The in-person beginning exposed participants to faces and personalities that they would then be able to match with names on e-messages and on electronic bulletin boards during the up-to-five years that some would take to complete the degree. Each subsequent semester, students spent a period of three to five days on campus, assigned to rooms and meal plans in university facilities. About 165 students, one-third of the library school's entire enrollment, participated in LEEP at any given time, 80 percent of them women. More than 70 percent of LEEP stu-dents lived outside Illinois, reflecting the extent to which the program served the needs of those who probably could not have easily commuted to a program, much less have become residential students. Most online programs, unlike the one in library science at the University of Illinois, have no residence requirement and students never meet in person. They deliver the content entirely away from a classroom.

Given the online future of library and information science, a program like LEEP was notable for using the content to immerse students in the very technology that would be at the heart of their day-to-day work in the profession. The skills they developed in pursuing the content of their education online would serve them well in their careers as librarians and information specialists. This was a hybrid course, presenting some content on campus and most of it online. Such courses represent an important part of the future of education. Graduates during the first five years of the program accepted such positions as an interface designer for Intel, information specialist with the World Resources Institute, archivist for the Museum of Broadcast Communications, hospital librarian in Pennsylvania, bank librarian in Florida, and school librarian in Japan.

The content of an online course, much like a classroom course, may originate entirely with the person teaching it. Or, the content may be the product of group planning so that students in the institution encounter the same material no matter who oversees the course. At the other end of the spectrum, unlike most classroom courses, the content may come, in part or in whole, from an outside provider who has little or no connection to the person teaching the course. Knowing that a course is delivered online does not reveal the extent to which the instructor created the course. And it is this idea, the possibility that someone other than the instructor produced the content, that adds to the controversy surrounding online education. Some institutions deal with this issue by having faculty adapt for e-learning courses of their own design that they have first taught in a classroom. Other institutions are satisfied to let instructors teach courses with content created by others. In the final analysis, the substance of the content and whether it provides students with what they need to learn should count most. Yet, some critics of online learning reject this proposition on the basis of tradition, holding fast to the idea that choice of content must originate with the instructor who interacts with students.

Designing Courses for Web Delivery

Online courses do not suddenly materialize from the ether. It is, in fact, possible that it can take longer, up to 66 to 500 percent longer, according to a study by the American Federation of Teachers,[7] to create an online course than to prepare a course to teach in person. Charles Kern, education technology manager for academic computing at Stanford University, warned against the shortcut of slapping together a lot of activities just because they are technologically feasible. Kern was talking about web-enhanced classroom courses, but his admonition was appropriate for courses fully online as well. He advised that each activity that an instructor asks a student to do online should fit with the rest of the course or else the instructor should not use it.[8]

The demands of course design resonate in ways that those unfamiliar with online learning may not immediately appreciate. The layout, illustration, and colors that appear on the monitor screen, the ways that links are displayed, the manner that lessons incorporate sound and video, the arrangements by which students move through the lesson, the instructions they receive for navigating the site, the decisions about how to incorporate electronic bulletin boards and chat rooms—all of these must be considered in designing a course for online delivery. If an instructor previously taught the course in a classroom, someone (possibly the instructor) must retrofit and adapt the content, very likely cutting it into modules suitable for learning that occurs in chunks, to enhance its effectiveness online. All aspects of the digital design should strive for simplicity to enable students to concentrate on learning. The Global Education Network (GEN) set out to design online courses based on the content of classroom-based courses of professors at elite colleges. Animators, illustrators, and technology experts sliced and rearranged the content in modules in which introductions, interactive features, and tests accompanied the lecture material. Course designers inserted streaming audio and video, added links, and compressed and digitized the whole kit and caboodle. "The backbone is the course itself and then we reproportion it," said Alexander Parker of GEN.

While critics may deplore the involvement of outside course designers, nothing inherent in an instructor's knowledge of the content equips him or her to package it in a design suitable for the web. In recognition of the need for expertise in both content and technological design, the development of content and the design of courses may move on parallel tracks. For the same course, different people may have responsibility for its content and for its technical design. Some institutions even contract with course designers to build online courses for them. Thus, designers with no particular expertise in content may take over much of this role at some institutions, using content that others provide.

Defenders of the practice of separating design from instruction argue that assembling a course for the web has little direct relation to content, that the process involves only technological and aesthetic concerns. Others contend, however, that design affects content by emphasizing some aspects of the content over other parts. There are parallels here to discussions about the power of the first draft, namely whether the author of the initial version of a paper frames the discussion, constraining those who later join the editing process. Fundamentally, the controversy revolves around this question: Is a new approach that apportions various responsibilities for a course appropriate for a new method of delivery? E-learning, to a degree greater than any previous way of formally distributing knowledge, offers the possibility of disaggregating content, design, and instruction. Just because all three parts have almost always resided in the hands of one person does not mean that is the best or only way of handling courses. Why should online courses have to follow and be measured by a paradigm born before the Industrial Revolution?

The former United States Open University had separate faculties—one to produce courses and one to interact with students as instructors. Those who produced the courses were not the teachers. Called professors, they were employed by the sister institution, Open University in Britain, where they created course materials. They reworked courses meant to be taught over an entire academic year at Britain's Open University, cutting them into units more suitable for the shorter course period of the U.S. Open University. In Britain, six of these year-long courses comprised all of the content for a bachelor's degree. Each course had an intricate interdisciplinary design from which the content had to be adapted for the single discipline approach of the U.S. Open University. Thus, this work demanded much more than merely "chopping," according to Richard Jarvis, the founding president of U.S. Open University, a noble effort that expired in 2002 for lack of students and insufficient funds.

On the other hand, the University of Central Florida decided when it embarked on e-learning in the middle 1990s to give regular faculty full responsibility for the content, the course design, and the teaching. The courses generally were ones that they had taught in regular classrooms. Technology staff taught faculty members how to adapt their courses for use online and how to teach those courses in this very different pedagogical environment. The people leading the faculty development course, in other words, modeled the behavior they wanted the faculty to learn for teaching their students. Ultimately, an instructional design team from the university's office of course development and web services worked on a course with each faculty member.

Thirty faculty members took this training each term, many seeking to create only web-assisted instruction for classroom-based courses, not fully online courses. They met in five-hour sessions once a week for the first five weeks. Then, during the next week or two, they completed the development of their first module, going through show-and-tell sessions with each other. They devoted the rest of the term to fashioning the remaining modules for a complete course. Officials said that almost all online courses at the University of Central Florida emerged from this process. While the training followed a set pattern, each course ended up having its own characteristics, though templates gave the courses a uniform appearance. Each faculty member controlled the content and methodology, deciding how the course used assignments, activities, chat rooms, and discussions.

Instructing Online

The University of Colorado at Denver and Penn State's World Campus also generally expected faculty to have taught courses in person before attempting to teach them online. But even when they have already taught courses in classrooms, teachers must adjust to working out of the sight of students. Online learning calls for fresh attention to the need to engage students, to respond to them properly and efficiently, and to ensure each step of the way that students understand the course work even though they are not in the room to say in person that they "don't get it." Some pedagogical techniques appropriate to the classroom are not as effective online; teachers must learn new approaches. The whole matter of pacing, for teacher as well as student, comes to the fore.

Teachers can use the technology to add new approaches to their instruction. For instance, e-learning opens the door wide to having students use self-assessment as an instructional tool. Customized tests taken periodically on the computer can acquaint students with the learning objectives of the course and allow them to gauge their level of mastery. For years, educators have spoken of "formative" testing and "summative" testing without honoring the dichotomy for its distinction between the uses of testing. Formative testing reveals to students what they don't know and what they still have to learn, free of the pressure of grades and sanctions. Summative testing should come at the conclusion of the process, after students are satisfied that they have mastered the content. Unlike summative assessments with high stakes, formative assessments use tests to convey content and let students challenge themselves without the sanctions that might accompany failure. Gradually, students can move through a series of electronic tasks, encountering questions of greater and greater difficulty. The questions expose them to what they are supposed to know, stretching them much like a good workout in the gym. Online education readily lends itself to this kind of learning, providing students with feedback without their having to worry about a mark until much farther in the process.

The implications are enormous when faculty examine their approaches to teaching, incorporating assessment as an instructional tool, and learning other methods for taking advantage of the virtual environment. Teachers must reconsider a lifetime of habits, replacing or at least modifying methods acquired in classrooms. They must adapt lessons to incorporate technology. Steven Sorg and Charles Dziuban, administrators at the University of Central Florida who helped faculty prepare to teach online, said that an important byproduct of the process is the reflection it causes. Faculty members who had taken their pedagogy for granted thought about their techniques as they sought to revamp their teaching to make it suitable to e-learning. "They told us they looked at every aspect of their face-to-face teaching to assess the appropriateness for online learning," said Dziuban, who conducted institutional research on e-learning at UCF. It was just such a process that Donald A. Schon[9] urged on academicians in his writings of almost a generation ago, before the advent of online learning, when he underscored the importance of discovering by reflection what one understands and knows how to do.

Julie E. Young's advice to officials at virtual schools, based on her experience directing such a school in Florida, was that they select their teachers with great care. Just as virtual learning is not for every student, it is not for every teacher, according to Young. She said, for instance, that teachers who enjoy performing and lecturing in front of an audience "may hate this," especially if they are obliged to follow a set curriculum. Young, who began her career as a teacher in a public elementary school, put it euphemistically: "There is not as much professional freedom in how to teach." She said that at her statewide virtual school the input of teachers into shaping the curriculum usually was limited to suggesting that maybe this or that should be added or dropped or that some part of the curriculum didn't seem to be working. After gathering such observations, it fell to a team to make the final decisions.

At United States Open University, those directly involved with the students were called associate faculty and assigned to handle up to 25 students in a section. Associate faculty supported the learning of the students by tutoring and mentoring them, though they had no control over the content that others had created for the courses. The associate faculty mostly had jobs at other institutions and worked on the side for U.S. Open University. This kind of moonlighting can truly be done at night, after completing other jobs. All one needs is a computer. The university paid associate faculty in the range of $600 to $1,000 per credit-hour for their work. A third group called "instructors of record" supervised the associate faculty. An instructor of record would review the electronic messages that passed between students and associate faculty in a particular course, providing a kind of quality control to ensure that the interaction promoted learning in the ways that the Open University believed it should. Instructors of record were to review those interactions more randomly after associate faculty had established themselves over a period of time with the Open University. But the institution ran out of time.

The policies of Art Institute Online (AOI), a chain of proprietary schools, illustrate how the expectations for instructors in some online programs differ from those in the usual traditional classroom. The very name that AOI gave to instructors, "facilitators," hints at the difference. These were not teachers in the usual sense. Their job was to oversee the provision of standardized courses developed by others. A project manager collaborated with an instructional designer and one or more content experts to create each of Art Institute's more than 100 online courses. The curriculum and the main ways to implement it remained the same regardless of who facilitated the course. AOI told prospective facilitators as they trained for the role that they were to teach to stated competencies and could not change those competencies. They had some latitude, though, in the way they used assignments to help students reach the stated competencies.

Good online learning requires considerable preparation. Just like education in the classroom, it begins with content, without which there would be no learning. Then, technology enters the picture and rearranges the elements in ways that make e-learning considerably different from the classroom. The design of the course, the way that it goes onto the web, the manner in which students access and interact with the content—all affect outcomes. The person leading the course becomes the intermediary between content and student. The role of these course leaders sometimes resembles that of the traditional teacher or instructor, but other times they may seem more like mentors, or tutors, or even like someone who has little more to do than answer e-messages from students. Students on the receiving end of knowledge delivered in this way must prepare themselves for a more active role than they have taken in the regular classroom. No passive vessels here.

CHAPTER 3

THE NATURE OF INTERACTION

Florida Virtual School strove to ensure that e-learning did not lead students to complete their courses in isolation. The school said that it analyzed each course to discover ways to have students interact with the web environment, with the community, and with each other. Interaction with the web environment for students in Florida might take the form of a teacher providing links to web sites to help students understand a concept or enhance a lesson. The teacher might ask students to use links to art museum web sites, for example, in art classes where a particular painter or style was discussed, audio links to an actor reading a poem to develop listening skills, and an animated link to a science site to allow students to "mix" chemicals and see the reaction. Interaction with the community included such offline activities as interviewing community members for reports, participating in community cultural offerings, and performing service in the community. Interaction with other students involved requirements to work with an online partner or in small online groups, as well as to use electronic chat areas and bulletin boards.

Moreover, the school asked teachers to contact students—and their parents—on a regular basis. Teachers were supposed to keep parents informed of the progress of their children. The school expected teachers to maintain contact with students, usually by e-mail, according to Julie Young, the school's executive director. The school hoped that at least once a month the teacher would speak by phone with each student and a parent. "We don't want a parent surprised if a student gets less than a C in a course," Young said.

There are yet other ways in which Florida Virtual School promoted interactivity. Teachers scheduled online discussions with students, sometimes as often as once a week. For these discussions, students engaged in synchronous online exchanges in chat rooms and participated in asynchronous threaded discussions on electronic bulletin boards onto which instructors posted questions. When they ran into problems, students could seek help electronically.

The school tried through these various interactive approaches to honor its motto: "Any time, any place, any path, any pace." Students in the Florida school said that the "any time" part of the motto mattered most to them. They liked the idea of not having to show up for a course at a certain time on a certain day, especially early in the morning when teenagers typically resist pulling themselves out of bed. Interaction has the potential to motivate students and enhance their learning, though this does not always happen. The motivational part is important because students who spend extended lengths of time online can grow lonely. Thus, online providers face the challenge of countering the possible negative effects of isolation in a classroom of one.

Considerable criticism was directed at the Internet during the 1990s as being a cause of isolation and depression. Then, in 2001,[1] came new evidence—from the same researcher who had earlier blamed the Internet for isolating users—showing that symptoms of depression had declined and that loneliness no longer was significantly associated with Internet use. Nevertheless, learning that makes extensive use of the Internet must face up to the dark side of solitary education. Able instructors of online courses try not to lose sight of the potential role of interaction in breaking down isolation that might otherwise undermine the morale of students. They hope to keep students who are out of view from feeling out of touch. Distance education evinced concern of this sort long before the era of online learning. Correspondence courses, which depend on postage stamps, not the Internet, to build connections, also have been subject to worries about isolation. An essayist in 1971 wrote of the difficulties of "compensating for the solitary situation in which the correspondence study student finds himself" and the "concern of the correspondence study center to find ways of establishing warm ties with the student."[2]

Online education has the potential to transform interaction into a learning task. Using the web to move from one link to another in a well-designed lesson allows for enrichment. Computer simulations introduce greater reality. Collaborative projects that students do online figure in the learning in many courses. The interactive nature of the best e-learning captivates students and makes them almost forget that the setting is a classroom of one. Beyond the quality of the content, interactivity probably attracts the foremost concern when it comes to online courses. Educators acknowledge the vulnerability of online programs in this regard. Along with trying to offer content that is at least the equal of what students get in a regular classroom, online courses have to give students opportunities to interact with the instructor and with each other. At their best, online courses can exceed classroom-based courses in cultivating discourse, albeit from afar. An online course, properly crafted, builds in many opportunities for students to advance their learning through responses and discussions. Ideally, this interaction is neither haphazard nor left to serendipity, though spontaneity may figure in it. A new domain demands new approaches to engaging and supporting students.

To Sheila Seifert, who taught at the University of Colorado at Denver, the interaction with students online was the best part of e-learning. She thought that not seeing each other removed possible prejudice and made discussion easier for some students. As a teacher of writing courses, she considered online learning ideal in this respect. "It forces students to reveal themselves through their words alone," she said. Seifert sometimes arranged for students to work together from a distance, requiring them to collaborate on projects with classmates whom they never saw. One time, however, members of the class chose to meet in person after completing an online assignment. "They were amazed at how they looked to each other compared to the personalities that had come across [online]," Seifert said. "We all enjoyed hearing about their perceptions and then the reality of who they were. They were given the gift of getting to know each other before attaching a name to a face."

Officials at the University of Missouri High School, also an online enterprise, said that they deliberately tried in their courses to draw out the students, apparently, for the most part, by emulating good classroom practices. The school provided students with learning objectives for each course, a list of assignments, and a study guide that expanded on the lesson and pointed students in profitable directions. Students submitted work online and instructors returned it online, with appropriate comments. "We make it as personal as possible," said Kristi Smalley, principal of the high school. Much of the contact through e-mail that the school maintained online with students apparently was written by nonteaching personnel, rather than actual teachers, presumably to save money.

The enhancement of online learning through interaction comes in both synchronous and asynchronous exchanges. Either way, an institution strives to give students a chance to test their knowledge, demonstrate what they have learned, and gain new insights. This electronic interaction via bulletin boards, chat rooms, and e-mail can enrich a student's education, much as good classroom discussions do. Interaction of this sort can also increase students' participation in the learning process. "Few university faculty have the interest or persistence to require every single student in their classes to participate in classroom discussions, much less answer *every* question posed or issue addressed," said Ronald Legon, provost of the University of Baltimore, speaking especially of undergraduate education but to some degree of the graduate level as well. "The typical situation in the vast majority of classes that even provide the opportunity for meaningful student discussion is that a relative handful of students avail themselves of this opportunity to demonstrate what they know, contribute to the learning process, and hone their speaking skills."

Some students who would be among the silent majority in an actual classroom shine in the virtual classroom, according to Legon. Students who are reticent in the physical presence of more assertive classmates who dominate discussions may welcome asynchronous interaction. Legon said that asynchronous online discussions to which students contribute at moments of their own choosing help them overcome shyness and give students time to mull over responses. Equally important, he added, this approach—allowing the benefit of some extra time—permits those who have lagged in completing an assignment a chance to catch up on the readings. They can weigh in with considered responses when they are ready instead of trying to bluff their way through, as they might try to do in a classroom in response to questions for which they are unprepared. Legon said: "Whatever their motivation, students who come out of their shells in online discussion soon discover that they have much to contribute, and the instructor typically watches their enthusiasm and confidence grow the longer they participate in online courses. This is particularly the case if the teacher encourages their efforts with the combination of public and private comments that web-based instruction makes so easy and available."

KEEPING STUDENTS ENGAGED
IN VIRTUAL CLASSROOMS

Courses created by the Global Education Network (GEN) were designed to poll students periodically for their opinions about one or another aspect of what they were learning. Students registered opinions electronically at the outset of an online lecture and again at the end, allowing them to see whether they had changed their minds. These were not right or wrong answers, simply opinions. The instructor was to gather the opinions of the individual students and feed back the collected responses to the entire class, allowing students to compare their own opinions at various points with those of classmates. This was one way that the Global Education Network tried to increase involvement. Online learning, in other words, need not—probably should not, given the capacities of the web—be a static process.

Some authorities maintain that students in online courses do not necessarily need special preparation to cope with the independence associated with this kind of education if they get enough interaction to keep them engaged and involved. Keith Anderson, who designed and taught online courses at Rio Salado College in Arizona, said that he and his colleagues thought that the facility to work online depends not so much on a learner's ability to handle independence as on the inclination of an online instructor to keep in contact with students, responding promptly to their questions and to the work that they submit. In other words, some people believe that online education can thrive with enough interaction to keep students' independence from becoming license for teachers to neglect their students. This puts pressure on instructors. Since e-learning can become a 24/7 activity, students may expect a quick turnaround on their electronically submitted work.

"We want them to have a sense that there is a person on the other end who is responsive to their needs," said Anderson. Instructors at Rio Salado were to phone students to inquire into the situation and to offer reassurance when students' online responses—or lack of such—indicated that they were dissatisfied or struggling. Such a philosophy underpins good teaching whether online or in a classroom, although teachers are entitled to reasonable limits on their workday. Katrin Tabellion, who completed her diploma at the University of Missouri's virtual high school, found that when she had a problem and raised a point by e-mail, a school representative almost always got in touch with her the next day. The Florida Virtual School tried to offset the isolation of students by offering them the chance to join clubs. The first two such groups formed were a Latin Club and a Science Club, with a Math Club added during the 2001–02 school year. Club members scattered throughout the state kept in touch by Internet. The Science Club organized a few face-to-face gatherings, scheduling outings in various regions of the state so that groups of students could explore natural phenomena of Florida together.

Students in online courses may yearn for such connections despite the convenience that spurred them toward e-learning. "I longed for verbal interaction," said Genevieve Kirch, a sixth-grade teacher who earned the first degree awarded by Western Governors University, an institution that uses various forms of distance education and has no classrooms of its own. She was most frustrated in a research methods course that she took online. "I wanted to be able to sit down with an instructor and have it explained to me," Kirch said. Her instructor and her mentor kept in close contact with Kirch to try to help her understand the underlying statistics, and she appreciated their efforts though she would have welcomed some flesh-and-blood contact. She lauded the role that mentors played from a distance at WGU in charting the progress of students and in keeping them focused on the learning goals. She was gratified that her course project, which called for engaging primary students in reading tasks, linked up so well with her professional work. It was just that sometimes during her academic struggles Kirch would have appreciated more human contact than e-learning typically offers.

In some other courses, probably not quite so rigorous as the course in research methods, Kirch found the interaction from afar more or less sufficient. She had textbooks and kept up her studies by way of self-paced modules. She submitted assignments online and got back online responses from the instructors. Kirch liked the contact with students through threaded discussions in which classmates left comments at their convenience and went online later to read the contributions that others made in the continually unfolding conversation. This kind of asynchronous communication happens with an electronic bulletin board that each student visits when time permits, reading messages posted by others, often in response to a question from the instructor, and adding their own messages.

Another form of interaction in online learning involves putting classmates in contact in "live" time. Synchronous approaches in which students are online concurrently—as in a chat room—replicate some of the spontaneity of the classroom. Lisa Neal of Electronic Data Systems, who taught and consulted in person and online, preferred this approach. She found asynchronous methods unsatisfactory for both herself and her students. The students, she said, felt disconnected from each other when they weren't online at the same time. Moreover, she, as the instructor, didn't really get to know them and establish relationships with them when the contacts weren't in real-time. "Something is missing that has always been there in a synchronous or face-to-face class," she said. "I have enormous reservations about asynchronous instruction."

Elinor Grusin of the University of Memphis used an exclusively synchronous approach in the graduate level course on communications law that she taught as a faculty member in the journalism department, not even bothering with asynchronous threaded discussions. The university's complete master of arts degree in journalism program was online, with all of the courses taught in synchronous style. Grusin said that the content and rigor were the same as the identical course that she taught in a classroom as part of the campus-based master's program at the University of Memphis. Students in the online version of the course sat at their computers in widely scattered locales for three hours one evening a week to take the course in real-time. A member of the class who lived in Germany apparently rose from his sleep or went to bed very late to participate.

Grusin thought that the students got more out of interacting in real-time in a chat room than if they visited an asynchronous site at times of their choosing. With a tiny class roster displayed at one corner of her screen, Grusin acted as the traffic cop, orchestrating the discussion by calling on the students in random order. They knew they had to be prepared when their names appeared on the screen. "Everything is removed from the interaction except the student's intelligence or lack thereof," Grusin said of her approach to synchronous online instruction. "There's no b-s-ing, no wasting time. No one knows how anyone else is dressed or their mannerisms or the color of their skin or their physical handicaps. It's all removed from the field of view." Enrollment in the online version of the class was capped at eight students and enrollment in the classroom-based version ran to 15 or 16. The online students paid a higher tuition for the smaller class size.

Many students, though, enroll in online courses specifically because they find it difficult to be at a certain place at a precise time. Online courses that have too many synchronous features, requiring students to be at their computers at the same time so that they can have a "live" chat, may not fit their schedules. Some travel in their jobs or live in different time zones from most of their course mates. It can therefore be a disadvantage if synchronous instruction vitiates the triumph over time and place that online learning usually provides through asynchronous instruction.

Written discussion replaces oral discourse in online learning, whether synchronous or asynchronous. Those who are less verbal may fare better in this format as every student is almost guaranteed a chance to say something. No one sits in the back row; no one has to wait long to be recognized. But some people with weak writing skills may feel self-conscious and less able to make their points when interactivity depends almost entirely on writing, not only in e-mail but also for electronic bulletin boards and chat rooms. For her part, Grusin maintained that "there's a lot more to communicating than the written word and that's lost when you're not face-to-face with students." Students have other objections, as well. Deborah Confer, a student in an online course on archives management at the University of Colorado at Denver, felt that discussions that had to be put into writing lacked spontaneity. She also thought that some classmates copied others' written contributions to the "discussion" and submitted them as their own words. She felt that they probably would have been less likely in actual conversation to try to pass off someone else's words as their own. "The instructor had to remind us that the e-mails should be our own thoughts, opinions, and observations *about* the readings," Confer said.

A PLATFORM FOR LEARNING

Most educational institutions depend on commercial companies to provide the technological expertise that enables them to offer online courses and to make them interactive. The software systems developed by these companies give instructors what they need to carry out the activities common to the virtual classroom—offering students a syllabus and online lessons, assessing students, and holding online discussions, as well as a range of such housekeeping tasks as registering and grading students and receiving electronic copies of their messages and papers. A so-called platform, literally an electronic foundation on which the course stands, tries to provide this underpinning within a secure electronic environment that resists hackers and cheaters.

A platform, simply put, is to an online course what a spreadsheet is to online stock monitoring. Whether called learning environments or platforms or some other name, software programs enable e-learning to flourish on more than a primitive basis that would amount to little more than posting lectures on the Internet. Educational institutions could create their own systems for operating online courses, and some do, but commercial companies have captured much of the market. Schools, colleges, and universities usually find it easier to concentrate on content and leave the rest of the work, including the round-the-clock technical and support service, to a company that exists for this purpose. In the master's of library and information science program offered online by the University of Illinois, for instance, the platform had a multitude of uses, described in the following four ways:

1. A syllabus section of the platform contained the outline and schedule for class events with links to assignments and to library material that was on electronic reserve.
2. A bulletin board section made threaded discussions possible and had the capacity to set up multiple bulletin boards for the same course.
3. A live event section gave access to synchronous presentations.
4. An archive offered audio recordings of previous lectures, relevant slides, and storage for online discussions.

A Closer Look at Platform Companies

Blackboard, eCollege, and WebCT were among the companies competing fiercely for business in the platform market at the start of this century. Tens of millions of dollars are at stake for companies providing platforms for web-based learning once the enterprise becomes profitable. The platform companies continually search for ways to gain an edge in the market, as Blackboard tried to do in 2001 by entering an agreement with Microsoft under which the two companies would promote each other's products. The growing pervasiveness of online learning generates increased business opportunities as e-learning spreads through more departments and more divisions of colleges and universities that already have a limited number of courses. Moreover, demand is driven by the desire of educational institutions to make their courses ever more sophisticated, thereby requiring more intricately designed platforms. Educators want platforms that have the flexibility to accommodate changes over time, the integrative qualities to make the various parts of the program mesh, and the ease of use—no matter how

complex its inner workings—to make e-learning friendly to students
and instructors. At the same time, an institution wants a platform that
can make courses cost-efficient so that online learning does not turn
into a fiscal albatross.

Blackboard, Inc., based in Washington D.C., began as a server software application designed by Cornell University students to promote
access to content and online interaction through chat rooms and bulletin boards. The company, privately owned, evolved into a management
system for building and running courses. Members of a class may turn
to Blackboard to conduct online conversations around the clock. A student might contribute a comment to an ongoing discussion or pose a
question at any time, and then a classmate can respond at a convenient
time. Instructors can post notices and present information to their entire classes. They might, for example, ask members of a class for the impressions they gleaned from an assigned reading. Based on students'
reactions, instructors can tailor assignments to respond to what students
did not fully comprehend or give them readings to advance concepts
that they had grasped. Blackboard extended its reach in 2002 by buying
one of its smaller competitors, Prometheus.

ECollege started in 1996 and by the end of 2001 grew to be the host
to 160 online programs in higher education with an enrollment totaling
58,600. It was a publicly traded company in a sector of the e-learning
industry where the inclination of other firms was to remain privately
owned. ECollege's revenues in 2001 grew to $19.8 million from $12.5
million in 2000. The company said that it offered educational institutions products to create, deliver, and administer online courses, to communicate with students, to provide technical support for students and
faculty, and to analyze and evaluate the e-learning process.

WebCT, a third company, said that its advantages arose from the
flexibility of its products in supporting numerous teaching and learning
methods, from having the largest course management system (28 percent of the market in the United States), the most online content (for
institutions that wanted to buy content), and the capability to integrate
its services with the institution's own student information system for
transfer of course and student data. Peter Segall, executive vice president
of WebCT, said that the company "focuses on professional development

for the faculty" to help them use the platform more effectively. In addition, he said, WebCT provided an orientation for students and a student help desk for them to contact. The company reported that 90 percent of students' problems had to do with logging in. The company also gathered information on students' use of the online site to assemble data that might correlate with the level of success a student achieved in a course.

Another commercial company, Apex Learning, boasted that its platform was developed specifically for K through 12 virtual schools, which the company said needed different approaches from platforms designed mostly with higher education in mind. The Apex platform permitted educators to track student enrollment, progress, and outcomes, as well as to generate reports for individual students, classes, and schools. Youngsters at the elementary and secondary levels could use the platform for multimedia tutorials, self-assessments, virtual science laboratories, chat rooms, and bulletin boards. Using online courses from Apex, for instance, the University of California College Prep Initiative tried to ensure that more of the state's high school students had access to Advanced Placement courses; Bloomfield High School in the extreme northeastern corner of New Mexico could offer four different AP courses to 36 juniors and seniors despite the retirement of five veteran teachers who were most qualified to teach the courses; and tiny Shanksville-Stonycreek High School in rural western Pennsylvania was able to give a second-year course in German to students who had completed the first year and had no other way to meet the state's graduation requirement of two years of a foreign language.

Started in 1997 by Paul Allen, a cofounder of Microsoft, Apex had contracts across the country by 2001 to help add virtual classrooms to existing brick-and-mortar schools. By mid-2002, Apex reached 90,000 students at 2,100 high schools in 30 states, according to Sue Collins, the company's chief education officer. Apex created such products as online Advanced Placement courses and foreign language courses, the kinds of offerings requiring teaching expertise not readily available in some schools and some school districts. Thus, Apex found its niche by squeezing into a void. Branching out, Apex entered a partnership with the University of Washington to develop ten new online high school courses—in chemistry, intermediate algebra, precalculus, introduction to American literature, U.S. history, earth science, geography, sociology, psychology, and study of the Internet. Apex's investors included Vulcan Ventures, Warburg Pincus, Edison Schools, Maveron LLC, Kaplan Ventures, and Michigan State University.

Schools, colleges, and universities want platforms that lend themselves to customization so that they can strive for their own identifiable electronic imprint, giving their online courses features that differentiate them from those of competing institutions. The ability to customize platforms lets educational institutions vary their approaches to teaching and learning in online courses within the same institution and even within the same department. Some educational institutions also tend to look to the platform companies to help faculty members develop and learn how to teach online courses. Platform companies claim to be able to analyze and assess the effectiveness of a particular online course by reviewing the interaction that occurred.

Adjuncts to Platforms

If one thinks of platform providers as contractors, then there are, in effect, platform subcontractors whose products work in conjunction with the main platform, performing specialized functions. Horizonlive, for instance, was such a subcontractor, offering a software tool to allow synchronous audio and/or video in connection with courses taught through one of the main platforms. Online learning has so many specialized functions that smaller companies such as Horizonlive can carve out niches for their products. Thus, Blackboard, eCollege, and WebCT all formed partnerships with Horizonlive to use its software for live video and audio. In turn, Horizonlive had a partnership with a company, Real-Networks, to integrate that firm's streaming audio and visual technology with Horizonlive's software.

A platform uses technological specialty tools from other companies to enhance its capabilities. An instructor might use Horizonlive in an asynchronous online course, for instance, to add an occasional live lecture that students may hear through the speakers and/or view on the screens of their computers. Or, an instructor might want a live, interactive lecture of this sort so that she can include verbal descriptions each time that students confront particularly complex material. Another instructor might use this interactive tool to allow students to send messages to a computer next to him during a live lecture to let him know whether they understand key points of the lecture, so that the instructor may adjust the presentation accordingly.

Yet another instructor, in a variation on the previous approach, might poll students on various topics in the course, gathering the results during the lecture and immediately feeding them back to the students. Students could use Horizonlive for live small group meetings to collaborate on a project regardless of their distance from each other geographically. At such institutions as California State University at Chico and Lehigh University in Pennsylvania, students used this software to meet faculty members for real-time conferences during which the professor was in his or her office and the student, at home or in a dorm room.

While Horizonlive marketed itself as a synchronous product for online real-time, it also promoted its asynchronous applications. Everything transmitted live through Horizonlive was saved automatically for possible future use, creating an instant archive for the course. Students unable to hear or view the original, live online transmission could go to the archive at a convenient time and hear or see what they missed. Moreover, even students who sat at their computers during the live presentation might later visit the archive to reinforce or confirm earlier impressions. This, of course, is impossible in a classroom-based course except on the unusual occasion when someone tapes the session. Instructors who liked the qualities of Horizonlive could also use it to make original recordings of lectures in which they wanted to include streaming audio or streaming video for asynchronous use by students.

An online institution can mix platform providers and software systems, along with various hardware providers, as seen in the manner in which Army University Access Online (AUAO) assembled its program for soldiers in the U.S. Army. The government allotted $453 million to get the Army University off the ground, hiring PricewaterhouseCoopers (PwC) to build an electronic portal to integrate the various parts of the program. PwC brought in many subcontractors for the web site, eArmyU.com, illustrating the potential for combining the expertise of several companies to deliver online learning. Two companies, Blackboard and Saba, provided the learning and learning management platforms, PeopleSoft provided the system to manage the support services, and Cognos provided the data warehouse. Fiberlink had responsibility for Internet access and Precision Response Corporation handled the technical help desk. Logistics support for the site came from LESCO and applications managing and networking, from Intel Online Services.

In addition, SMARTHINKING provided online tutoring and academic assistance. GALILEO provided a digital library. Laptop computers and printers that the Army gave to participating soldiers came from Hewlett-Packard and Compaq. The contributions of the various vendors testified to the extent to which providers can combine software and hardware from various companies to build a full infrastructure for a functioning online university. All that was left was the content. The Army University turned to colleges and universities across the United States for the courses and paid the tuitions for the soldiers who enrolled through one central portal.

COLLABORATION

Proponents of the virtual classroom speak often of learning communities, students working together in groups to advance their knowledge. Advocates of collaborative inquiry[3] maintain that this approach stimulates and supports students, motivating them to learn. Also, they say, by working in groups, students get a chance to act as teachers (of each other) as well as learners. These statements and most other endorsements of collaborative learning pertain to students who attend courses in classrooms. Online education may multiply the advantages for students, many of whom welcome interaction that helps overcome some of the isolation. Some proponents of e-learning would have people believe that online education, perhaps even to a greater extent than real courses that meet in real classrooms, can facilitate interaction through collaboration among students. They base this proposition on the idea that students on campus go their own way at the end of each class session, generally not to have contact with one another until the next session.

Paradoxically, the world wide web, which critics say depersonalizes education, presumably might help overcome this separateness. By providing students with virtual spaces where they can meet electronically and share comments, a bulletin board or chat room could lead to more personalization and interaction for students outside of classrooms. Tina House taught a course entitled "Developing and Implementing Parent Involvement Programs," at the University of Colorado at Denver in which she tried to take advantage of this idea. The course combined 32 hours of face-to-face teaching with time that students spent online developing plans for parent involvement projects. In addition, House used the web to describe assignments and expected students to turn in their work online. Originally, this course consisted of 45 contact hours in a classroom and required no project.

The online program (LEEP) leading to a master's degree at the University of Illinois's Graduate School of Library and Information Science prided itself on trying to inculcate a sense of community among students. They entered the library science program in cohorts, organized into groups of classmates with whom they were encouraged to form bonds and collaborate online, though ultimately not all went through the program at the same pace. This effort helped underpin the goal of building a sense of community. An electronic bulletin board containing information about campus events, which few online students were in a position to attend, helped them to identify with the university and campus life.

Requirements for a face-to-face session on campus each semester—though 70 percent of the students lived out of state—played an important part in pursuit of community. Each group of students had to start the program with a nine-day stay on campus. Each course also had a weekly live-session time slot during which students and faculty gathered in the web-based virtual classroom, with students listening to a faculty member speak via RealAudio and responding via Text Chat. The program made available online recordings of campus events so that LEEP students could learn from the guest speakers even though they did not attend in person. In addition, students visited a directory with photos and biographical notes of classmates whom they had come to know online. The dean of the school had a live online session with the students once each term. Even career aspirations got attention; practitioners offered students information on professional opportunities by way of threaded discussions online. Finally, the web provided a broadcast of the May commencement ceremony to ensure that students experienced this campus ritual.

Techniques for promoting collaboration—e-mail, bulletin boards, and chat rooms—all figure in efforts by online programs across the country to create communities of learners. Sometimes instructors make specific assignments that require groups of students to confer electronically. An instructor might, for instance, consider no joint project complete until each of those assigned to a group sign off on the work. Such an expectation means that no one can fulfill the assignment in splendid isolation. The Learning Lab at Stanford University in its research on asynchronous discussions that augment classroom lectures said that the findings "confirmed the importance of social engagement and informal contact between participants in collaborative and distributive learning environments." The lab said that it had come to recognize and was addressing the challenges of forming communities among geographically dispersed students.[4]

In spite of such lofty aspirations, group learning online still has many of the same strengths and weaknesses as group learning by students who attend courses in person. On the one hand, students can learn from each other. Working as part of a group also gives students time to burrow into one segment of knowledge if they know that others in the group will carry out the same kinds of explorations in other segments and that members will then share their findings. Yet, just as in cooperative learning in the classroom, online groups bog down if inept or lazy members do not carry their full share of the load. This problem may be exacerbated in online courses, in which fellow students don't have to face the reproach that comes with looking into the eyes of those whom one has just let down.

Another impediment to online collaboration may involve the size of the class. In a large class, the length of the online discussion can overwhelm possibilities of collaboration. One instructor told of having a whole-group online discussion with a class of 35 students. The experience of trying to get so many people involved in an online discussion felt to her as if they were all talking at once, messages speeding in on top of messages, the conversation devolving into a jumble. She and some other instructors with large classes took to breaking the students into smaller units for purposes of online discussions. She made the online conversations of each small group available for members of the other groups in the class to peruse, contributing to the cohesion of the entire class. The value of creating smaller units to promote online collaboration could be seen at Teachers College, Columbia University, where an instructor told of dividing her online class of 21 into three groups, each consisting of 7students, and letting each group have its own separate online discussion. "There are fewer messages and this makes it more manageable," she said.

The ethereal nature of e-learning provides the greatest restraint on collaboration and interaction. All of the hosannas aside, this is not flesh and blood. Interaction from a distance cannot be the same as a series of substantial face-to-face encounters over the length of a school term, though online contact can be frequent, meaningful, and instructionally enriching. One student's experience in the online courses offered by the Center for Talented Youth of the Johns Hopkins University showed the attenuated nature of this kind of instruction and the difficulties of bringing about proper interaction. In the first two courses she took through the program, precalculus and physics, Morgan Arenson said that she was never once offered the chance to interact with other students taking the courses.

In each course, she was assigned a tutor, a graduate student at Hopkins. The tutors communicated with her almost exclusively by e-mail, the exceptions being infrequent phone conversations. She conceded that perhaps she might have had more contact with the tutor by phone if she had initiated the calls. But even the interaction by e-mail fell short of her expectations. Given the limits on her schedule and that of the graduate student, Arenson found that e-messages often sat for a day awaiting a response. "This all held back my learning," she said. "I learn best if I can go right to the teacher and talk or ask a question." She also felt that the lack of contact with other students was a setback. "I take great joy in going to a group of peers and working out a problem together. It's a great learning tool. It also means you don't have to go to the teacher and say you don't know something."

Interaction, so taken for granted in the classroom that it may not even occur, becomes a vital vehicle for online learning, where its absence can prove an impediment. Instructors use online discussions and exchanges to convey concepts and ideas and to get students to reflect and elaborate on their learning. Software written for this purpose creates a platform that enables students to interact with instructors and with other students. The platform delivers the course to students through their computers, allowing educational institutions to perform administrative tasks for students from a distance. Online learning communities, connected by software, enable students to collaborate with classmates whom they never see, an effort to emulate in virtual settings one of the features of well-organized courses that meet in person. Without adequate interaction, a classroom of one can be a very isolated place—and learning can be compromised.

CHAPTER 4

FACILITATING THE CONVERSATION

A look at an online course offered by the State University of New York (SUNY) provides a glimpse of how an instructor organizes an online course to promote electronic interaction between himself and the students and among students. The course, Abnormal Psychology, given through one of SUNY's community colleges, was organized into modules, a typical way to assemble an online course. Usually, a module represents a self-contained body of work for a student to complete over a period of a week or so, the equivalent of several classroom meetings and the associated out-of-class assignments. An instructor may present some lecture material on screen in the module, but most of the reading comes through books that students must acquire, material found at sites linked to the course web site, and what appears in the online discussions. The web site for the course gave an overview of the sections in each of the eight modules. Every step of the way, the course called for e-mail exchanges and online discussions. Interaction, in other words, was a vehicle of instruction.

The web site gave an overview of the chapters in each module, lists of learning objectives, self-test quizzes, links to pertinent web sites, and video clips to view on the monitor screen. Each module called on students to read assigned material in the textbook that accompanied the course, locate and summarize/analyze the contents of other web sites pertaining to topics covered in the module, create and submit a discussion question for each chapter in the module, respond in the online discussion to some or all of the questions submitted by classmates, and discuss online with other students and the instructor questions posed by the instructor.

The student-led, online discussions were a particularly important part of the course, counting for 40 percent of the entire grade. The instructor cautioned students that the questions they posed for others to consider should be thoughtfully developed and carefully worded. The questions were supposed to address issues and concepts from the readings. The instructor said he would evaluate the questions by their relevance to the materials, importance to significant issues in the chapters, ability to provoke thought, originality, and timeliness. He rated the responses by students to each other's questions according to whether they were correct, thorough, focused, well organized, well written, and original. "A high quality response," he said, "contains information from the textbook or another valid source, or applies a concept from the text in a meaningful way, or facilitates understanding of the course material."[1] Students did not have to participate in every online discussion, but the more they did so, the more opportunities they had to improve their grades.

There were examinations at the ends of four of the eight modules. The instructor told students to treat the essay tests as they would a take-home, open-book exam in a classroom course. He said he would award the best grades to essays that carried documentation, used examples, were not too short, and cited other students' comments from the discussions. In this connection, he encouraged class members to keep logs to record the most important comments that fellow students made online in discussing each chapter. The instructor told students at the outset that they must submit three research papers of at least 1,000 words, each based on investigations conducted via the Internet. He directed the students to locate at least five web resources relevant to the chosen topic for each paper, read the resources, organize the information, and summarize the findings. They were to include citations of students' comments from the pertinent online discussions.

At the end of each online document was an "Ask a Question" button that students could use when assignments gave them pause. These were not discussion questions, but nuts-and-bolts inquiries about the logistics of the course. Such questions went to a site at which the instructor and other students could answer them. For questions that they wanted to ask of the instructor only, students were told not to use regular e-mail. Instead, students had their own private online folders in an Online Office Hours module, where they could leave questions for the instructor who, in turn, would send a response to the inquiring students' private folders.

INTERACTING ELECTRONICALLY

Distance education has always meant delivering learning to students from afar. Correspondence by mail sufficed for generations, eventually supplemented by the technology of the telephone. Instructors and students could hear each other's voices even if they could not see one another. This facilitated dialogue about assignments. Most of today's cyber learning builds on that relationship and, in some ways, represents an elaboration on the ways of correspondence—providing an ease, speed, and capacity for the written word far exceeding what was possible by mail. Instructors of online courses say that cyber learning has electronic dialogue at its heart. A key component of the learning flows from the discussions that electronic bulletin boards, chat rooms, and e-mail make possible. These communication methods hold the potential for turning online courses into seminars.

For many students, the level and success of the interaction seems to contribute to their satisfaction with the course. This could be seen in the courses of World Campus of Pennsylvania State University, an entirely online program. Surveyed in the spring of 2001, students in 30 of the courses praised the technology for allowing them "to actively participate in online discussions about the course material," for making it possible "to actively monitor online discussions about the course materials even when I didn't participate," and for supporting "the discussion of ideas and concepts taught in the course with other students." More than 80 percent of the students agreed or strongly agreed with the propositions of the three questions. Seventy percent were satisfied or very satisfied specifically with the interactions with the instructor, and 76.9 percent felt this way about interactions with other students.[2]

Interestingly, students at Penn State, while positive, were less favorably disposed when it came to interaction in behalf of collaborative assignments. One hesitates to make too much of this finding, but it is worth pondering the possible implications as online students around the country seem to have similar feelings. It could be simply more difficult to get students to work together in behalf of online projects than to get them to engage in discussions. As mentioned in the previous chapter, this would, more or less, be an extension of the experience in classrooms, where collaborative learning and group projects sometimes fail when a lack of cooperation impedes group work. Is there any reason to expect people to behave differently online?

Experiences so far in elementary and secondary e-learning somewhat mimic those in higher education. For all of its successes, the U.S. Department of Education's Virtual High School, a five-year pilot project that ended in 2001, did not achieve the quantity or quality of interaction in its courses that it sought. This was true in both student-to-student and student-to-teacher contacts, according to an evaluation of the program.[3] The teacher of an Advanced Placement statistics course said that students' online dialogue was minimal. The teacher of a pre-engineering course said that there was little or no student-to-student interaction and that even the students' interaction with him was limited. The teacher of a modern classics course estimated that student-to-student contacts accounted for two-thirds of the interaction in his classroom-based course but only one-third of the interaction in his online course, where, presumably, he had to do more of the communicating.[4] The evaluation attributed this lack of interaction to the students not signing into courses frequently enough, reducing the sense of conversation. This held down the amount of feedback that students got on their ideas and on their work products and reduced the sense of community among the students.[5] Thus, in spite of assurances about online learning producing interaction, practitioners apparently still have much to learn about how best to achieve it.

E-Mail

E-mail, like the Internet itself, existed for quite some time before it became *de rigueur* in academia. For one thing, the exponential growth of
e-mail had to wait until Internet access was a standard feature of faculty
offices. From e-mail's origins in the 1960s until some 30 years later,
most faculty members outside the sciences made scant use of this new
technology. It became essential to the academic community as computers proliferated and Internet connections became more prevalent in the
1990s, and with its ubiquity, e-mail rapidly grew indispensable to communications on campuses. Now, while online learning would be unthinkable without e-mail, it serves also as a vital resource of many
courses that meet entirely in classrooms.

One of the most important roles of e-mail in online learning is the
access to the instructor that it provides for students. It is a portal that
remains open regardless of a student's distance from campus and
whether or not instructors are actually in their offices. E-mail has carved
a new door into the office of each professor, whether the person teaches
online or in person. As a matter of fact, e-mail may be a vehicle for dealing with what has become a vexing problem on campuses, namely the
unavailability of faculty members who seem to curtail their office hours.
In one notable instance, the administration at Boston University became so concerned over what it considered the failure of faculty members to maintain sufficient office hours, it floated a controversial
proposal to require them to be on campus and in their offices at least
four days a week. The idea provoked a firestorm of protest among faculty, and the administration backed off. Defenders of the status quo
maintain that professors must be free to be away from their offices to
pursue their research and writing. Moreover, some faculty can attest to
spending time in their offices during announced hours and having no
students show up.

"Although I am in my office Monday through Friday from 8 A.M. to
5 P.M. students who need to talk with me are more likely to e-mail me
than to phone or stop in," said Martha A. Townsend, director of the
campus writing program at the University of Missouri at Columbia.
Townsend conducted a survey[6] to determine if colleagues had similar

experiences. She sent the questionnaire to faculty members and graduate assistants in the English department at Missouri, as well as to writing program administrators around the country. Seventy-seven percent of the 147 respondents reported that students most frequently contacted them by e-mail. Freshmen and sophomores were most apt to get in touch with their teachers this way, while juniors, seniors, and graduate students were less likely, presumably preferring to speak to teachers in person. Moreover, students at larger universities in the north were the most likely to use e-mail to maintain ties with faculty. One of Townsend's conclusions was that besides the convenience of e-mail, "it appears that some use it to avoid confrontation." Apparently, some students preferred to don an electronic cloak when broaching sensitive topics.

This way of communicating interweaves the schedules of morning people and night people, those who travel and those who remain on campus. Americans who send e-messages to colleagues in Europe and Asia can readily appreciate how electronic communication overcomes the problem of determining the best time to try to reach someone abroad, which is always an issue when telephoning. Fax was an earlier solution to the time difference and e-mail makes communication even easier and more personal. Whether they take courses on campus or online, students do not have to worry about finding an instructor's door locked; e-mail, in turn, frees instructors from the confines of rigid office hours. E-mail is truly the win-win device for solving the persistent problem of keeping in touch outside the classroom and it is a *sine qua non* of online education. Furthermore, e-mail probably leads to more frequent communication between teachers and students, providing more contact than would occur on campus, though quantity does not necessarily replace quality.

Perhaps educational institutions should not despair if e-messages sent between students and instructors do not always receive timely responses. E-mail garners no better reactions in some other sectors. One might expect, for instance, that the business world with its incessant bottom-line approach would have smoothed out problems in communicating with customers by e-mail, but this is not the case. Just 30 percent of all retailers respond to basic customer service requests online within six hours, according to the results of a survey released in 2002.[7] Forty percent of retailers took more than three days to respond to e-messages from customers or did not respond at all. Many instructors of online courses seem to do better than this.

E-mail is of particular consequence in an era in which part-time and adjunct faculty teach at least one-third of all undergraduate course hours. Their time on campus may consist of little more than the hours spent in the classroom. These freeway fliers, as they are called in California, drive from institution to institution trying to stitch together enough teaching gigs to equate circumstances somewhat resembling those of a full-time assignment, though they receive anything but a salary approximating that of a regular faculty member. E-mail has greatly added to their ability to keep in touch with students, as it has for instructors of online courses.

Can the ease of e-mail lead to too much interaction? Kathy S. Gresh,[8] an instructional designer at the Bloomberg School of Public Health at Johns Hopkins University, recommended that those who teach online courses should take steps to not let a flood of e-messages inundate them. She suggested, as a first line of defense, that instructors require students to post their queries—if they are not of a personal nature—on an electronic bulletin board so that fellow students could initially attempt to answer each other's questions and spare the instructor this task. (This was the practice in the SUNY course described at the opening of this chapter.) Then, if no one provides a satisfactory answer, a teaching assistant could respond before turning over the most difficult questions to the instructor. An ominous sign in the concern about too much e-mail is the development of a program by EchoMail that, based on certain key words and phrases, can provide boiler-plate answers to e-messages. Online instructors who resort to such software to save time in interacting with students risk undermining the interactivity vital to e-learning.

Creating too much interaction is not the only potential drawback of e-mail between instructors and students. For all of its advantages, electronic communication, of course, ultimately lacks the fullness and serendipity of face-to-face meetings. Frank W. Connolly,[9] a professor at American University in Washington, D.C., was wistful about what he felt students and faculty lost in communicating largely by e-mail. He thought that today's students and younger faculty members, for whom e-mail is and always has been the principal mode of out-of-class communication in higher education, don't even know what they're missing. Connolly longingly recalled the conversation and bonding that he said grew out of the spontaneity and informality of office meetings that used to take place with students. He said: "The teachers asked questions. They offered suggestions. They knew people in their fields and would suggest contacts for summer jobs, internships, full-time employment . . . It doesn't work that way these days. When students send e-mail requests for references now, I must dig out old grade sheets before I can start writing. Our connections are based only on classes and e-mail, of course."

Bulletin Boards and Chat Rooms

The discussions that occur through electronic bulletin boards and chat rooms are vital to online learning, as illustrated by the Abnormal Psychology course described at SUNY. Much of e-learning depends on more than reading the lessons. Instructors use electronic discussions to extend and elaborate on what students have read. Furthermore, students use these electronic devices to collaborate in small groups. Bulletin boards are asynchronous, in that they do not depend on everyone being online at the same time. Students visit bulletin boards at their convenience, usually within a specified period of time. They read what others have written and post responses. The messages are sewn together, incorporating the entries in chronological succession: a threaded discussion. Chat rooms, on the other hand, allow for synchronous discussions, everybody sitting at their computers at the same time, messages flying back and forth in live time.

Terri Hedegaard, a vice president of the Apollo Group, which owns the University of Phoenix, said that the "heart and soul" of the institution's approach to education was always "connecting students to faculty and students to students" for dialogue. She played a key role in creating the University of Phoenix Online in 1976. From the start, she said, the aim was to replicate the dialogue that was a cornerstone of Phoenix's classroom-based learning. "Online technology supported our interactive teaching model, which is dialogue-based and critical to the success of our program," she said. And so it was that bulletin boards figured importantly in online courses at the University of Phoenix. Peter Navarro,[10] a professor of economics and public policy at the University of California at Irvine, told of how he used the electronic bulletin board with his students. He posted several questions each week pertaining to articles appearing in online editions of such publications as *Business Week*. Links from the bulletin board took the students to the articles. He said that the articles usually related to his lecture topics. Students had to post at least two responses per week to the questions, and they could choose to remark on the postings of classmates as well.

Typically, an online instructor posts a discussion question on a virtual bulletin board and directs students, based on their readings, to provide responses by a certain date. Sometimes the whole class engages in one discussion; other times, as mentioned earlier, the class breaks into groups or teams, each with its own separate electronic discussion. Students in the learning group read the accumulating responses and often add comments based on what classmates have written. The instructor may use the various responses to frame a new approach to the topic and, once again, ask students to contribute to the evolving lesson. Contributions to such online discussions are not supposed to be a written version of talk radio. The readings and what classmates say online should inform the threaded discussion, ideally leading to fresh understandings and deeper insights. Online discussions provide an opportunity for reflection on the comments of peers, as well as on one's own comments.

The University of Phoenix Online said that it based its approach on findings showing that online discussions involved a dynamic and extensive sharing of ideas, opinions, and information among students. The university, in an internal document on how e-learning affects students, equated this online dialogue to what might occur in a face-to-face classroom environment. An instructor ends up with a written record that exceeds the product of classroom discussions, which generally have no life beyond the utterance of the words.

The experience of Patricia Cranton as an online instructor at Teachers College, Columbia University, recorded in a personal journal that she kept, bears consideration. The course, Fostering Transformative Learning, was offered in the fall term of the 2001–02 academic year, her first involvement in e-learning as either student or teacher. Let's set the stage. In June, prior to the course, Cranton, who taught the course from Canada, where she was a professor at the University of New Brunswick in Fredericton, got a three-hour overview of the Blackboard platform that delivered the course. She had little opportunity for hands-on practice, making her hope that she could figure out what to do when the course began—a bit of unrequited optimism. After a less-than-smooth dry run in August, when she couldn't seem to log onto Blackboard, she fired off a few e-messages reporting her problem and finally got access. It was a daunting experience, leaving her wondering how she would ever set up discussions for students or have them do group work. Still the optimist, and still August, she began planning the course, creating the first five weeks of lessons to post for students but leaving much of the rest of the work to be done after the course began. She wanted to let the students, once into the course, decide on topics for the remaining lessons.

September 5, the first day of the online course. But how was she to launch it? "I eagerly went to the site, but there was nothing," she wrote in her journal. Slowly, apparitions of students appeared electronically over several days—an e-message here, an item on the discussion board there. Thirteen had signed up for the course, but only six had made online appearances and five of the first postings on the discussion board were from the same guy. Cranton noted to herself: "What is interesting is that the teaching is continuous. Since there is no 'class' per se, there's always class. So I 'teach' this course all day in some way." By the end of the first week in October, she realized how difficult it was to keep track of students when she had no visual images of them. The activities Cranton had assigned for them to perform in small groups were not working out as well as she had hoped. She asked the students why they weren't using the electronic forum more and thought to herself that perhaps they felt threatened discussing ideas in small groups. The discussion board for the whole group discussion was going well. The idea arose for a real-time chat, something different, but Cranton saw complications in that two of the students lived in Japan.

At about this point, Cranton mused on the success she had generally had in face-to-face classes, where she felt she always knew "what happened and why." She thought something was missing in not being able to see the students in her online course. Near the end of October, she felt that a sense of community was developing even though the students never saw each other and she never saw them. The small groups had not worked well enough to sustain them and so she had abandoned that approach. On the other hand, the all-class discussion board had good results despite the fact that some students followed a pattern that alternated between full engagement and no engagement. The students were still trying to schedule a synchronous online meeting, a goal that was important to a number of them.

It was November 6, a Tuesday evening. The long-discussed "live" meeting of the class took place in an electronic chat room, their first virtual gathering in real-time. It occurred via computer screens, omitting the possibility of simultaneously using a voice connection because the equipment of some members of the class would not accommodate voices. There was an electronic discussion of how to foster transformative learning, with attention to appropriate learning styles. Students gave examples from their experiences as learners and as teachers (this was a graduate course and most of the students already worked in classrooms). The messages flew furiously from computer to computer as students' fingers raced across their keyboards to keep up with the chat. Cranton noted that the real-time format did not allow for the longer speeches that some students might have made in an actual classroom, which wasn't an altogether bad thing. This meant to her that no one could very easily dominate the discussion but, on the other hand, the students didn't necessarily present deeper arguments that take time to make.

In looking back on her first experience with online learning, Cranton conceded that she struggled, but enjoyed the process and thought it went well. "I received the most amazing comments from students about how the course changed their lives, and the evaluations of the course were outstanding," she said, gratified by the work. The challenge of facilitating electronic conversations is never far from the minds of most instructors of online courses.

The University of Massachusetts's Pam Whitehouse used AOL's Instant Messaging and an AOL chat room for her women's studies courses. She also offered office hours through a chat room. In addition, she found that the shared learning environment provided by Groove Networks fit the collaborative atmosphere that she tried to create for her courses because it enabled her and her students to review each student's paper together at the web site. The site also allowed Whitehouse's class to brainstorm as a group.

In yet another group activity, using the free portion of Active Worlds, each of Whitehouse's students received an avatar that he or she could move around a virtual town hall during class discussions. Masking their identities with electronic avatars permitted students to engage anonymously in intellectual repartee, asking questions and making comments without restraint.

The anonymity of online interaction can cut two ways. Physical features of people who might be subject to bias in person—based on gender, race, ethnicity, or outward signs of sexual preference—are not apparent, as the experience with the avatars showed. Yet, there is a downside to removing signs of physical difference. Like the default in a computer program, the anonymity introduces a situation in which many participants simply assume that the other party is white and male. Part of learning ordinarily involves the intermingling of students of various backgrounds. Many blacks and Latinos, for instance, bring a particular perspective to a learning task, and it is often beneficial for others to appreciate that perspective for what it represents in that person. So, exchanges devoid of personal identification have their advantages but raise some fundamental questions about the fullness of the interaction.

While bulletin boards and chat rooms facilitate interaction, instructors have no assurance how the discussions will end. Sheila Seifert, who began teaching magazine writing and creative writing at the University of Colorado at Denver in 1998, found in the years afterward that each online course seemed to have its own personality. One semester the students were unusually aggressive, and she felt that they were challenging every word she put online, apparently taking advantage of not having to face her in person. Another semester the students were so chatty that the threaded discussions seemed to go on for miles, the 24/7 environment providing no cutoff to the conversation as the clock does in a classroom. And yet another class bonded so well online that they wanted their discussion to last beyond the course; consequently, they created online critique groups in which they could continue to give feedback to each other after the course concluded.

Online discussions, lacking face-to-face encounters and physical proximity, lead to unpleasantries in some courses. Students and instructors relate instances of outright aggression in which one or two participants, bristling with negativity, intimidate and insult others. Techno-lingo labels such behavior "flaming," and for good reason. The eruption, like a fire on the prairie, quickly spreads anxiety through the course participants. Despite possible abuses, chat rooms and bulletin boards are immeasurably valuable for promoting interaction in online learning.

Video and Audio

Even in the era of e-learning, other forms of distance education continue to prove preferable and appropriate under some circumstances. National Technological University (NTU), for example, never abandoned the use of satellite to deliver courses by television. CD-ROMs also served an important function at NTU even after the advent of web-based learning, and videotapes remained a vital part of the university's delivery system as well. The live, televised broadcasts of classes were taped or put on CD-ROMs so that students could view them at convenient times, thereby making what would otherwise be a synchronous course asynchronous. By 2002, almost two decades after the founding of the university, online learning still accounted for only a minority of the courses taken—a reflection of the needs and desires of the students.

Distance education at Ohio University, as recently as 2002, seemed to have been barely touched by the cyber era. Ohio continued to cling to interactive video and correspondence as the crux of its program while offering only a limited number of online courses. The Ohio University Learning Network, a service that began in 1983, linked the institution's main Athens campus in the foothills of Appalachia with its five regional campuses by television. Courses used microwaves that travel through the air and compressed video that moves on phone lines to connect teachers and instructors. The continuing dependence on video and correspondence by such institutions as Ohio University reminds one that even as online learning proliferates, it does not hold a monopoly on distance education.

Instructors can enhance e-courses with streaming video and streaming audio, as well as videoconferencing to allow students in many different locations to participate in the same class. Cameras and/or microphones mounted on computers can heighten the interaction. Students enjoy the possibility of examining each other's data via these devices and sharing graphics, slides, and spreadsheets while connected by telephone wires. In fact, students these days need not be wired to participate in some aspects of this kind of interaction. Officials at the University of Minnesota at Duluth explored the idea of providing students with hand-held wireless computers. "I think there's a strong interest in mobile computing—mobile in the sense that you can move around more or less anywhere, and you don't have to worry about whether there's some outlet you can plug into," said Linda Deneen, director of information technology systems and services at the campus in Duluth. "And the idea of not having to wire every seat in a large classroom is very appealing."[11]

Even education in the performing and studio arts may benefit from video and teleconferencing, sometimes in combination with computers. Some colleges and universities use these methods to teach students to play the cello, dance ballet, sing lieder, or paint watercolors, for instance. It is the next best thing to student and instructor being in the same room. Instructors give instant feedback and students adjust technique and get quick reappraisals. Video- and audiotapes, CD-ROMs, and DVDs add to the mix and may augment or substitute for online activities.

Videoconferencing could well remain an important technology despite the availability of the web. In the wake of September 11, such an approach looms as a practical alternative to asking people to travel long distances by air in order to attend meetings. Not only does this method save time and money that participants would otherwise spend to gather in person, but it enables them to remain at home locales where they feel secure. It seemed more than appropriate, for instance, in the wake of the fears engendered by the World Trade Center disaster that Internet2, a national group for campus computing officials, abandoned its plan to meet in Austin and held the meeting via videoconference. Also, in the aftermath of the terrorist attack, the New York State Legislature considered a bill to develop a contingency plan to hold its sessions by video-conferencing in case of further attacks. Another offshoot of September 11 was the new-found interest of corporate recruiters in conducting interviews from afar by videoconferences. Videoconferencing for distance learning may grow more prevalent as it becomes a more accepted part of the business world. About 150 Kinko's locations offer videoconferencing facilities, perhaps a harbinger of a business that may figure increasingly in education.

The decidedly low-tech telephone remains a tool of distance education during the cyber age. Dorot, a social service agency assisting primarily the elderly, operated what it called a University Without Walls via telephone conference calls. Hundreds of elderly people around the country had signed up for courses with the New York City–based agency by 2002, paying nominal fees or nothing at all if they could not afford it. Typically, a course met for 50 minutes once a week for 14 weeks, though some were of shorter duration. Much like a business conference call, a course would begin with phone calls to the students to link them to the course. After everyone was on the line, the instructor began the session. Printed materials were sent to students to augment some courses. Another testament to the technological brilliance of Alexander Graham Bell was the Migrant Student Program operated by the University of Texas at Austin. It offered Algebra Across the Wire, a course by telephone hookup to students at five locales. Groups of youngsters, usually eighth- or ninth-graders, gathered in speaker-equipped rooms in parts of the state where their parents had gone to find work in fields and in factories. The Migrant Students Program also used CD-ROM and the Internet to teach other courses.

In many of the best online courses, electronic conversation is an important vehicle of learning. This means not only teacher-to-student conversation, but also student-to-student. E-mail, bulletin boards, and chat rooms serve as proxies for face-to-face contact. Ideally, such discussions allow students to test ideas, share insights, critique each other, and demonstrate the extent to which they grasp the material. E-mail puts students in touch with instructors despite the geographic distances that separate them. In many ways, conferences by e-mail place students in online courses on a par with their classroom-based peers, who may also initiate most of their contact with instructors by e-mail. Online learning has not displaced previous forms of distance education despite its quick ascent in the academic world. Educators continue to finds uses for video, audio, CD-ROMs, and even correspondence in reaching students from afar.

CHAPTER 5

ADAPTING TO THE NEW

A classroom of one requires that a student gain comfort and facility with technology. This is not so rigorous an expectation to place on people, especially those of high school and college age. Computers, cell phones, fax machines, and other artifacts of the latest technology have surrounded them since infancy. Information technology and computer gadgetry are as natural to them as eating and sleeping. They find it perfectly reasonable that sometimes you can't reserve an airline seat or buy a concert ticket because "the system is down." They have no memories of Underwoods or Royals; the keyboards with which they are familiar accompany computers. Their earliest toys contained chips to make dogs bark and dolls talk, and they are no more intimidated by technology than they are by an automatic teller machine or a VCR that needs programming.

Their music has always traveled with them and they think it ridiculous to fetter themselves to a telephone by a wire. They are plugged-in 24/7, never craving silence, never wishing to be far from the glow of the screen of a television set, the voice on the other end of a cell phone, or a computer—miniaturized or full-sized. They even attend virtual college fairs, no longer visiting in person all of the campuses that interest them, but browsing electronic exhibit booths at college web sites to gather the information that they need to make choices and then to submit applications online. They arrive on campuses across the country with their own computers, toting other accouterments of the cyber age—cell phones, graphing calculators, DVD players, MP3 files, and perhaps Palm organizers, as well. Remember: most young people getting their bachelor's degrees in 2003 were born in the same year as IBM's first personal computer.

Connected, connected, connected. They wonder why older Americans care about the rules of spelling when spell check can address those concerns. They seldom crack the pages of such tomes as the *Encyclopaedia Britannica* or *World Book* when they have only to go on the Internet to find what they want to know, not worrying about its veracity. They glance at news reports online, eschewing newspapers and obtaining the smattering of current events that sate their curiosity. The possibility of adapting to an online course does not faze them. "They come to college with an understanding of the tools of technology," said Bruce Chaloux, director of the Electronic Campus of the Southern Regional Education Board. "They bank this way; they shop this way; they learn this way. When this group floods higher education, you will see signs of change."

When it comes right down to it, many people of all ages today, not just those in their teens and their twenties, spend considerable amounts of time in the solitary pursuit of information or entertainment, with and without technological assistance. Some of them may not be fully at ease in the cyber age, but the very idea of learning on their own, a predisposition that makes it easier to adapt to online education, is not an alien concept to most of them. Even reading newspapers, magazines, and books prepares people for learning alone, as does watching television and films, and listening to music. A growing number of Americans of all ages send and receive e-mail daily, and one in five has access to the Internet. The country has more than 136 million cell phones. It would hardly be a stretch to use technology to take a course on the web. The biggest adjustment, perhaps, would be to acknowledge the legitimacy of the classroom of one—that bona fide learning can occur despite the absence of classmates, despite not walking into a campus building to take the course.

Students who already learn online defy categorization. What they share is a desire to make education more convenient. At Rio Salado College of the Maricopa Community College District in Arizona, for

instance, Keith Anderson, a faculty member in the English department, estimated that 60 percent of the online students were mothers,
many of them home-bound with children when they are not at jobs.
"They have little time to commute and to find parking and get into
the rigamarole of a campus," he said. At the University of Colorado at
Denver, Diana Wheat, who taught a basic biology course in which she
put the lectures online, had the chance to meet one of the students in
person. He told her how grateful he was for the course. He was a fire-
fighter, who worked a staggered shift, four straight days on and four
straight days off. Regular attendance at classroom lectures was impossible for him. He said that without online courses he could not have
pursued a bachelor's degree.

Elsewhere, Arna Clark lauded online learning for its flexibility. She
had graduated from the University of Utah and was working toward a
master's degree in learning and technology at Western Governors University, an online institution. Clark lived in a suburb of Salt Lake City
and was able to adapt her schedule as an English teacher in a public
school to the demands of online graduate study. A measure of students'
adaptability to online learning is the persistence they show. At the University of Baltimore, students in the online M.B.A. program that began
in 1999 remained enrolled at rates equal to those in the classroom-based
program, according to officials.

HOW ELEMENTARY AND
SECONDARY STUDENTS ADAPT

The inclination of young people to make a smooth transition to online
learning may have contributed to the quick start-up of online precollegiate programs in states across the country. Indications are that many
more students in elementary and secondary schools would take courses
online if supporters promoted the concept and more spaces were available to enroll. This is a market waiting to be tapped. William J. Bennett,
a former Secretary of the U.S. Department of Education, recognized
this opportunity and took a lead role in trying to entice younger pupils
online. His program, K12 Inc., was designed especially to help parents

in home schooling their children, as well as to supplement the education of those who attend regular schools.

K12 was online by the beginning of 2002 with curriculum material for children of kindergarten, first-grade, and second-grade ages, with the next three grades to follow in September 2002 and, presumably, curriculum for the upper grades in the ensuing years. In marketing its curriculum to families, K12, Inc., said that parents could customize the learning of their children and chart their progress, and it stressed that with a significant portion of the curriculum delivered on the web, the program provided access to tools that made it easier to plan lessons. The company intended to market its online curriculum directly to parents and to establish cyber charter schools in various states, providing another vehicle by which to reach home-schooling families and others to whom the curriculum and its special features appealed.

The first two such schools were Pennsylvania Virtual Charter School and Colorado Virtual Academy. K12's Pennsylvania school claimed an enrollment of 633 by the spring of 2002 and expected an additional 850 students in the fall, when three more grades would be added. It said that 41 percent of its students were from families poor enough to qualify for free or reduced lunch (which, of course, the school didn't provide), and that many of those youngsters lived in rural poverty.

The web's attraction extends beyond home schoolers. Adolescents are notorious for their late-to-bed and late-to-rise habits that make it difficult to get up for school in the morning. After-school employment causes many of them to work into the night and do homework (if they do it) afterward, exacerbating the problem. They do not want to harness themselves to society's clock. Some secondary students need more time, some less, than the regular schedule allows to make their way through a course. At least some online courses may appeal to high school youngsters in these circumstances.

Florida Virtual School recognized these vagaries and scheduled courses accordingly. Students indicated upon enrolling in each course whether they wanted to pursue the work on a traditional schedule, an accelerated schedule, or an extended schedule. Those choosing the second or third option could take less or more than the usual time to complete a course. The school said that it required students to obtain the permission of parents or school counselors to pursue the extended schedule, which added several months to the time allotted for the completion of the course. The executive director of the Florida school readily conceded that online studies were not appropriate for all youngsters. Her simple three-part test for potential students to administer to themselves called for them to ask whether they could manage time, summon up motivation, and work without a teacher in the room.

The ability of young students to adapt to virtual classrooms could be seen at the Daniel Jenkins Academy of Technology, a combination middle school and high school near the center of the Florida peninsula, a rural portion of the state between Tampa and Orlando. After proceeding through a classroom-based middle school program rich in a curriculum infused with technology, students continued into a high school at the same site in which the main subjects were offered online through Florida Virtual School. Four out of five days a week they attended a high school in which there were no teachers teaching courses; they did not have to bother showing up on the fifth day. Though no actual courses were taught in the classrooms during the four days they attended school, students had to go to the building because state regulations generated per pupil funding based on their attendance.

"If it were up to me," said Sue Braiman, principal of the combined school, "I would ask them how many days they want to come to school and leave it at that, but Florida has a funding mechanism tied to the time students spend sitting in seats, not to learning objectives. It's absurd." But so long as they had to attend school, even though they did not have to pursue their studies while there, the school promoted their socialization. These were young people who were not apt to feel isolated just because they accessed their courses online. Despite taking no classes in the building, the students had a student government, proms, and other activities. Furthermore, their presence in the building was considered a boon for the middle school students, as the older youngsters served as role models and mentored the younger ones.

Students spent some of their time while in the school building helping the middle school students solve the mysteries of technology. They devoted as much or as little time as they wished to their online courses at computers during the normal school day. Many waited until the official school day ended before going online to pursue their studies at home. Those who wanted to enroll in gym, art, music, or other electives attended a nearby brick-and-mortar high school for those electives. If they decided not to enroll in the electives, that was okay, too.

Originally, only a middle school had stood on the site in Haines City occupied by Jenkins Academy. The old middle school was closed for a year of renovation in the late 1990s, after its facility showed signs of serious deterioration. Officials promised local residents that the school would reopen as a charter school, housing both a middle school and a high school. But a funny thing happened on the way to completing the renovation—some parts of the building were beyond repair and had to be razed. Left with only 13 classrooms on the site, education officials in Polk County pondered how to fulfill their promise to the taxpayers. There was no way that two schools—a middle school and a high school—could fit into what remained of the original plant.

Then, someone had a brainstorm. Since the middle school was devoted so extensively to technology as a tool of education, the students obviously felt comfortable working on the Internet by the time they entered high school. As there were not enough classrooms to accommodate them on site, why not let them attend Florida Virtual School? The school gave high school students laptop computers to take home and told them that none of their courses would be taught in the building. It was an adaptation on a scale that few high school students have ever had to make. The first group of high schoolers, distributed among all four grades, embarked on this grand adventure in the fall of 2000. When four students were finally graduated from Daniel Jenkins Academy, they all headed off to college, one with a scholarship to Georgia Tech's nuclear physics program, according to Jenkins officials.

CHALLENGES IN ADAPTING TO ONLINE LEARNING

The success of online education depends on more than getting learners of all ages to change their attitudes and behaviors. If the content of the courses is unsatisfactory, e-learning will lose potential adherents no matter how many people turn on, plug in, dial up, or use some other means of access to learn outside the formal classroom. Some of those who drop out of online courses have not adapted, though this may be through no fault of their own. It can happen when courses bore students, faulty technology overwhelms the course, or instructors do not interact responsibly with students. But students may also abandon online courses, however valuable the content, however effective the technical design, and however competent the instructor. They may simply discover that this mode of education does not suit them. How does having to adapt themselves to online learning affect students' achievement? Are they satisfied with the experience? Do they have to alter their learning styles? Are there yet further ways in which students must adapt to online learning?

Achievement

A basic question, one not fully answered, has to do with the extent to which online courses promote learning. Can students adapt successfully to this mode of instruction? Some insist that the question is whether e-learning leads students to achieve at higher levels than they would in a classroom. Why should this be necessary? It ought to be enough if students learn just as much on a computer on their own as they do in a classroom with others. The Graduate School of Library and Information Science at the University of Illinois had as its stated policy for students getting their master's degrees online that the courses "be comparable in quality to those taught on campus" and that online students "should have the opportunity to gain the same knowledge, skills, and sense of professionalism." The school reported a 95 percent retention rate.

Proponents of distance education, including online learning, have been so focused on the question of whether the process leads to the same achievement levels as classroom-based instruction that they even had a web site—"no significant difference"—dedicated to the issue. The site contained hundreds of research reports, summaries, and papers on the topic, organized year by year. A companion web site—significant difference—was later established to make available studies that found that e-learning and classroom-based education do not have the same outcomes. Such evidence continues to accumulate as online learning grows more widespread and researchers try to determine its impact.

Rio Salado College's Keith Anderson had taught composition courses online and in person. He did not believe that learning was sacrificed in the online version of the course. He said that assessments of the writing of online students yielded results comparable to those of students who took the course in the classroom. "The quality depends on the personnel involved," Anderson said. "The classroom is not innately superior." Perhaps there is nothing inherent in online learning that makes it better or worse than classroom-based instruction. Much of the impact on student achievement may depend on the implementation of the courses—the quality of the content, the manner of presentation, the value of the interaction—not unlike education in a classroom, which certainly varies in the performance outcomes it produces for students.

A review of findings on student achievement by one group of researchers concluded that there were no significant differences in achievement among students taught through various delivery systems. The authors of the study decided "that distant and local learners will achieve at the same level, and that distance education is an effective method for delivering instruction that works."[1] Elsewhere in their book, the authors offered the following summary statements that, they said, were supported by the literature: distance education has as effective outcomes as traditional education; distance learners generally have a more favorable attitude; interaction should not be added to distance education without real purpose.[2]

Given the multitude of studies showing no significant difference between learning online and in the classroom, a research study on student outcomes in sections of a microeconomics course at Michigan State University attracted considerable attention in early 2002 when it found that students fared significantly better on tests if they took the course in the classroom. "The results strongly suggest that the virtual course represents an inferior technology compared to the live sections," the study said.[3] In addition, students in the online section reported investing less effort in the course, which might have accounted for their lower achievement. At the end of the course, 51 percent of the e-learners said that they ordinarily spent less than three hours a week on the course and none claimed to devote more than seven hours a week to it. Meanwhile, students who took the course in a classroom attended at an 80 percent rate throughout the term, with 52 percent of them not missing a class, which in itself meant giving the course at least three hours a week before doing the homework. The researchers concluded that differences in test scores were most pronounced (with students in the virtual section scoring lower) for exam questions that tapped the students' ability to apply basic concepts in more sophisticated ways. The bottom-line conclusion was this: "Choosing a completely online course carries a penalty that would need to be offset by significant advantages in convenience or other factors important to the student."[4]

When it comes to achievement, one must also consider the extent to which the web environment itself has an effect. The traditional classroom is a known and familiar setting. Students understand how such classrooms operate, and whenever they enter a new classroom, they usually quickly recognize the mores and expectations. They know, for instance, just how much work they must perform to get by, the extent to which they must complete homework, when to talk and when to remain silent, and how to get in the instructor's good graces. Their achievement levels tend to be a function of how they fit together the pieces of this puzzle. Online learning presents an altogether different context, though some characteristics overlap. Achievement in this setting depends on the ability of students to adapt to what begins as an unfamiliar situation for many of them.

Satisfaction

Educators paid little attention to student satisfaction in their classrooms until college students of a generation ago began rating their professors. Sometimes students published these ratings, and professors and institutions were forced to take notice. Satisfaction tends to be a fuzzy and imprecise measure of courses and/or instructors. Clearly, though, students who are consistently dissatisfied are apt to get the word out on a course or an instructor through ratings and by word of mouth. The reputations of courses and professors are well known on campus.

Among research findings are some indicating that interaction between students and instructors tends to increase satisfaction with online learning. The more satisfied that students are in online courses, the more apt they are to think they have learned something, whether or not they actually have. The discussions that students have online and the feedback they receive tend to lead to positive feelings about courses and, apparently, make them feel that they learned more than if they were left to pursue e-learning without this kind of interaction. Students also seem to like it if online discussions count significantly toward their course grades. Such findings do not seem to support the idea of offering online courses that consist of little more than having students do their work in isolation, without interaction, no matter how rich the course materials.[5] Not surprisingly, students are less satisfied when technical difficulties and poor course design complicate their work on the computer and interfere with their online studies.

Satisfaction with almost all aspects of online learning was high among students who responded to a survey of those enrolled in 30 courses of Penn State's World Campus during the spring of 2001. World Campus was an entirely online program, and fully half of the enrollees said that without the program they would have been unable to pursue their education. These were adults, equally divided between males and females, and almost all, presumably, caught up in the daily demands of work and family. More than 80 percent were from 25 to 54 years old. Four out of five students rated the course they had just taken as excellent or above average, a finding reinforced by the fact that a virtually identical portion said they would recommend the course to others. A whopping 85 percent said that they were likely to take another World Campus course. Only 7.7 percent considered their course below average or poor, and only 9.7 percent felt negatively about recommending the course.[6]

The reasons for the high levels of satisfaction with e-learning could be seen in the responses to other questions in the survey of World Campus students. Eighty-eight percent said that the course would help them meet their education objectives, and 87 percent said both that it would help them meet other professional objectives and that they were satisfied or very satisfied with the new knowledge and information they had gained. More than 80 percent said that what they learned in the course would make them more effective in their work setting, and about the same portion were satisfied or very satisfied with what they had learned about analyzing and solving problems. Students' favorable responses to the interaction that the course fostered with peers and with the instructor bolstered these high satisfaction levels, as did their satisfaction with the technical support that they received. In general, students who adapt themselves to e-learning argue that it breeds satisfaction because it offers more convenience than classrooms in terms of time and place. One can only speculate as to whether these feelings prevail also because online courses are easier and higher marks more attainable.

As for the faculty, the questions of their satisfaction with teaching online courses are also pertinent. During 1999–2000, the second year of Penn State's World Campus, 15 faculty members who had taught e-courses were surveyed. Fourteen of them indicated that, overall, they were satisfied with their involvement in World Campus. They cited such factors as increased access to students, increased knowledge and experience with educational technologies, increased opportunities for interaction with students, and positive student outcomes.[7] Other studies show that faculty who teach online courses are more satisfied if they think their students are satisfied and prospering in the courses, especially if the students do better or at least as well as they were apt to do in a classroom.[8]

Learning Styles

Most students hardly think about their style of learning, but when pressed and asked to reflect on it, they can probably identify the factors that facilitate or impede their learning. Online courses demand adaptation simply because the approach differs from the familiar. When computers became widely available in classrooms, proponents hailed the potential for individualizing instruction. This is no less true of online learning, though one would hope that online learning exceeds the unfulfilled promise for individualization of classroom computers. Instructors can use streaming audio, streaming video, graphics, animation, volume, voice recognition, and text size to satisfy various learning styles, and students control pacing to meet their individual needs. Time and place fade in significance, allowing students the time they require to complete the work at their own speed, within reasonable parameters.

Jennifer Hardy recognized that she was a visual learner who fared best with one-on-one interaction. Online courses claim to offer interaction of an electronic nature, but Hardy discovered that making contact this way did not satisfy her. A 22-year-old psychology major at the University of Colorado at Denver, she found it more difficult to learn without the actual interaction of a classroom. Also, the timing of synchronous discussions in chat rooms was not always convenient to her full-time job as a claims adjuster with State Farm Insurance. Her course in behavioral genetics was the second she had taken online. Simultaneously, she was enrolled in several classroom-based courses. The temptation, she said, was to put off the work for the online course and concentrate, first, on completing assignments for courses that met in person. She had to prod herself to avoid falling behind in the online course. Ultimately she adjusted, a process helped by an instructor who generally made himself accessible online to answer questions and clear up confusion.

While researchers have much to learn about how online learning meshes with learning styles, one study on this question found that students with sequential learning styles, that is those who organize information in a linear fashion, showed more preference for online education than did other kinds of learners.[9] This study, however, involved only 40 freshmen in economics. There are some less obvious ways in which e-learning affects learning style. One professor found that online students were more apt to engage in recursive reading, going back to reread sources they had studied earlier. This, he said, was because they could conveniently return to these readings on the course web site and did not have to ferret out the books again in a library.[10] On a less favorable note, they do not experience the serendipity and sense of discovery that can accompany time spent in the stacks.

The evidence does not persuade all researchers of the fruitfulness of trying to match learning styles to teaching styles. Lenna Ojure and Tom Sherman argued that researchers need to know more about what teachers do to mesh instruction with learning styles and with what results.

The benefits may not be so obvious as proponents think. The researchers said that teachers want to believe in a connection between learning styles and teaching styles and that they attend many workshops on the topic.[11] If such a link exists, then surely e-learning is positioned to take advantage of it—or, perhaps, to dissuade some candidates from enrolling in online courses on the grounds that this mode of education will not match their learning styles.

Another aspect of learning styles has to do with differences between males and females. While some people hail online education for injecting an anonymity that melts away some of the variations in treatment between the genders, a report from the American Association of University Women said that online learning can burden some women who already have to attend to family and home after working all day. The report, "The Third Shift: Women Learning Online," said that online education adds another shift to the schedule of females who still must meet the demands of the other two shifts—home and job. Many of the women surveyed were anxious about their ability to fulfill other obligations if they assumed the responsibilities of studying, conducting research, and writing papers for online courses, which compete for a limited amount of unscheduled time. The report noted, though, that women appreciated the flexibility of online learning, the money they could save in not having to commute or pay for child care, and the chance to more readily fulfill personal goals.[12]

Other Considerations

Students in online courses appear to have more staying power than those in the earlier form of dominant distance education, correspondence. Michael Lambert, executive director of the Distance Education and Training Council, estimated that, historically, 15 percent of students who enrolled in correspondence courses never even bothered turning in a first assignment. He said that about 35 percent of correspondence students completed the typical course for which they enrolled. Lambert was on the council staff for 30 years, becoming director in 1992. From what he saw of the organization's member institutions after the advent of e-learning, Lambert considered it rather unusual for a student to enroll in an online course and not at least begin submitting assignments. Moreover, he estimated that 55 to 60 percent completed the typical online course.

Online learning extends great independence to students, requiring them to have motivation and to summon up more self-discipline than the usual classroom course demands. Some students quickly find themselves struggling to stay above the surface in a body of water in which they thought they would be able to stand. It should come as no surprise that a number of them figuratively go under, becoming dropouts. Technology, when it goes awry, exacerbates the problem, creating disincentives that courses in classrooms can avoid. Computer quirks can exasperate students and drive them away from courses.

Flaws in the program itself, not the learner's shortcomings, may prevent still other students from adapting to e-learning. Gary Natriello, a professor at Teachers College, Columbia University, and editor of *Teachers College Record*, wrote an article about his sons' dismal experience in a distance-learning course.[13] The family wanted to give them, a third-grader and a sixth-grader, a boost in mathematics. The youngsters received a CD-ROM containing a placement examination to help them find the right levels at which to start their work. Then, based on the results of the test, the programs provided materials with lectures and exercises to do on the computer that, once completed, they were to e-mail to their tutors, who were to mark the answers and e-mail back comments and suggestions.

The program had hired university students and recent graduates as tutors, who it turned out gave up the tutoring jobs as quickly as one can log off a computer. Every few months the Natriello boys had new tutors, a development that diminished their allegiance to the program. "What was striking," Natriello said, "was how my sons came to pay less and less attention to the advice of their tutors each time a new tutor came on the scene. I think they were very disappointed when the first tutors said goodbye online and so decided to withhold their full attention from subsequent tutors." It did not help that it took 24 hours to get responses from the tutors, a period of time that the boys took to be a mark of unresponsiveness. The parents found that the only way to sustain the boys' attention was for them, the parents, to get more involved in tutoring them. "A process might be 99 percent fine," Natriello said in retrospect, "but that 1 percent of the time when it is not fine undermines the credibility of the effort. The online environment is very unforgiving. We have a much greater margin for error in classroom-based teaching because we are there to recover when we sense a mistake."

As the home tutoring advanced, the Natriello family found that, despite the generally high quality of the program, some material in the lessons sent by the online provider was wrong or incomplete. This was a discovery made after long sessions during which the entire family tried to figure out why answers did not compute. Gradually, the two youngsters lost their will to work on the program despite the willingness of their parents to continue to help them. "One evening after spending a long time trying to understand the answer the program was expecting only to discover another flaw, we decided that, like our children, we, too, were losing the motivation to continue," Gary Natriello said. That was the beginning of the end as the boys used the program less, finally dropping out. The experience underscored the difficulty that students, particularly younger ones, may have in adapting to online learning when they perceive a lack of consistency at the other end of the e-mail and when confidence in the program grows shaky.

ADAPTATIONS BY THE FACULTY

While online learning calls for obvious adaptations on the part of students, it also requires much the same of faculty, almost all of whom have spent their careers—whether consisting of 3 years or 30 years—meeting with groups of students in classrooms. Teachers face pressures that are no less complex than those confronting students. They complain of having to make extensive adaptations in their teaching. They have to learn how to motivate students in an online environment. They have to spend large amounts of time responding to e-messages and to points raised in online discussions, and in total often feel that such courses demand more of their time than teaching in a classroom.

Nonetheless, some faculty members make an easy transition to this mode of instruction. Sheila Seifert, a teacher at the University of

Colorado at Denver, found that her adjustment to e-learning was
largely uneventful. The biggest change, she said, was that she had to
type out her entire lectures to put them online and could not merely
deliver them from notes, as she might in a classroom-based course.
The flexibility of teaching online satisfied her, making it possible for
the course to continue uninterrupted regardless of her circumstances
on a given day and whether or not she felt like leaving home and
going to class. She felt that e-learning made her available to interact
with students to a greater degree than she did on campus.

Helping Online Instructors Adapt

Commercial software that helps create content, manage courses, and
carry out interactive activities eases the transition to e-learning for faculty members. Matthew Pittinsky, chairman of the board and cofounder
of Blackboard, said that his company's software allows the teacher of an
online course to emulate the live classroom and, in some ways, to sur-
pass it. "The traditional course meets a couple times a week and then the
classroom fades away and it's hard to logically connect everything," he
said. "We create a 24/7 learning environment, a third dimension. The
interaction is totally virtual; it's the grass roots." Presumably, with this
kind of assistance, a teacher may have even more involvement with students than in a real classroom. Whether online learning always fulfills
this idealistic vision is another matter.

At Stanford University, the Learning Lab, established in 1997, acted
as a research and development unit, trying to ensure that e-learning solutions would have wide application across the campus. The focus was
on using technology to enhance classroom-based courses, but the
Learning Lab's approach would suit purely online courses as well. The
Learning Lab sought to build a knowledge base and infrastructure to
help faculty, teaching assistants, and students to create their own web-
based content. Stanford constructed six experimental classrooms in
2002 in which to observe and measure the impact of technology on day-
to-day instruction. The university expected to hold 15 to 30 courses per
quarter in the specially equipped classrooms and will encourage faculty
to visit and observe courses in these rooms, hoping to entice them to

shift from lecturing to hands-on and peer-to-peer learning through web-supported exercises and online discussions.

Educational institutions that want to put programs online owe teachers the chance to undergo professional development. Then, the institution should provide them with technical support, both in the development of courses and as a service during courses. In Maryland, 23 colleges and universities banded together as the Faculty Online Technology Training Consortium to prepare faculty for the transition to online instruction. Baltimore City Community College (BCCC), a member of the consortium, sent two people for the summer training— Diana Zilberman, who taught English, and Carolyn Dabirsiaghi, who taught biology. They, in turn, trained their colleagues at BCCC. The experience of the two women was probably typical of what happens when institutions offer special preparation to faculty members who want to teach online courses. Said Zilberman: "We learned mostly about the pedagogy of online learning, setting up courses, communicating online, integrating interactivity, technical support, assessment strategies, and such. We took notes and had the opportunity to discuss various aspects of distance learning. We had a chance to connect and share stories with faculty from other colleges in our state, which is a rare opportunity. We stayed in touch and found that we gained a network of support. For example, since no math faculty showed any desire to design an online course at BCCC, we called on a technology fellow from another college whom we knew to be a math professor. He came and presented his course to our math faculty, and he successfully swayed a few."

Zilberman wrote an online course in which faculty at BCCC and other participating institutions could enroll, the idea being that it would give faculty members the experience of being online students before they attempted to function as online instructors. They took the equivalent of a three-credit graduate-level course with three two-hour, face-to-face sessions scheduled monthly, in addition to the instruction they got online. Zilberman believed that time, training, and technical support were essential prerequisites to online courses of high standards. She thought that not all faculty members were ready to accept a challenge of this magnitude. "Even to start thinking of teaching online, one needs a high confidence level," she said.

The Center for Educational Technologies at the University of Illinois provided faculty with support for online programs, though some parts of the institution—the College of Engineering, for instance—had their own separate support resources. The center grew out of the Sloan Center for Asynchronous Learning Environments (SCALE), one of a number of such endeavors established at Vanderbilt, Berkeley, the State University of New York, and elsewhere around the country in the 1990s by the Alfred P. Sloan Foundation. Many campus-based courses at Illinois used the web to supplement classroom instruction, and the center helped faculty members prepare materials to put online. There was even an experiment employing streaming media online to replace large lectures. Pressure for space in the science laboratories at Illinois led to putting online some of the preparatory studies for freshmen and sophomores that might otherwise have consumed scarce lab space.

Learning the Steps to a New Dance

Gary Bedore Sr. formed Socrates Distance Learning Technologies Group in 1996 to help organizations understand how to use technology as a communications medium in educating students. Bedore was a pioneer in online learning at such places as the University of Phoenix and the UCLA extension division, and the program he created ended up training hundreds of online learning instructors. Education Management Corporation acquired Socrates in 1998 to use as the basis for training its own facilitators—the institution's title for course leaders—for the new Art Institute Online that it had established. Once it converted Socrates to its own purposes, Art Institute Online required its facilitators to complete a six-week, web-based training course unless they already had extensive experience in e-learning. The training, in effect, modeled the teaching—just as the program in Maryland tried to do—and a mentor monitored each facilitator in training. Of course, it didn't matter where prospective facilitators lived, just as long as a computer and an Internet connection were available to them for the course, as would be the case with the students they would teach.

Art Institute Online set out to sell its Socrates training to other organizations. This effort began with two courses. Introduction to Online

Education was designed expressly for organizations with little or no experience in web-based instruction, providing a primer in how to develop, implement, and support an online program. The other course, Online Facilitator Training, was for new e-learning instructors such as those at Art Institute. Each of the six weeks of Online Facilitator Training had a different focus: Week 1, An Overview; Week 2, Creating a Learning Community; Week 3, Facilitating Learning Through Discussion; Week 4, The Role of Feedback in Facilitating Learning; Week 5, Developing Instructional Strategies; and Week 6, Administrative Issues and Procedures.

During the fourth week of the course, for instance, the future facilitators learned about the importance of electronic feedback in a teaching environment without face-to-face contact. The opening lesson told them that online feedback could have an advantage over in-person contact in that students must write to communicate online, and that this process more readily exposes strengths and weaknesses in analysis and critical thinking. During the week, the prospective facilitators received lessons in promoting a productive relationship with students, fostering learning, and assessing performance. Some of them had taught in classrooms, but Art Institute Online expected the future facilitators to recast their experiences to deal with online education. Like the students they would eventually lead, the novice facilitators had to complete readings and assignments each step of the way. They also had to participate, sometimes several times a day, in threaded discussions intended to get them to focus on ideas—their own, those of fellow students, and those of the course facilitator. There were short written assignments and essays to turn in electronically, joint projects to pursue in teams with other students, and tests to take.

A typical written assignment, for instance, might call for identifying and discussing methods for providing effective feedback to students, or the techniques for successful group and team activities, or the role of the facilitator at different points in the online learning process. Their entries in the threaded discussion illustrated both the advantages and disadvantages of education that depends on interacting solely online in the absence of face-to-face contact. Some entries in the threaded discussion by the facilitators-in-training lent no insight or illumination to the learning process, as might well be the case with courses they would teach. "Very good idea." "Thanks for sharing this." "Students can offer great ideas." There seemed to be a compulsion among online learners to use brief messages to cheer each other, slogans to keep them attached to people they could not see. This may be what happens when people are unable to reaffirm their presence and participation by the nod of a head, a smile, or just being there. This is not to say that electronic discussions in this course or other online courses necessarily lack substance, but the mundane comments—sometimes providing needed reinforcement for the learner—figure more prominently than they probably do in the real classroom.

The type of assistance that Socrates offered those who would preside over online courses is essential for the acceptance and success of e-learning. It is wrong-minded to assume those who have taught in traditional classrooms will automatically be able to do the same in the virtual classroom. This kind of education requires instructors to learn the steps to a new dance. The majority of faculty want someone to help them gain this facility, according to the senior technology officers at 590 colleges and universities, who identified this need as "the single most important IT issue confronting their campuses."[14] Whether the goal is to put entire courses online or to provide Web-based support for classroom courses, successful change of this nature seems to depend on faculty recognizing value in e-learning and adapting their course design and pedagogy to make use of it.

CHAPTER 6

RESPONSIBILITY FOR LEARNING

The experiences of youngsters at the online high school that is part of Daniel Jenkins Academy of Technology in Florida offer a case study of the degree to which students are equipped to take on the responsibility of learning online. When it admitted its first class in the fall of 2000, all 50 applicants were accepted without any attempt to sort out those whom the school considered the most promising candidates for e-learning. The district, Polk County Public Schools, had been under court-ordered desegregation for some 30 years and thought it could not screen applicants as that might smack of racial discrimination. But, in avoiding screening because of race, they were unable to screen for other aspects of students' backgrounds, with the result that online learning was unsuitable for some students admitted to the program. Only 34 of the students remained in the school by the end of the academic year; the rest having transferred to the school system's traditional high schools.

Principal Sue Braiman said that the school lost students who could not cope with taking six online courses at once. Others just weren't accustomed to working without close supervision. "We told them they would have to take responsibility for their own education and that was a huge leap," Braiman said. "They were used to teachers bringing learning to them." While the high school had none of its own teachers teaching the courses offered at the web site, two teachers at Jenkins served as facilitators, leaving it to the students to take much of the responsibility for their learning. Essentially, the job of facilitator was nonacademic, normally not involving tutoring students. Instead, a facilitator guided students in setting learning goals for themselves and in managing their time.

In 2001, after the high school had existed for a year, almost all of the students completing the middle school level at Jenkins Academy decided to enroll in the virtual high school, which had its headquarters in the building. Students entering ninth grade liked what they had seen and wanted to be part of the grand experiment. The online school, trying not to leave as much to chance as it had the previous year, decided to prepare students when they were still in the eighth grade for the possibility of their continuing into the virtual high school. The goal was to equip them to resist the seductions that accompany independent learning, kind of like Odysseus lashing himself to the ship's mast and plugging the ears of the crew to fend off the alluring but dangerous call of the Sirens. Thus, their teachers had encouraged the eighth graders, one year away from online learning, to handle autonomy. This is no small matter for adolescents, youngsters at an age known for its turbulence. A buddy system paired middle school students with high school students who could share their experiences as virtual learners and show the middle schoolers the online course work at the high school level.

Many courses in Florida Virtual School had an interdisciplinary flavor, and Jenkins sought to prepare students for this approach by organizing more of the middle school courses along interdisciplinary lines. Project-based learning figured strongly in the virtual school and this, too, was replicated in the middle school courses. Teachers encouraged students to set goals and taught them to pace themselves, just as they would have to do once they no longer sat in classrooms with teachers to urge them on in person. The middle school students were also introduced to an option that Florida Virtual School offered its students— submitting work for a review and not for a grade. Teachers would then return the work with corrections and suggestions and expect students to go through as many as four revisions, helping them, ultimately, to strive for higher quality work when it was ready for a grade. "We started weaning them from needing so much help from the teacher," said Braiman. "It was great to see kids make an investment in their learning instead of passively waiting for a teacher to tell them what to do."

Some institutions try to help students determine if they can exercise the responsibility that distance learning demands. San Diego State University provided online guidance for students who contemplated enrolling in distance courses. Students could scroll through pages that allowed them to evaluate themselves as potential students in the program, visiting web pages with such titles as "Are Distance Learning Courses for Me?," "The Online Learning.net Self-Assessment Quiz," "Are You Ready to Take an Online Course?," and "How Do I Learn Best?" A self-administered quiz asked candidates to answer the following questions so that they could assess their readiness:

- Do I like working and learning on a computer or television?
- Am I comfortable resolving technology problems when they arise?
- Would I want to learn new software, or a set of online procedures, just to access the course materials or to chat with the faculty and others who are taking the course?
- Do I work well alone?
- Am I self-disciplined enough to follow the lessons on my own without peer pressure or pressure from the course instructor?
- Will I be comfortable if I don't get to see the instructor in person?
- Will I be comfortable if I have to ask questions via e-mail?[1]

Macomb Community College in Warren, Michigan, also offered prospective e-students an online self-assessment questionnaire, in this case calling for multiple-choice responses to ten questions. The questions allowed them to gauge their need for the course, their comfort with taking responsibility for their learning, whether they could complete tasks on time without reminders, their facility in written communications, their ease in figuring out directions, the importance of feedback from the instructor, whether they found word processing on a home computer easy and fun, their receptiveness to using technology, their facility as readers, and the ease with which they could find a time and place for studying.

The flexibility of online learning is motivation enough for some students. Katrin Tabellion, for instance, found that the University of Missouri's virtual high school met her needs because her father's job kept the family relocating around the world. "I wanted to get my high school diploma," she said in an interview by e-mail from Ghana, her residence at the time, "but since I was moving quite often I got the idea of a long distance course. I just looked up some schools on the Internet and the University of Missouri was most appealing to me. The biggest advantage is that you can choose the time to study or to take your exams. You don't have to be at one place at a certain time. You can do it from anywhere you like." She conceded that despite these incentives "it is also hard sometimes to make yourself sit down and study. It is easy to say, 'Oh, I'll just wait until tomorrow.'"

TRUST

What can be done about students with less motivation than Katrin Tabellion, those who cannot or will not take responsibility for their own learning? The formal classroom, in part, is predicated on the assumption that many students lack initiative: someone needs to prod them. A teacher must watch over them and shield them from distraction. The idea is that sitting in a classroom will prevent them from doing something else during time assigned for their learning. Classroom teachers usually take attendance to ensure that students do not cut classes. For the most part, a lack of trust pervades the traditional system.

A system of Carnegie units evolved for secondary school students to provide a kind of guarantee that high schools would expose them to a certain regimen of courses. Carnegie units represent seat time. The Carnegie unit, which helped put education on a solid footing in the early decades of the twentieth century, transformed itself by the final decades of the century into a restraint on teaching and learning. The fealty to seat time can undermine high schools that try to improvise and can hinder the ability of students to take control of their own education. The hours devoted to a course assume greater importance than the content of the course. Many schools give little consideration to the fact that some students could complete the course more quickly and that others would benefit from having the content stretched over a longer time frame. The National Association of Secondary School Principals[2] advocated in the 1990s that officialdom redefine or replace the Carnegie unit so that high schools no longer equate seat time with learning.

Education policymakers tend to adhere to the fiction that time equals learning and shun a Pandora's box filled with questions about the nature of the knowledge that students acquire along with amassing Carnegie units. A similar situation exists in higher education. It was, in fact, pressure from colleges and universities almost 100 years ago that forced high schools to adopt Carnegie units to make it easier to compare applicants for admission to higher education. Shot through the assumptions is the idea that formal education would hardly occur if students did not sit in the presence of teachers who deliver course content to them. Yet, the experiences of students who attend classes and nonetheless achieve at low levels demonstrate that such provisions guarantee nothing about the amount of learning that occurs. Every term in the classrooms of schools and colleges, an appreciable portion of students seems not to comprehend the material, baffled by lessons that teachers offer in the classrooms where they assemble. The fault may rest with the student, with the teacher, with both, or even with the course material.

Some put the onus on the teacher to engage the student's interest. Teachers in elementary schools take this expectation most seriously, and those at colleges and universities feel least responsible for rousing the interest of students in the subject at hand. High school teachers fall somewhere in between in their inclination to engage students. The consumer orientation that ought to be part of the mission of schools and colleges gets short shrift. Whether or not one approves of making money from education, many for-profit education providers seem more oriented toward an obligation to try to keep students engaged than not-for-profit educational institutions. They recognize that students deserve treatment at least as solicitous as that bestowed on the customers of dry cleaners and florists.

The standards movement sweeping the United States today represents one more effort to make time devoted to education more productive. It tries to improve on the Carnegie unit by going beyond seat time to have students demonstrate achievement. Controversy dogs attempts to gauge that achievement, however, and the notion of divorcing the measurement of achievement from seat time is not a central tenet of the standards movement. By and large, students in elementary and secondary schools still must endure courses for prescribed times before submitting to assessments, which critics denounce as inserting unnecessarily high stakes in the learning process.

Online education revolves around trust, placing the destiny of students in their hands, an approach that may motivate some learners. Admittedly, an irresponsible student may exploit this trust relationship. Sloth and dishonesty are enemies of online learning. For that matter, they are not friendly to in-person education either. It is just that everyone is used to some students being lazy and cheating in traditional classrooms. Perhaps students slough off work more readily when the teacher and other students are out of sight, but this hardly warrants the rejection of online learning.

Bob Weight, who taught at the University of Phoenix Online, trusted his students to assume more responsibility for their education than they would in what he called a "traditional teacher-directed model." In a short paper he distributed to students at the outset of each course, Weight said: "We assume that you are motivated to learn, otherwise you wouldn't be here." Given the largely working-adult enrollment in both classroom and online courses at Phoenix, Weight said that he credited students with being "accomplished adults who have achieved some level of success" and told them that he was not about to check up on them. He expected them to ask questions electronically of him and of fellow students if they failed to understand something in the course. "I don't track them down or hold their hands," he said in an interview. "I expect them to be responsible adults, just like workers in the real world." He saw his role as mentor and facilitator more than expert or authority. He strove to establish a peer relationship with members of the class and said that he "will fall all over himself" trying to help students when they ask for it. This trusting attitude translated into flexible deadlines for turning in assignments.

MOTIVATION

E-learning, as discussed throughout this book, is just another vehicle for education. Motivated students make obvious candidates for online courses, but perhaps this kind of education also suits *some* less-obvious candidates, students who have not previously taken responsibility for their learning in traditional classrooms. They might fare better with more latitude for independence, while receiving the backup and support that good distance education ought to offer. Motivational research in traditional classrooms shows that—to the extent that students choose to perform a task as opposed to *having* to do it—they are apt to be more motivated. Making more of the decisions about their education may spur some students to learn. E-learning, which offers greater possibilities for empowering learners in this way, might appeal to some students who have enjoyed limited success in classrooms, where they chafe under authority.

On the other hand, freedom alone may not be sufficient to motivate students who have failed in other settings. Monitoring and support should accompany the availability of online education for such students. Otherwise, they may show little diligence, as occurred at a virtual high school operated by the Cincinnati public school system. The school made a special appeal to youngsters who were previously unsuccessful in the classroom-based schools that they attended. But the cyber school dropped hundreds of students from its rolls at the end of the 2001–02 school year for what it said was their failure to do the work.

Solving the Motivation Puzzle

The desire for a measure of control over one's fate affects many endeavors, not just education. A fairly substantial body of research underscores the notion of giving students as much discretion for learning as they can handle productively. "Sometimes the students who are disaffected the most from school and would benefit most from practices that enhance motivation are given the least amount of autonomy," wrote Deborah Stipek in *Motivation to Learn*. Some of her recommendations for providing this autonomy lend themselves to online learning: allow students to participate in the design of their academic tasks; give students choices in how tasks are completed; let students have some choice in the difficulty levels of assignments or tasks that they complete; and give students some discretion about when they complete particular tasks.[3]

Peer pressure prevents some students, especially in secondary schools, from working diligently on their studies. They attend schools in which they risk losing social acceptance if their classmates consider them grinds; these casual attitudes toward academic achievement foster a milieu unsupportive of hard work. Secondary schools exacerbate the situation when they fail to recognize and reward effort and achievement. Online courses, pursued in private, might offer respite from these pressures, but this is not an easy solution as some teenagers have little inclination to study on their own—a *sine qua non* of e-learning. One has to wonder about the motivation of some secondary school students as autonomous learners, when, as the research literature shows, they do not even see the value of taking notes when they read assignments.[4] Yet, in light of past failures, schools need to find something different for alienated students.

Instructors at all levels should recognize the need to motivate students. Preparation to teach, in person or online, is incomplete without attention to what teachers can do to prod students to learn. Good teachers take this responsibility to heart and try to draw students into the lessons. Some follow the entertainer route. Some titillate. Some pepper their presentations with nuggets of information designed to make students take notice. Some target individual students, taking a harder stance with those they think need it and softening the approach for those they think require cushioning. In the hands of a good teacher, motivation is the stealth weapon, designed to sneak up on unsuspecting students, capture them, draw them into the lesson, and impel them to battle with all their fiber to conquer the material.

The computer and access to the Internet—perhaps even some entirely online courses—might motivate students who have not responded to previous opportunities to learn. Those who design online courses can bring the far-ranging resources of the Internet to academic tasks that are both creative and filled with substantial learning experiences. Students may complete tasks by selecting, for example, from among simulations, threaded discussions that they lead, and essays that they write on the word processor. Branched learning on computers moves students through tasks of increasing levels of difficulty; and, surely, one of online learning's great virtues is the ability it gives students to complete tasks at their own pace. So, online learning with its potential for a do-it-yourself approach is replete with motivational possibilities.

Since some students show more motivation than others, Western Governors University (WGU) let potential students assess their readiness for online learning through a self-administered questionnaire similar to San Diego State's quiz. The former asked students about their need for face-to-face interaction with instructors and other students, their ability to prioritize tasks, the degree to which classroom discussion helps them, the extent to which they need someone to provide instructions for an assignment, how much feedback they need on their progress, how much desire they have to take distance courses, the amount of time they have available for such courses, their receptiveness to new software and new technologies, whether their predominant learning style is auditory, visual, or tactile, and the predictability of their personal and professional schedules.

In helping candidates evaluate their responses and weigh their own readiness for online learning, WGU advised that "some distance delivered classes are even more highly interactive than some classes that occur on campus," "you must be fairly self-directed and conscientious about completing assignments to succeed," you could do well "if classroom discussion is not particularly helpful to you," and if you are a tactile learner "it may be somewhat difficult to select distance-delivered classes that will fit your learning preference."[5]

Officials at Art Institute Online said that they found that online learners, a self-selected group to be sure, were self-motivated and typically focused on meeting specific goals and objectives. These officials said that e-learners value convenience and understand how to use technology as a viable way to learn. "A successful online student has the desire to want to learn and is willing to make the sacrifices of time and effort to do so," said a school official. Maturity seems linked to motivation. At the University of Phoenix, which served principally working adults in both online and classroom-based courses, the age and life experience of the students seemed to help motivate them. Craig Swenson, a Phoenix vice president, said that pursuing learning in adulthood leads students to be more self-directed, makes learning more meaningful, and makes learners more effective when their pre-existing competencies are taken into consideration by the instructor. He said that adults want a useful education. "They expect immediate practical relevance," Swenson explained. "They want theory married to practice and they shy away from instruction that doesn't bridge the gap between theory and practice."

Life experience and maturity provide perspective that may help motivate certain learners. One of the most responsible students in Ohio's Electronic Classroom of Tomorrow was a woman who had dropped out of a regular high school several years earlier as a pregnant 16-year-old. She had never returned to a classroom to complete her studies for a diploma because she had a small child and felt that an 8 A.M. to 3 P.M. program was not compatible with her family obligations, not to mention the fact that she would have been older than the other students in the building. She thought that virtual high school, which she could complete from her home, was a blessing, a chance to obtain a diploma that had more meaning than an equivalency certificate and could open doors to a brighter future for her. She passed all five parts of the state's proficiency test with honors and showed sufficient promise to win a scholarship to Ohio State University.

Given their limited life experience and the fact that they have not yet embarked on careers, younger students probably have different motivational issues. A revealing study of eighth-grade math students from three ethnically diverse middle schools in two midwestern school districts identified the key role that teachers play in spurring motivation. It was important to the students' confidence that they perceived their teachers as caring about them and supporting them. As teachers are more invisible in online learning, one must have some concern about the prospects of precollegiate students in e-learning. Another finding in the same study, also having apparent implications for online education, dealt with the connection of interaction to motivation. Students saw instructors as supportive (which, in turn, presumably motivated the students) if instructors promoted interaction and let students collaborate with each other.[6] This finding seems to underscore the value of incorporating online discussion and group assignments into online learning.

Two experts, who have consulted widely to help faculty members prepare to offer online courses, said that their reading of the research indicated that students who enrolled in distance education tended to be older and more serious, and to share such characteristics as self-discipline, higher expectations, and motivation.[7] Another expert, Lisa Neal, found when she consulted with the University of Puerto Rico on the feasibility of a program targeted for economically disadvantaged 18-year-olds that the group of potential students lacked maturity and self-discipline, as well as the technical skills to work online. She wondered, in this connection, about the advisability of online learning for secondary school students in general.

Katrin Tabellion, the student who got her diploma online from the University of Missouri's virtual high school, devised ways to motivate herself in both the short term and the long term. In the short term, she set specific times for study and, in the long term, she focused on how good she would feel, finally, to complete the work and earn her diploma. "That helped me sit and study," she said. She conceded that it was probably easier to do schoolwork in a classroom over which a teacher presides in person. Such a setting, she said, would be an advantage to students who need actual teachers to force them to study and to provide immediate explanations when they cannot grasp topics.

Ultimately, whether in classrooms or online, students need to take greater responsibility for their own learning as they advance beyond the elementary grades. Those fortunate enough to be caught up early in the learning game start pushing themselves more and more, realizing that they cannot count on coddling. They gradually gain a sense of delayed gratification and come to see a connection between what happens in the classroom and their later lives. These students endeavor to complete assignments, turn in homework, and come to class regularly and prepared. Many others, for a whole range of reasons, do not push themselves and float through school on the raft called social promotion. One might characterize online learning as an experiment in the degree to which students can take responsibility for their own education. Like all experiments, it is subject to failure under certain conditions, and chances for success may be worst with precollegiate youngsters.

LEARNING HOW TO LEARN

The idea that students should learn how to learn has been a fundamental principle of formal education, though honored mostly in the breach. Education at its best equips students to recognize what they need to know for a particular task and to understand how to go about gaining that knowledge. Those who can teach themselves, in effect, take control over their own learning. Whether working online or in a classroom, they use the material as a starting point and the instructor as a coach who does not have to hold their hands each step of the way. In the book *How People Learn,* the National Research Council said that students must learn to recognize when they understand the material at hand and when they need more information. The book proposed three key questions about students that go to the core of self-directed learning:

1. What strategies might they use to assess whether they understand someone else's meaning?
2. What kinds of evidence do they need in order to believe particular claims?
3. How can they build their own theories of phenomena and test them effectively?[8]

Knowing how to learn means coping with unanticipated situations and finding solutions to problems. One aspect of this ability involves pacing oneself, as if intuiting how fast to run each quarter-mile lap in a mile race. Those who can regulate the rate of their learning, especially online, have a better sense of how much effort to expend along the way. "If they haven't developed those skills, online learning will probably be hard for them," said Stanford University's education dean Deborah Stipek. "Online learning can be great for a disciplined person, but many people don't finish what they start. They may need the discipline of a teacher and a classroom."

All too many recipients of diplomas and degrees do not join the company of competent independent learners, and the fault is not entirely theirs. Educators fail to move students toward the self-sufficiency of knowing how to learn when they don't stress the importance of examining evidence, of determining how it is that we know what we know, and of recognizing where to turn to enlarge one's knowledge. This imperative looms ever larger in an era replete with instant and abundant telecommunications and the challenge of sorting through the information overload. Talk radio with its all-opinions-are-equal format has captured an audience of millions. The Internet has added enormously to the glut of information by establishing an instant repository of facts, so-called facts, pseudofacts, untruths, and lies in a format in which anyone can post whatever he or she wants. Schools and colleges often flunk the test of teaching their students how to sort through this information and how to learn, not preparing them to become discoverers of knowledge, not arming them with the intellectual tools that would give them firm footing to explore unfamiliar intellectual terrain.

The cyber world, at least initially, is part of this unknown ground. Regardless of the content of an online course, a student has to figure out how to navigate through new avenues and to recognize landmarks never before encountered. Those who know how to learn enjoy an edge when they go online. In addition to technological facility, life experience itself provides some advantage. Perhaps that is one reason why some observers say that online learning works best for older students. That is only partially true, though. Young people who have learned how to learn and revel in technology may prosper in online courses; older people may fail if their life experience has given them nary a clue about how to cope with new demands and if they are also technophobes.

Genevieve Kirch, an older student who enrolled in Western Governors University, thought that one reason that she was able to move through the online program as quickly as she did was because she knew how to conduct research and look for answers. She recognized when to take a detour and how to recognize when she had reached a dead end. She could turn to another avenue of pursuit when the one she first took led her into a wall. Roadblocks, she said, are a feature of online learning. "Because the interaction with others is diminished, you have to have your own resources for finding answers," Kirch said. She felt that a person who has learned how to learn can more readily cope with the frustrations of online learning.

STUDENT SUPPORT SERVICES

The support that students take for granted in a school or on a campus has relevance as well for online learners. Support for students who attend classroom courses means the availability of tutoring and remedial help. In addition, faculty maintain office hours during which they meet with students, the library remains open late at night, students can get ailments treated at the health center, food services keep them sated, and an office of student services points them toward any other kind of help they cannot readily find. Glenn C. Altschuler, a dean at Cornell University, underscored the importance of this extra attention when he observed that "support services are as important as course content."[9] Expecting online students to take responsibility for their learning should not absolve educational institutions of certain obligations, especially in terms of both technical and academic support.

Online students need assistance with hardware and software problems. An institution imperils the success of students in e-learning if it does not lend this kind of aid. An institution that doesn't plan to offer steady and reliable technical support to its students ought not to bother with online learning. There are enough frustrations in online education without having to deal with glitches in equipment and software. Schools, colleges, and universities should follow the best examples from business in this regard. Dell, for instance, has a popular product that owes some of its success to the quality of the technical support that accompanies the purchase of the company's computers. Underscoring this attraction was Dell's increase in sales in the first quarter of 2002, a time when sales by its rivals sagged. Genevieve Kirch, the first student to get a degree from Western Governors University, ran into technical difficulties that probably exceeded those faced by students who followed the path she blazed. There was, for instance, the time when she was using one word processing program and her instructor was using another, leading to incompatibility. With experience, Western Governors and other institutions presumably learned to anticipate problems of this sort.

Technical Support

Difficulties that have nothing to do with the content of the lessons can readily undo online learning if left unattended. Just making sure that students have the requisite equipment can be challenge enough. A good example of one such a pitfall from the very start was seen in the first year that Ohio's Electronic Classroom of Tomorrow operated, when, according to the school, the company chosen to provide a computer, a scanner, and a printer to each student ran late on deliveries. "It was a nightmare," said Tom Baker, who oversaw the school from his position as head of the Lucas County Education Center. Equipment deliveries were two to three months behind for some students. Exacerbating the situation was the collapse of the e-company that was to have served as the portal connection for the program.

Technological shortcomings limited the impact of the U.S. Department of Education's Virtual High School in several ways that were identified by evaluators. Technology "had serious liabilities in the two courses for which student products required visual inspection by the teachers," concluded a report.[10] These two courses, photographic vision and pre-engineering, were among the handful subject to intense evaluation for the purposes of the report, so there was no telling how many of the other courses in which students submitted work for visual inspection might have faced the same problems. In the photography course students were to discuss compositional elements of photographs that they submitted to the teacher via the world wide web. The students were to view each other's photos on the web, but the software did not permit students to see the photos at the same time that they commented on them, according to the evaluation. Similarly, in the online pre-engineering course the teacher said that the software limited his ability to inspect and comment on images of the designs that students had created as the culminating activity of each unit in the course.[11] "These limitations seriously jeopardized the quality of their whole learning experience in the course," the evaluation said.[12]

Assistance, of course, is almost always delivered from a distance for those who learn online. The ease and facility with which this occurs goes a long way toward determining the success of students, particularly older ones. Technology is a foreign country for some adults who venture into online courses. They need skills and confidence to negotiate this journey, regardless of their maturity. Some institutions fail to deliver the technical support that learners of all ages crave in times of trouble. "Many of the students had to make major adaptations, considering some didn't even know what a mouse is, don't have e-mail addresses, and are only moderately savvy on the computer," Tina House said of the students she taught at the University of Colorado at Denver. "I have not lost any students yet, and out of 24, only one person does not use the web site for the course. She uses her team partner instead to help her get information and turn in assignments."

Technical support takes on special proportions in an online course in the studio or performing arts that uses the web, as when someone studies art or music from a distance. Images and sounds require an added level of excellence to convey the totality of the experience. As Art Institute was preparing to establish an online arm for its program, its developers anguished, for example, over whether students would have fast enough computers and whether there would be problems related to the size of the images that could appear on the screens of their monitors.

Academic Support

Online education tends to give less attention to academic support than to technical support. Students pursuing courses from a distance do not as readily have access to the tutors, reading and writing centers, and other forms of assistance that have become widespread on campuses during the past generation. A computer in working order and 24/7 technical support to help deal with oddities in surfing the Internet may not be enough to get students through courses. A lack of academic support can exacerbate feelings of isolation and undermine online students.

An example of the possibilities of online academic support comes from a company that specialized in this area, leaving it to others to offer the actual courses—online or classroom-based. SMARTHINKING, Inc., based in Washington, D.C., had some 250 contracts by the end of 2001 to provide online academic support for students at institutions around the country, especially at community colleges and for-profit educational institutions. Another of the contracts involved tutoring Army and Navy personnel in online degree programs. Under a typical contract, students in designated courses at a particular institution could go online 24 hours a day, seven days a week, to reach one of SMARTHINKING's tutors, called e-structors.

Students communicated with tutors in real time, not having to leave e-messages and wait for responses. The company was able to offer the service around the clock by including on its staff English-speaking tutors abroad, whose daytime hours coincided with the overnight hours in the United States, where all of the company's customers were situated. The e-structors were college instructors, graduate students, and house-wives, 90 percent of whom the company said had master's degrees. The company said that each tutor underwent six hours of self-paced training, followed by a practicum with a lead tutor, and a battery of tests to confirm the skills of the tutor.

SMARTHINKING's contracts for 24/7 academic tutoring were available to cover courses in math, business studies, Spanish, chemistry, and writing. The company billed the institution for the actual number of minutes that tutors spent online with students. A student might also electronically submit an essay to the tutors at the company's online writing lab and receive a critique within 24 hours; a flat 30-minute charge was assessed to the institution for this service. Typically, an institution purchased a bulk number of hours of tutoring in advance from SMARTHINKING and then students drew down the minutes each time they turned to the service, much like using a prepaid telephone card.

While SMARTHINKING did not offer courses of its own, its approach in assisting students underscored the role that academic support can play when the tutoring as well as the course is online. Academic support of this sort could very likely raise retention rates and course completion in online courses, where students sometimes give up in frustration. Christopher Gergen, the president and chairman of SMARTHINKING, who cofounded the company in 1999, saw another role for online academic support. "Ultimately," he said, "this kind of support will drive enrollments more than course content." According to Gergen, there is just so much variation in course content possible from institution to institution, but the amount of academic support lent to students varies widely. The availability of academic support, he said, can be the service that determines where a prospective student enrolls.

Penn State's World Campus, a nonprofit online entity with a carefully crafted business plan, took a close look at the provision of student services. In a sort of fiscal triage, the institution categorized services as essential, desired, and not needed. World Campus was guided somewhat in these considerations by its experience with correspondence courses. For instance, online opportunities for registration, preadmissions advising, and academic advising are necessary and essential, according to Gary E. Miller, who headed both distance education and World Campus at Penn State. He placed career planning in the second category as exemplifying the sort of service that may not be necessary, even if students want it. The desire for career planning apparently stemmed from the fact that so many online students are adults with thoughts of using their e-education to look for new jobs. The kinds of services that Miller labeled as not needed for online students, unsurprisingly, included intramural sports, dorm life, and social services.

Online programs may have to consider other services as well. Miller pointed out by way of example that if a faculty member in a regular class has a student whom he recognizes as obviously afflicted with emotional problems, then the faculty member will probably refer the student to the counseling center. "But what do you do if you are teaching online and you detect the possibility of emotional problems?" he asked. "This will arise and we will have to grapple with it." World Campus planned to create an e-student union as another route for interaction between the university and its online students. Miller thought this might be a mechanism to address some of the daily life issues that online students share with on-campus students.

CHAPTER 7

THE BUSINESS OF ONLINE EDUCATION

Education has not been immune from the mania for profits that swept the digital world and fueled the dot-com phenomenon. Visions of dollars danced through the heads of some educators as they weighed the prospects of virtual learning. Most online education ended up in the hands of traditional colleges and universities as part of their mainline nonprofit mission, and some of the for-profit providers were spin-offs from these institutions. A sizable portion of online providers, though, were commercial enterprises with no links whatsoever to nonprofit education. In 2001, one-quarter of the providers of courses that were fully online were for-profit entities.[1] Often they focused on career training for business employees.

Even for providers that have limited their programs to the nonprofit sector, there is a Wild West aura about the business of e-learning. This is a frontier of educational experimentation, replete with trial and error, as in any laboratory in which a new product is put to the test. The pursuit of enrollment growth and the accompanying revenues stimulates colleges and universities in this endeavor. Institutions harbor vague hopes that somehow online courses will eventually lead to lower per-student costs and larger per-student revenues. Providers, both nonprofit and for-profit, concede in their less giddy moments, however, that they don't really know whether a substantial and enduring market will develop for their cyber wares. Putting entire courses online is no more of a sure thing than the groceries, job searches, toys, discounted automobiles, books, or other goods that drove dot-coms into bankruptcy. The billions invested in start-ups could not save many of them that ultimately found no lasting market for their services or products, a fact that haunts those who hope education will be different.

COMPETING FOR STUDENTS AND MONEY

One must distinguish hybrid or blended courses that incorporate features of both the classroom and the world wide web from courses that are wholly online, requiring no classroom attendance. Traditional educational institutions embraced fully online courses to protect their franchises, fearing a loss of their "customer base" if they failed to expand their course inventories to include such offerings. Implementing e-learning was for many educational institutions a defensive action, not unlike that taken by hundreds of newspapers around the country that created web sites during the 1990s to ensure that their publications would be able to deliver readership numbers if readers turned to the Internet for news and classified advertisements. The moguls of journalism discovered that the costs of these operations were excessive and the profits elusive. By 2001 they deemed web sites an extravagance and many sharply reduced outlays for such activities.

The clashes over cyber learning are but battles in a larger war. Competition of all sorts has plowed its way into education like a cyclone, leaving havoc in its wake. Elementary and secondary schools have had public charter schools inserted in their midst. And a ruling by the U.S. Supreme Court in 2002 means that school systems will also have to cope with vouchers that allow children to flee the public sector for private and parochial schools, including those operating online. Meanwhile, more and more high school seniors vie for places at the nation's finite number of selective colleges and universities, which accept a lower percentage of applicants each year. At the same time, less prestigious colleges and universities face competition from commercial enterprises that sell education as just another commodity. Add the wild card of on-line learning, shattering geographic monopolies as it pours out of computer terminals, and competition is honed to a keen edge.

Questions arose at the elementary and secondary level as states and local school districts went online with cyber public schools, often operating under charters, in the late 1990s and early 2000s. From where should such schools derive their revenues? Should they be funded at the same levels as brick-and-mortar schools? Could they become vehicles for saving money? Pennsylvania's experience was instructive. The state passed a charter school act in 1997 under which cyber schools were founded. The law provided charter schools with 80 percent of the amount that the home district would have spent on the child in a regular school. Students in Pennsylvania gained the ability to attend charter schools anywhere in the state, a regulation of particular advantage to the cyber schools, though observers said that they weren't aware when the regulations were written of the potential benefits to the not-yet-existing cyber schools.

The provision meant, however, that the per-pupil amounts following each child to a cyber charter school varied, according to the spending of the child's district. For example, the Western Pennsylvania Cyber Charter School estimated that the funds it got in behalf of individual pupils ranged from about $4,600 to $10,800. The charter school spent an average of $6,000 per pupil. Some public school systems refused to pay the invoices that cyber charter schools sent for the children who resided in those districts. Then, the cyber charter schools turned to the state for the money, and the state education department deducted the funds from the state aid earmarked for the public school systems that had withheld the payments. Lawsuits ensued. Public school districts contended that they had a right to hearings before the state took amounts from their state aid. Furthermore, the districts maintained that cyber charter schools were illegal anyway, not having been envisioned in the authorizing legislation for charter schools.

The idea that proponents of online learning have taken advantage of charter legislation to establish schools should offend no one. A cyber school is as legitimate a charter school as one that classrooms provide.

What has proven disturbing, though, has been the failure of some such schools to monitor the progress of students and to maintain educational quality. Cyber schools in such states as Ohio and Pennsylvania have sometimes been their own worst enemies, enrolling more students than they could reasonably handle and failing to document students' progress. In one instance, after an investigation, Ohio authorities ordered the Electronic Classroom of Tomorrow to pay back $1.6 million to the state because it could not document that its students were receiving instruction.

One study of the financing of virtual K through 12 schools proposed a two-stage implementation strategy for states across the country. In the first stage, states would heavily subsidize the cost of online courses used by public schools as a way of encouraging growth and innovation. In the second stage, public schools districts would gradually assume the costs of online courses and would not—in turn—charge regularly enrolled students. Online courses, like those students take in classrooms, are presumably part of the free public education to which they are entitled. The report was less charitable when it came to home schoolers and youngsters attending nonpublic schools. "Charging private or home-schooled students or their schools would appear to be broadly consistent with public policies," the report said. It warned of a burden on resources and a loss of enrollments if students outside the public school systems can take tax-supported online courses without paying for them.[2]

Nick Trombetta, superintendent of the Midland (Pennsylvania) School District and chief executive officer of the Western Pennsylvania Cyber Charter School operated by the district, said that while he was pleased to see the school thrive, he worried that the rush to create such online K through 12 schools would drain dollars from school districts across Pennsylvania, undermining public education in regular schools. He proposed that the legislature develop a plan under which a uniform amount of money would follow each child to a charter school, regardless of per-pupil expenditures in the child's home district, and that the state would provide some sort of financial relief to those school systems to offset their lost funds.

Meanwhile, for-profit companies pushed to win contracts to operate schools of all kinds in Pennsylvania and other states. By the beginning of 2002, 36 of these private educational management companies ran 368 public schools, most of them charters, in 24 states and the District of Columbia, according to the Education Policy Studies Laboratory at Arizona State University. Business could use e-learning as a vehicle to strengthen its beachhead in elementary and secondary charter schools, a prospect certain to arouse concern in many circles. Together, pre-collegiate and postsecondary education comprises a $700-billion-a-year enterprise that entices commercial providers. The kind of money at stake can be seen in the pay of executives in the for-profit sector of education. The top-ranking officers at both DeVry Inc. and Career Education Corp. got total compensation of more than $1 million each in the 2000 fiscal year. More than $500,000 was paid to each of the executives of Education Management Corp., Apollo Group, Corinthian Colleges, and ITT Educational Services.[3]

Revenues that make it possible to pay such salaries in education's for-profit sector come mostly from classroom-based education, not e-learning. Some critics have noticed for-profit education largely in connection with the arrival of online learning, failing to recognize that such ventures existed long before education on the Internet was much of a factor. The on-the-ground activities of for-profit providers have been far more lucrative. The number of such companies has proliferated and their enrollments have soared. The Education Commission of the States said in 2001 that the number of four-year, college-level for-profit institutions increased by 266 percent during the 1990s and that the enrollment at both two-year and four-year for-profits swelled by 59 percent, to 365,000 students.

While traditional colleges and universities may appear to be detached from the world of profits, the demarcations are not so clear. The traditional institutions may not profit from courses, but they get involved with business in other ways. For many years, prestigious universities have nurtured relationships with Fortune 500 companies in behalf of research, for instance. By the beginning of this century corporate partners underwrote almost 10 percent of all of the research at America's colleges and universities, according to the Association of University Technology Managers.

Precollegiate education, too, has connections to the world of profits. Venture investments by business in elementary and secondary education reached $723 million in 2000–01, according to *Education Week,* which projected a sharp drop in such investments in 2001–02.[4] Two of the commercial companies operating charter schools merged into other corporations in 2001, a possible harbinger of consolidation in a field that holds more challenges to those seeking profits than was originally thought. One of the most visible companies trying to make money from operating schools, Edison, still struggled in 2002 to get its ledgers into the black. Its lack of profits was exacerbated that year by a rebuke from the Securities and Exchange Commission for inadequate information about revenues and inadequate financial controls. Another sign of the struggle for profits could be seen in the experience of Princeton Review, the upstart tutoring company that competed fiercely with its older arch rival, Kaplan. Princeton Review sold its stock to the public in 2001, attracting investors who sought to join the search for educational riches. The stock was issued at $11 a share and promptly sank and settled at a lower price.

One of the difficulties facing those who seek gain from online learning and even not-for-profit providers has been a paucity of reliable information about the field. Robert Zemsky of the University of Pennsylvania said that "missing data, inadequate definitions, and woeful assumptions" have led to unduly optimistic projections. Said Zemsky: "No one knows how many students take an e-learning course in any given year; nor how much colleges and universities spend in pursuit of e-learning initiatives; nor what their students themselves spend."[5] Thus, with the support of the University of Pennsylvania and Thomson Learning (another not-for-profit–for-profit collaboration), Zemsky took up the directorship of the Weatherstation Project. The effort dedicated itself to developing a data collection strategy and set of measuring instruments pertaining to e-learning generally.

Despite the setbacks during the first years of the twenty-first century, the prospect of profiting from education remains. At the elementary and secondary level, the Bush-backed education bill that will allot money that can be spent on private tutoring for lagging students will mean revenues for such providers as Sylvan's Educational Solutions division. Also, charter school laws that allow such companies as Edison to assume operation of public schools may eventually lead to profits. In higher education, online courses have proliferated in the pursuit of enrollments by both for-profit and nonprofit institutions. Brandon Dobell, a senior research analyst for Credit Suisse First Boston, a firm that invested in such enterprises, told attendees at a 2001 seminar on online universities, sponsored in Arlington, Virginia, by the Institute for International Research, that venture funds serving the field look for the following characteristics in online learning:

1. quality offerings, especially ones that are accredited and serve job needs;

2. long-term students, particularly those enrolled in bachelor's and master's programs;

3. the right mix of technology for the courses—not too much, not too little, and easy to use;

4. control by the provider over what goes into the online learning environment, a quality that could be interpreted as not giving veto power to the faculty.

Elaborating further, Dobell said that investors in online education want to see predictability in terms of demographics; multiple revenue streams from such sources as courses, services, and customizing; superior value position reflected in customer loyalty and barriers to competition from others; and a record of profitability. He said that companies selling online learning should be able to show that they can retain students and that they understand the needs of customers. It all amounts to a sound fiscal approach appropriate for most any product—which, in this case, just happens to be education.

Speaking at the same conference, Stephen G. Shank, chairman and chief executive officer of Capella Education Company, a for-profit provider of online learning, predicted that by 2006, 25 percent of the adult higher education market would pursue courses online. He marveled at the progress that the industry had made since Capella's founding in 1992, a time when, he said, it was difficult to convince perspective students that online learning was a credible form of education. He urged the industry to concentrate on "learning outcomes," which, he said, matter most to customers. "E-learning provides tools that fit ideally with the needs of adult learning," Shank said. "It is a superior way to learn for most adults." He said that he was obsessed with two objectives: "demonstrating the quality of educational outcomes" and "demonstrating the vitality of our business." It was clear that he considered the two goals compatible.

Some companies involved in online education profit from the infrastructure, not from the courses. They sell the technology associated with the services and systems that make e-learning possible. They license software, build portals, provide platforms and adjuncts to platforms, offer 24/7 support hotlines, train students and faculty for online activities, integrate systems, and consult with educational institutions. Other companies create and sell courses and even offer courses that generate tuition revenues for accredited institutions, which then award the academic credits. The network underlying and connecting e-learning is no less intricate than the one involving the farms, truckers, processing plants, and marketing associated with the food sold in supermarkets.

EARLY MISHAPS ON THE PATH TO PROFITS

As in the larger dot-com world, online education has had its flops. The treacherous waters into which universities sailed in the pursuit of profits contain shoals and reefs that skilled helmsmen can avoid only with careful planning before embarking on their adventures. Higher education may prepare future leaders for the Fortune 500, but institutions are sometimes less adept at keeping their own ships on an even keel. The demise of early online, for-profit start-ups at Temple University and New York University serve as sober reminders to those at colleges and universities who might lose sight of the need for adequate preparations and good judgment.

Temple University in Philadelphia was among the pioneers of traditional institutions that set up a for-profit arm to sell education in 1999, and then, in 2001, one of the first to withdraw. A new president, David Adamany, said in abandoning the venture that his predecessor, Peter J. Liacouras, had established that he didn't see profit potential in online learning. E-learning's death at Temple did not even warrant a formal announcement, coming to light in the manner of a newborn abandoned at a church door. Adamany confirmed the action as an aside in a conversation with James M. O'Neill, higher education reporter of the *Philadelphia Inquirer.*

Virtual Temple, as it was named, was depicted at its launch as a possible money machine to buffer a hard-pressed inner-city university from fiscal woes. When he eventually released a public statement after dropping the venture, Adamany called it "an uncharted sea," and went on to observe that "it is already apparent that no one has yet found a way for online learning to be economically viable." He conceded, however, that many universities had found online courses "educationally effective for some students in certain kinds of educational programs."[6] Those who promoted the concept as a moneymaker seemed to think that investors could hardly wait to place their money on Virtual Temple, but the anticipated rush to the betting windows by entrepreneurs who liked the odds never materialized. A faculty that had been skeptical from the outset was not terribly surprised when word leaked out that Virtual Temple was a victim of Adamany's act of euthanasia.

Temple, constantly strapped for funds and with scant endowment income, was financially trapped between an inner-city student body that could not readily afford tuition increases and a state legislature unsympathetic to funding increases. As a "state-related" university, Temple depended on the legislature for about one-third of its revenues and had to raise the remainder on its own, mostly through tuition. Virtual Temple was supposed to liberate the university from some of these pressures, but it turned out to be a far more expensive undertaking than the decision makers apparently anticipated. If there was a pot of gold waiting to be found at the end of the rainbow by folks at Temple, it was somewhere far from the gritty streets of North Philadelphia. The enterprise stalled along with the dot-com madness that produced it. The university apparently discovered that it could not afford the steep costs associated with creating online courses, marketing them, and building and maintaining an infrastructure to support the online enterprise. Such an epiphany may yet strike home at some other universities that have embarked on this yellow brick road to cyber education's Oz.

Virtual Temple's main legacy was a disgruntled faculty that felt that the administration had not properly consulted them about the plan. They wondered from the beginning what Virtual Temple's impact would be on the university's reputation. They worried about whether there was sufficient concern for the integrity that, the faculty said, only they could bring to the project. The business side of the university had rushed past the academic side only to stumble early in the race. In the wake of the death of Virtual Temple, Adamany propounded a vision for Temple's future online pursuits. In June 2001, in a document entitled "President's Self-Study and Agenda," he proposed that distance learning at the university take three forms: 1. courses taught simultaneously at several locales by interactive video; 2. online courses and programs developed by academic units; and 3. online courses in educational niches where Temple has unique strengths.[7] Online learning in Temple's future would figure apparently only in the context of the regular academic program and not with the expectation of profits.

New York University, however, thought it had figured out a way to avoid the perilous side of online learning when it created NYUonline as a wholly owned business in 1998. The separate for-profit unit, formed in conjunction with the university's School of Continuing and Professional Studies, planned to find a spot for itself by offering programs in which NYU had already established a firm reputation in the classroom—real estate, hotel management, risk assessment, and publishing, to mention a few. The idea, not unlike the route that Cornell University later took with its for-profit subsidiary, was to operate from a position of proven market strength. Furthermore, with the online programs under the aegis of the School of Continuing and Professional Studies, the effort could emulate that division's policy of retaining ownership of the courses and assigning the teaching to interchangeable adjuncts.

NYUonline envisioned a two-prong initiative in which individuals would enroll in courses and companies would contract for courses for groups of students. There was even an effort to enlist corporate partners. Considerable ballyhoo accompanied the formation of a so-called strategic partnership with the Lifetime Learning division of the McGraw-Hill Companies, which was to provide an outlet for the distribution of

NYUonline's certificate-bearing management courses to the corporate marketplace. How well NYUonline gauged the needs of corporations was an open question.

Very quickly, though, NYUonline felt pressure from the university's board members and others to offer courses related to other parts of the university, especially the Stern School of Business. Such a shift in mission would rob the cyber program of its distinctiveness and subject the courses to intense competition from many other providers of online business education. Moreover, the business school faculty had its own notions of who should own the courses, which had been less of an issue so long as the program stayed within continuing studies. Meanwhile, one of the visionaries behind NYUonline, Gerald A. Heeger, left his post as dean of the School of Continuing and Professional Studies to accept the presidency of the University of Maryland University College, which was building an online presence of its own.

NYUonline soon found itself spending what some insiders estimated was up to $1 million per course to develop offerings of uncertain appeal because of their resemblance to what was already available elsewhere. Connections between NYUonline and the School of Continuing and Professional Studies grew tenuous. The virtual sinkhole that opened at Washington Square quickly swallowed up the original $10 million investment of the university's board and apparently absorbed millions more before New York University pulled the plug on its losses. The university declared the cyber program dead at the end of 2001. NYUonline was said to have produced fewer than 10 courses during its short, well-financed life.

The demise of NYUonline and Virtual Temple holds several lessons for other institutions of higher education. First, the experience shows that it helps to have a tight focus in cyber programs and not try to do too much. Operating from a position of strength with long-established programs that have already distinguished themselves in classrooms can help an institution compete effectively. Second, a provider reduces chances for success when program development costs mount too high to amortize over a reasonable period. Third, an online program may not get the help it needs from other sectors of the institution if those sectors are not enlisted as allies early in the process, or at least neutralized as possible opponents. Those contemplating or pursuing cyber programs should look closely at the sad tales of NYUonline and Virtual Temple.

A BUSINESSLIKE APPROACH

Businesses have characteristically been more aggressive innovators than traditional institutions of higher education simply because survival in the for-profit sector demands bold action. Public colleges and universities almost never shut down, no matter how hapless their performance, and private institutions of higher education, though more vulnerable to market forces, have a Houdini-like ability to survive.

Colleges and universities have historically had to compete with for-profit businesses only at the margins of what people in the field refer to as postsecondary education. Technical institutes to train truck drivers and technicians, secretaries and data entry specialists, tellers and cashiers, and employees for a host of other occupations have taken up squatter's rights to offer programs that traditional institutions of learning largely eschew as outside their orbit. Now, though, businesses are pushing toward the center—seeking profit in some of higher education's more conventional areas, especially through courses offered both online and on-the-ground at learning centers spun off in a multitude of states. At the same time, traditional colleges and universities are trying to adopt some of the attributes of the entrepreneurs that they formerly disdained. Eighteen institutions of higher education decided in 2001, for instance, to let an agency sell advertising to appear on the screen savers of computers used by the 250,000 students, faculty, and staff on their campuses.

Traditional higher education's fascination with the goal of profiting from online ventures had its counterpart in the trend by for-profit businesses to extend themselves into conventional learning. In fact, a study by the Education Commission of the States said in 2001: "Once considered well outside the mainstream of America's higher education system, for-profit degree-granting institutions have emerged as an integral and increasingly influential part of the system." The study categorized these for-profit ventures in postsecondary education as small, local enterprise colleges; publicly traded supersystems; and Internet-based institutions.[8] While the third category consists of for-profit institutions that offer their programs entirely online, it is worth noting that a growing portion of schools in the first two categories are building up their online offerings. On top of these categories, business and industry have developed internal online training systems for their employees. The magnitude of this corporate training may rival that of formal postsecondary institutions.

The profit motive has long lurked in the wings of traditional learning. Publishers and test makers reap fortunes from schools and colleges. Contractors and members of the building trades line their pockets with construction revenues from these institutions. Everything from school furniture to computers to buses to laboratory equipment to footballs and band uniforms has been sold to schools and colleges for a profit. And faculty members seldom turn down the lucrative consulting contracts that come their way. This is the nature of a free market society and there is nothing evil about it. As a matter of fact, the *Chronicle of Higher Education* observed in 2002 that state governments were pushing public universities to seek revenues by collaborating more closely with business and industry in research and technology-transfer programs.[9] Promotion of such links came at a time when legislatures around the country were restraining the growth of allocations for higher education.

Furthermore, institutions have tailored courses to the specifications of individual businesses in order to generate tuitions by training their employees. Institutions of higher education, especially community colleges, have a lengthy history of collaboration with business and industry. Colleges and universities have established many certificate and degree programs designed specifically to serve the needs of particular corporations and industry groups. If online learning now facilitates more such links, then that relationship will not deviate much from what has been commonly found in classrooms. Programs that Rio Salado College set up in cooperation with individual companies and with employer organizations indicate the scope of these ties. Rio Salado, a community college, had partnerships with four police academies in its region of Arizona to provide education leading to either a certificate of completion or an associate degree in law enforcement technology.

Another program was offered in conjunction with the Arizona Dental Association to train dental assistants. Students took six months of courses online or with videocassettes, then spent two weekends learning skills in a clinic, and, finally, served a 200-hour internship with a dentist who belonged to the association.

Collaborating with individual employers in what the college called an "educational service partnership," Rio Salado also set up a customized multitrack program to train new employees of America West Airlines. The college sent faculty to their work sites so that airline employees could earn certificates in one of five specialties—reservations, passenger services, vacations, initial flight attendant, and ground operations. Students could apply the credits they earned toward an associate of applied science degree if they wished to continue their studies. By 2002, some 1,500 employees of America West had received certificates from Rio Salado and some had gone on to take other courses toward degrees at the college.

Three universities that took a businesslike approach to online learning are Penn State, Cornell, and Columbia. While Penn State shunned profits in creating its World Campus, a fully online entity, the university nonetheless developed a business plan for the not-for-profit enterprise and tried to adhere conscientiously to established commercial practices. This meant tracking fixed and variable costs; budgeting for faculty costs, course design, marketing, and administration; and outsourcing certain parts of the program. A rate structure for salaries was established and monitored for each phase of the operation. Costs included pay rates for dedicated marketing managers, plus 7 percent of the operating budget to cover access to a pool of researchers, account specialists, and client development specialists. Costs for student services were calculated on a per-student basis. Penn State's World Campus tried to avoid the haphazard business practices that too often characterize the operations of not-for-profit higher education.

Programs leading to certificates and degrees at both the undergraduate and graduate levels were added to the World Campus based on enrollment potential and then marketed to target audiences of potential students. For example, the certificate program in noise engineering was marketed through corporations and trade shows; the program in turfgrass management was marketed through an association of golf course superintendents; and an associate degree program in dietetics was marketed through an organization of dieticians and restaurant associations.

Each of the 30 fully online certificate and degree programs established by the end of 2001 had its own program team. On each team were a program manager, a senior faculty coordinator, an instructional designer, a program marketing manager, and a specialist in student support services. Only the senior faculty coordinator was a faculty member; the rest were nonacademic staff. Every program manager had under his or her jurisdiction all of the programs offered through the World Campus by two or three of the colleges at the University Park campus. Behind this approach was the idea that every college would have a program manager well acquainted with its offerings and its faculty.

For its first foray into online learning, Cornell University took on career development, gearing up to offer courses that built on existing classroom programs in industrial and labor relations and in the hotel and hospitality field. These noncredit courses each ran for about a month. Tuition for each course ranged from $700 to $1,000, with about 20 students in a class. Members of the regular faculty and adjuncts developed online versions of courses that they had taught in person in the classroom. Those from the hotel school were assured of royalties for their work. Teaching associates employed by e-Cornell and others who were not part of Cornell's regular faculty took on much of the responsibility for interaction with the online students. A smaller online program was mounted in continuing medical education.

For example, officials described a course, Human Resources and the Law, in which the subject-matter expert was the faculty member who had created the course. She was scheduled to work with teaching associates who would keep in touch with students through e-mail and other electronic means. This was a course that used case studies to teach about the relationships of federal, state, and local laws pertaining to employment. A complete online certificate program in Human Resources Studies comprised six courses, including this one and Fundamentals of Employee Benefits, Selection and Staffing, Fundamentals of Compensation, Building and Managing Employee Relations, and Performance Appraisal and Management. E-Cornell said that it set out in most courses to achieve a straightforward design, avoiding adornments that would dress up what appeared on a monitor screen but needlessly complicate matters for students whose main objective was learning, not entertainment.

The university committed $36 million to the for-profit business plan for e-Cornell and hired Francis Pandolfi as chief executive in 2000. Pandolfi, former head of the U.S. Forest Service and former chief executive officer of the magazine division of Times Mirror Company, brought a marketer's sensibilities to the job. The university was sole owner of e-Cornell, an arrangement that the trustees hoped would reassure critics by keeping outside investors from buying a piece of the Cornell name. By the summer of 2001, the company had 50 employees, with offices in Ithaca and New York City. Forty of the 50 were what e-Cornell called "content architects" and "learning designers."

Some faculty members registered their distrust of this commercial extension of the university, but as a freestanding business, e-Cornell enjoyed flexibility and autonomy that it never would have had as part of the regular program. "Some folks think that this is probably not a place for us, distance learning of this kind, and they are not about to be convinced otherwise," Pandolfi said of the dissenters. "It is up to us to prove that there is a business here and that it is not in conflict with what they do as faculty members." Mitigating the possibility of such conflict was the fact that e-Cornell, while offering certificates, would not confer degrees. Pandolfi said that ultimately e-Cornell's acceptance by the faculty would depend on the program's ability to bridge the "culture gap" that he felt separated the for-profit entity from the rest of the university.

E-Cornell counted on its brand name to carry the day. Almost as important as name recognition in the marketing was the strong reputation of the career-oriented programs that provided the university's first online courses. Cornell's schools of hotel administration and industrial and labor relations are among the most widely known in the country. Success with these programs might lead to certificate offerings from Cornell's schools of veterinary medicine and engineering, according to Pandolfi. In keeping with the solid business practices that Pandolfi tried to adopt for e-Cornell, ideas for the program were subject to market research. Proposals for online courses were tested, revised, and retested, especially to discover the motivations of potential students. Market research led e-Cornell to tightly focus its offerings in certain areas of career education rather than to pursue an array of courses across the curriculum.

Another Ivy League institution, Columbia University, chose a different route in pursuit of profits. Columbia was the moving force in the founding of Fathom, a portal to courses and reference information made available by a consortium of universities, research organizations, and museums. Fathom itself awarded no certificates or degrees and offered no courses. Rather, it directed users—most of whom were expected to be adults—to courses at the web sites of its member institutions. And a prestigious group of institutions they were. Columbia's partners in Fathom were the London School of Economics and Political Science, Cambridge University Press, the University of Michigan, the British Library, the New York Public Library, the University of Chicago, American Film Institute, RAND, Woods Hole Oceanographic Institute, Victoria and Albert Museum, Science Museum (UK), and London's Natural History Museum.

Ann Kirschner, president and chief executive officer of Fathom, said that the consortium had turned away other institutions that sought membership. There were, however, some nonmember institutions such as the State University of New York at Buffalo, the University of Washington, and the University of Iowa whose courses were also available through Fathom. In a different sort of arrangement, Fathom agreed to makes its services available to members of AARP at a 5 percent discount, giving the company entree to 35 million middle-age and senior citizens, who would also have access to online learning through a part of AARP's web site that Fathom was helping to create.

Aimed at what Kirschner called "the average intellectually curious person," Fathom planned to draw on its abundant resources to assemble a package for its users that, otherwise, they would have to spend a great deal of time aggregating on their own. In the fall of 2001, for example, this might mean something like piecing together an online package that included a lecture on terrorism that had been delivered by a visiting diplomat at Columbia's School of International and Public Affairs, a full profile of Afghanistan from, say, the New

York Public Library, a semester-long course on the region from the London School of Economics and Political Science, and a briefing paper on women's rights under Muslim governments from another of Fathom's member institutions. The site could offer online copies of one-time lectures, interviews with and articles by faculty and staff of the member institutions on pertinent topics, virtual performances and exhibits from the member museums, and the latest research findings from the institutions. At least this was the plan in one of Fathom's incarnations.

Fathom sought to position itself as a high-end provider of online learning and information, a sort of equivalent of public television. Fathom pursued this goal with a marketing program that included a full-page advertisement inside the back cover of the upscale *New Yorker* in the fall of 2001. Kirschner estimated that 11 million Americans formed Fathom's potential hard-core demographic center, along with untold others around the world. Alumni and members of the institutions in the consortium were seen as an important starting point for building a following for the company's offerings. Almost $30 million was invested in Fathom as a start-up venture, with the lion's share provided by Columbia, which perhaps is appropriate for a university that has a lion as its mascot.

Only time would tell whether Fathom, which situated itself in the glossy midtown offices of a Manhattan high-rise several miles south of the campus, could succeed with the select audience that it coveted. Progress was halting and Fathom sought to reinvent itself each time it encountered obstacles. The web site itself was revised and simplified, allowing for more customizing to meet the individual needs of users, after early users found it needlessly convoluted. Originally Fathom saw itself primarily as a repository of free content and intended to sign up corporate partners and advertisers for its site to generate additional revenues, but put that plan in abeyance when advertisers did not emerge. Officials at the university and at Fathom had notions of taking the company public and making it self-sustaining. Later, some representatives said that Fathom was never meant to make money but to give Columbia a prestigious online presence. For their part, some students had reservations about the university spending its money on such an enterprise. Writing in the *Columbia Daily Spectator*, a columnist said: "It is very ironic that a university that claims never to have enough money for clearly needed academic enhancements—i.e., more faculty for an increased number of undergraduates—would be so willing to throw money at something whose benefits are unlikely, if ever, to materialize."[10]

Under the plan that prevailed by late 2001, Fathom's profits were to come—*when and if* they came—from a percentage of the tuitions and fees that the member institutions charged those who signed up through Fathom. Much of what Fathom made available could be obtained directly from the member institutions, but Fathom counted on its attractiveness as a portal for one-stop shopping. The "customers," and that is what Fathom called them, paid no more for a course by registering through Fathom than by going to the member institutions' web sites.

While Fathom ran the risk of defining its potential audience too narrowly to turn a profit, the company may have been on to something in its elite positioning. The Internet, after all, is filled with junk. Columbia was wagering that potential learners might find benefit in a portal that intended, in effect, to vet its offerings and relieve users of the worry that they might be signing up for courses of questionable value. The heavy-duty brand names associated with Fathom spoke to quality. Furthermore, Fathom's goal was to assemble the courses and other information for its upscale audience in a user-friendly manner that would make it unnecessary for them to visit the web site of each participating institution and wend their way through lots of superfluous information. What Fathom sought to deliver along with its quality content was convenience, comfort, and peace of mind. This kind of mix has sold lots of Mercedes automobiles and Tiffany jewelry. But the formula remains unproven for online learning.

BUSINESSES IN EDUCATION

For businesses, the web represents just another method for trying to boost profits. An example of an extension by business in this direction was the creation of Barnes & Noble University, which offered free enrollment in online courses that, in effect, promoted the retailer's books.

Sylvan Learning Systems, however, was already in the education business. As one of the for-profit sector's major players in education, it set out during the late 1990s to add online courses to what had been essentially a classroom-based program. The company, listed on the NASDAQ, operated at both the K through 12 and postsecondary levels. Sylvan Learning Centers and Sylvan Education Solutions were its two main efforts in elementary and secondary education. The learning centers, perhaps most frequently associated with Sylvan in the public mind, have more than 850 locations in North America and almost 1,000 in Europe, where youngsters go for after-school tutoring and test preparation for which families pay. Sylvan Learning Centers gradually expanded its repertoire with online tutoring and expected to become less dependent on opening centers in physical locations as it increased its online activities. Sylvan Education Solutions contracted with school systems to provide tutoring services in schools at no charge to students and to help school systems with staffing.

In higher education, Sylvan's main online programs were Canter & Associates, which offered graduate courses to teachers; Walden University, which had been accredited since 1990 to provide graduate degrees in management and social and behavioral sciences; Sylvan Teachers Institute, formed in 1999 to prepare candidates to obtain teacher certification and to provide professional development for teachers; OnlineLearning.net, a company it acquired in 2001; and National Technological University, acquired in 2002. In addition, Sylvan Ventures was formed in 2000 to invest in companies providing Internet technology to K through 12, higher, and corporate education. Sylvan's other two areas of operation in higher education, which at first had the least connection to the company's emerging online presence, were Wall Street Institute, which taught English at 360 centers in 20 countries, and Sylvan International Universities, through which the company bought stakes in proprietary institutions in Mexico, Spain, Switzerland, and other countries.

OnlineLearning.net was founded in 1996 as the exclusive, worldwide online distributor for the extension program of the University of California at Los Angeles. As a part of Sylvan, OnlineLearning.net apparently is to use what it gleaned as an independent company to assist other Sylvan divisions. "People have learned in the last few years that online learning is a lot harder and more expensive to do than they thought," said John Kobara, senior vice president and general manager of Online-Learning.net. His division's goal is to help strengthen Sylvan's corporate infrastructure for online education in a way that allows for customization in the various units of the company.

MIXING FOR-PROFIT AND NOT-FOR-PROFIT ENTITIES

There are other nexus points in online endeavors between commercial enterprises and traditional institutions. Hungry Minds University, a decidedly profit-oriented business, operated a web site in conjunction with Yahoo that sold links to colleges and universities with online programs. Listed as "featured university partners" were such institutions as Michigan State, New York University, Penn State, Rochester Institute of Technology, and several campuses of the University of California. Among those listed simply as "partners" were MIT, Teachers College of Columbia University, and Virginia Tech.

The history of Hungry Minds University exemplifies the fragility of e-learning. Starting with grand ambitions to make money from online courses and enlisting some of the country's leading institutions of higher education in that pursuit, the company fared no better than Icarus. Hungry Minds University was launched in 1999 and within three years barely a trace of the company remained. In the beginning of the wild ride on which Hungry Minds and others embarked, the company expected its portal to lure thousands of students who would enroll in online courses offered by its prestigious partners. Circumstances proved otherwise. Prospective students could shop the Internet themselves, going directly to university web sites. The demand for e-learning never fulfilled the soaring expectations, and the collapse of the dot-coms wreaked collateral damage on almost everything associated with the Internet. Moreover, Hungry Minds was sold and the new owner really wanted only the " . . . for Dummies" books that were part of the same company. All that remained of lofty ambitions by the spring of 2002 was a site on the web that said: "We regret to announce that Hungry Minds University will be discontinued in November 2002."

Portals like the one Hungry Minds set out to become are points of entry that lead web surfers to sites that then seek to capture their attention. Purveyors of e-learning, both for-profit and not-for-profit, value "sticky" sites that will draw in computer users, hold them for awhile, and possibly lead to course enrollments. And so it is that any number of schools and colleges have joined consortiums that offer their courses at a portal. Why, one may ask, does an educational institution want to list itself alongside competitors that also want to enroll students? Simply because it thinks, like a store among competitors in the same mall, that the comprehensiveness of the portal offerings may attract potential students more readily than a stand-alone web site. Portal owners like Hungry Minds University expected to grow rich charging rent to universities for which the portals would serve as conduits for students seeking information and courses. It may or may not be a good marketing tool, but some people still find merit in the portal approach.

Hungry Minds was one of many businesses allied with traditional institutions. The Community College of Denver contracted with Eduprise to expand its virtual course offerings. New York University arranged with GP e-Learning Technologies and Centra to facilitate such features of online courses as chat rooms and live discussions online between teachers and students. The University of California at Irvine teamed up with the National Investor Relations Institute to offer courses online on capital markets and investing. Clemson University agreed to provide some of its courses to RedVector.com, an online learning company.

Universitas 21, a consortium of universities around the world, was initially a kind of forum for convening meetings and for sharing information among administrators, staff members, faculty, and their international counterparts. It included such institutions as Canada's McGill University and University of British Columbia, the United Kingdom's University of Birmingham and University of Edinburgh, Australia's University of Melbourne and University of South Wales, China's University of Singapore and Peking University, and the United States's University of Virginia.

It wasn't long before Universitas 21 saw a new role for itself as a player in international online learning. Universitas 21 formed a 50/50 partnership with the Thomson Corporation to create U21global, a for-profit company based in Singapore and capitalized at $50 million, that announced its intention to offer higher education online beginning in 2003. Initially, it intended to offer courses in English and then to phase in courses in Mandarin and Spanish over a five-year period. Chris Robinson, managing director of Universitas 21, said that U21global would obtain online course content from a variety of possible suppliers including Thomson and the member universities of the consortium. U21pedagogica, a subsidiary of Universitas 21, was charged with overseeing content quality assurance and the academic operation of U21global.

E-learning has become a vehicle by which some universities take on more and more attributes of business, with interlocking subsidiaries and infusions of venture capital. Thus, business and education have come closer together. Online courses, particularly those offered for a profit, fit within this tradition. Students should have choices. Time and place often needlessly complicate the pursuit of an education, especially for older students who need some flexibility to accommodate demands in other parts of their lives. It remains to be seen, though, whether traditional not-for-profit educational institutions can meet this desire for convenience. For-profit online learning has appeared on the scene at a time of intensified competition in almost all phases of education. Its arrival coincides with an era of greater receptivity to the idea that making money from education may not be all that objectionable, so long as the product offers quality and fills the needs of students. Online courses are as much a product of this era as they are a factor that helped produce the era.

CHAPTER 8

FOCUSING E-LEARNING ON CAREERS

They are among the elites in graduate business education and they jealously guard the use of their good names—Columbia Business School, Stanford, University of Chicago Business School, Carnegie Mellon, and London School of Economics. So, when the names and logos of these institutions turned up on the web and in glossy printed materials in association with UNext's subsidiary, Cardean University, it gave instant authority to an obscure online entity unknown to most people in higher education. Potential students were told at Cardean's web site that "faculty members from these leading institutions work with us to convey their knowledge in an online environment." Adding weight to Cardean's instant standing was a board of directors that included two Nobel laureates in economics, Kenneth J. Arrow and Gary S. Becker, as well as George P. Schultz, former U.S. Secretary of the Treasury and U.S. Secretary of State.

How could so much prestige attach itself to so obscure an entity? The story of UNext and its Cardean subsidiary indicates the extent to which visionaries regarded the Internet as a perfect locale for students seeking to further their careers. For one thing, UNext apparently contracted to pay each of the illustrious business schools projected sums of $20 million over a period of years. How much they promised to pay members of the board of directors is anyone's guess. Cardean's business and management studies were expected to generate the revenues to make possible such payments. UNext launched Cardean in 1999, in the midst of the craze during which observers expected anything touched by the Internet, in Midas-like fashion, to turn to gold. Michael Milken was one of the investors, and the glamorous new cyber university captured attention in *Fortune, Business Week, Newsweek,* and the *New York Times.* Cardean would offer an M.B.A. in its own name—a name, incidentally, borrowed from a Roman goddess who protected doorways and, presumably, portals, their virtual equivalent.

Cardean was to adapt courses taught by distinguished professors at leading brick-and-mortar universities to the Internet, redesigning them with the input of cognitive psychologists and information technology experts to produce problem-based learning using hypothetical cases. Animation, video clips, self-assessments, and interactive electronic discussions were part of the adaptation, with development of a single course costing reputedly hundreds of thousands of dollars. The university projected that a student would spend 25 to 30 hours over a period of six weeks to complete a one-credit course, with 45 such courses needed for an M.B.A. degree. UNext was apparently prepared to spend tens of millions of investors' dollars on its Cardean enterprise. Courses were to be taught largely by trained facilitators, called "faculty," with limited authority to supplement the content.

By 2002, though, a battered UNext and its Cardean University subsidiary were on life support, like so many other surviving start-ups that fell to the ground when the balloon burst. The payroll, not counting faculty, had shrunk from a high of more than 400 to about 100. Payout agreements to the big-name university partners were restructured and much of Cardean's marketing staff was fired. The company contracted with Thomson Learning and Knowledge Universe to act as exclusive sales and marketing partners for Cardean programs. In addition, Cardean would use Thomson's courses for some of the students below the M.B.A. level.

THE SPECIAL CASE OF PROFESSIONAL AND CONTINUING EDUCATION

Chances for signing up students for online learning are perhaps greatest in job-related fields in which courses tend to be more about training than about theory. Requirements from states and from professional organizations that people engage in continuing education help boost enrollments. The constituencies for the courses are working men and women with positions that make it difficult for them to meet campus residency requirements and sometimes even to break away from work to attend courses. Courses online can have great appeal to them. And these students, in turn, are an attractive group for higher education. Unlike undergraduates, they have money and are not as dependent on loans or grants, and they need to overcome problems of time and place. Anthony F. Digiovanni, chief executive officer of the University of Phoenix Online, maintained that what gave his program a kick start was that the online component simply targeted the same audience that the university pursued in its campus-based courses: midcareer professionals.

Duke University had roughly the same audience in mind but with a slight twist when in 2000 it began the Cross Continent M.B.A. program at its Fuqua School of Business. As one of the country's elite graduate schools of business, it was still seeking primarily students with work experience, in this case with about six years on the job and, typically, in their late 20s. Duke tried to lure them with this message at the Fuqua web site: "You want to enhance your career by earning an M.B.A degree with an international perspective from a prestigious university, but you're not willing to relocate and stop working for two years to go back to school." The bait, of course, was a Duke M.B.A., which students could earn without moving or having to take leaves. Students could complete the degree online and with CD-ROMs by taking 16 courses over 20 months, two courses during each of eight terms, in such subject areas as management, marketing, operations, economics, finance, and accounting. Duke cautioned them that they must devote 20 to 25 hours a week to the online courses, which included real-time chats, bulletin boards, and digital access to the university's libraries.

The Duke program had the distinction of a residential requirement along with the online learning. Students satisfied the requirement by spending time at either the university's main campus in Durham, North Carolina, or at Duke's Fuqua School of Business Europe campus in Frankfurt, Germany. Each of the eight terms making up the program lasted a total of nine weeks, beginning with a week of readings, followed by a week of traditional classes in residence at one campus or the other. Students then worked online for the next seven weeks, with a one-week break in the middle during which they had no assignments. Each January, half the students who normally spent their residential week in Durham went to Frankfurt for their one-week residence, and half the Frankfurt students went to Durham. In March, the other half of the students followed the same pattern.

The program used both online and classroom-based learning to bring students in contact with each other. Part of this interaction came when they collaborated on virtual teams for course projects. The program provided the kind of networking—on an international basis in this case—that business people crave. Approximately 150 students in each 20-month group were based around the world, flying to the Durham or Frankfurt campuses from far-flung locales. Donna Spinella, assistant dean and director of the Cross Continent Program, said that the two pedagogical approaches, live and virtual, combined to suit different learning styles. The two programs equipped students with knowledge that they could apply immediately in a relevant laboratory where it mattered and had consequences: the workplace. In addition to the Cross Continent Program, Duke also had its Global Executive Program, following a somewhat similar online and classroom pattern, but geared to senior executives with about 15 years' experience.

Close Ties to Technical Education

The National Technological University (NTU) represented one of the better examples of distance learning tapping into the market for continuing technical education. NTU was founded in 1984 as a nonprofit institution to provide graduate-level engineering education to working professionals at leading technical companies. The program began with videotapes and television broadcasts downloaded from a satellite, and later added online learning from the web. The focus throughout was on helping people enhance their knowledge and advance their careers in engineering and engineering-related occupations. The courses came from more than 50 academic partners including Arizona State University, Columbia University, Illinois Institute of Technology, Massachusetts Institute of Technology, Michigan State University, Rensselaer Polytechnic Institute, and the University of Minnesota. Among the corporations sponsoring the enrollment of their employees were Alcoa, Boeing, Digital Equipment Corporation, Du Pont, General Electric, IBM, and Whirlpool; in most cases they offered the courses at work sites. For years, Motorola provided more students for NTU than any other corporation.

NTU, which called itself the largest distance-learning consortium in the world, listed 1,400 graduate-level courses in its catalogue, though it did not offer all at the same time. By 2002, the university had granted 1,600 master of science degrees in 19 separate programs and thousands of certificates for graduate study, almost all of these credentials going to students who studied part time while holding full-time jobs. The academic credits and the degrees were awarded in the name of National Technological University, which was accredited in 1986 by the North Central Association, one of the eight main regional accrediting organizations.

Students selected among courses that originated with the campus-based universities, and NTU reimbursed the institutions for students who took their courses through NTU. The technological university also paid stipends to professors teaching the courses at the universities. In the late 1990s, the university spun off a for-profit entity, eventually called Stratys Learning Solutions, to open the door to greater growth and to the possibility of profits. NTU hoped to expand its constituency beyond the big corporations from which it got almost all of its students and also to move toward enrolling students who came to the university on their own, not through corporations. The form that NTU will assume in the new century became an open question in 2002, however, when Sylvan Learning Systems bought the university to make it one more folder in its expanding portfolio of higher educational institutions.

Interest in yoking education to careers is not limited to the professional audience that National Technological University served. Blue-collar and service workers, too, comprise a potential audience. Job skills appear to be the key, whether the courses are in classrooms or online. These skills seem easier to teach and more in demand than the ideas and arguments of the liberal arts. The 16 institutions that made up the Wisconsin Technical College system, part of the University of Wisconsin system, joined forces in late 2001, for instance, to establish a collaborative online presence, etechcollege.com. The venture represented a first step in lending coherence to what until then had been separate, disparate online offerings. The 16 colleges continued to determine their individual fates in e-learning, but in addition to their separate home pages there was suddenly a single portal to deliver all of the system's online courses to potential students in one place on the web. "Our presidents expect us to coordinate this so eventually there aren't 16 versions of the same course," said Jeff Larson, who was charged with pulling together the project for the system. This was also the beginning, some in the system hoped, of higher standards and more quality control in the online courses.

Not scheduled to change was the orientation of the courses toward adults looking to change jobs, retrain, or earn certificates essential to getting and retaining their positions. For instance, there were certificates in clinical coding for specialists who analyze health records and assign diagnosis codes, for office workers who use Microsoft software, for wastewater operators, business managers, legal assistants, and information management specialists. There were associate degrees in microcomputer programming, emergency dispatch, and developing web sites. It was a matter of Wisconsin's technical colleges doing online what they already did in classrooms. Students arriving through the Wisconsin Technical College system's portal were to choose a home campus for purposes of matriculation and for the granting of a credential. Then, the student could select online courses from any of the 16 institutions.

Policymakers have often regarded education as the engine that drives economic development. Some people in Michigan had the novel notion of harnessing that engine to the Internet. It all began in the mid-1990s as an idea that appealed to the University of Michigan,

Michigan State University, and the Automotive Research Center. They wanted to use online courses to accelerate work-force development. Governor John Engler embraced the approach and helped persuade the Big Three automakers to commit themselves to buy $5 million each of professional development from what was dubbed the Michigan Virtual Automotive College. By 1998, the idea had snowballed into the creation of Michigan Virtual University (MVU), a private, nonprofit, market-driven entity that contracted for the delivery of programs and services by Michigan's colleges and universities and by private training providers. Michigan Virtual Automotive College was absorbed into Michigan Virtual University as part of the Michigan Manufacturing Training Network.

In all, MVU by 2002 was carrying out three missions, all linked to its original goal of economic development—operating Michigan Virtual High School, providing online career guidance, and offering corporate learning services. Eight thousand Michigan workers, from private companies and government agencies, trained under contracts with Michigan Virtual University in 2001. MVU brokered the contracts under which educational institutions and private trainers provided both credit and noncredit online courses. MVU was not authorized to grant degrees, which students earned through the educational institutions that offered the courses. The courses were not only for workers in manufacturing and information technology; hundreds of schoolteachers throughout the state took professional development courses online via Michigan Virtual University. A feature available to educators was a program to help them learn to develop their own online courses. MVU's online career guidance was used by employers and by individuals seeking jobs and internships, as well as by high school students trying to plan careers and choose colleges and universities. Michigan Virtual High School, like the online university, brokered courses for students whose brick-and-mortar high schools did not have such courses or whose regular schedules could not accommodate certain classroom courses.

The emphasis on economic development by Kentucky Virtual University (KVU) provided another example of using online courses for nonprofessional education. In 2002, KVU directed the largest portion of its students to the institutions of the Kentucky Community and Technical system. The virtual university itself offered no courses, instead facilitating enrollments and providing various support services to students who found their way into online programs through its auspices. KVU worked with other state agencies to carry out this mandate. The Kentucky Department for Adult Education and Literacy, for instance, contracted with the virtual university to create, deploy, and maintain online literacy courses for people learning to read, as well as professional development courses for literacy instructors.

The nation's strong interest in information technology exemplifies another aspect of the appeal of technical education. Microsoft, which has an extensive internal training program for its employees, offered no courses directly to the outside world despite the clamor to learn more about how to use its products, which, among other things, helped make online learning possible. Microsoft instead collaborated with 2,500 private centers that trained candidates for tests that certified their ability to use the corporation's applications. Supplying each student with a kit that it bought from Microsoft, the corporate training "partners," as Microsoft called them, offered courses, usually five days in duration. Microsoft created more than 400 different courses to enable outside trainers to teach about every phase of the corporation's products.

Microsoft did not get directly involved with the more than one million students that it estimated had been trained through these programs by 2002. Each student got Microsoft in a box—a typical kit containing printed instructional materials, a CD electronic version of the materials, and the software that was the subject of the course. In 2002, Microsoft was increasingly creating online versions of these materials. Microsoft even wrote the tests for the courses and its name was on the certificates of those who successfully completed the courses. At the highest level, a student could become a Microsoft Certified Systems Engineer (MCSE). In turn, Microsoft expected its partners to use only teachers with MCSE certification for the various courses. Job ads in newspapers are filled with initials for the various Microsoft certifications that employers require. An emerging question in 2002 was if and when Microsoft might decide to circumvent the partners, develop modules that conform more closely to the traditional academic progression, and make itself a player in providing technical education to the general public. Surely such a step would mark the arrival of an 800-pound gorilla to online technical education.

The Pursuit of Career-Oriented Students

Both for-profit providers and traditional institutions of higher education have recognized that one of the best chances for early acceptance of online courses resides in offering them to people who most need them for instrumental purposes, courses with content to advance their careers or allow them to embark on new careers. Some of the shrewdest, profit-oriented education entrepreneurs have seemed, in the best tradition of business, to coalesce around these career-oriented, professional-based courses tied to the needs of employers. Certificate and advanced study in business and other vocationally oriented offerings figure prominently in e-learning. Not surprisingly, online courses in the humanities and the social sciences do not enjoy the same appeal. Working students, whether they attend classes in person or online, usually want courses that will advance them in the workplace, not in the marketplace of ideas. Philosophy, literature, and art history, for example, have a much smaller online following than management, finance, and marketing.

Does this mean that online providers seek to cream off the easiest part of the market? You bet. In this regard, e-learning differs little from the freelance entrepreneurs who prowl the bus routes of the outer boroughs of New York City, picking up waiting passengers before the municipal buses arrive, leaving public authorities with the headache and expense of maintaining the infrastructure. Not many potential online students crave a course in anthropology or poetry. Some traditionalists dismiss the emphasis that e-learning places on career-oriented education. Yet, how different is this approach from the situation that prevails on campuses, where students flock to majors in business, communications, health care services, and other applied fields that they think will lead to the surest employment? Colleges and universities often sustain enrollments in the liberal arts only by compelling students to take these courses to satisfy degree requirements.

On the other hand, cautious providers realize that even courses in business do not *guarantee* enrollments. The *Chronicle of Higher Education*, which usually does a good job tracking trends, observed in the fall of 2001 that universities around the country were pulling back from what they had expected to be a booming market for online master of business degrees.[1] The downturn in the economy and the shakiness of the e-business industry caused institutions to reevaluate grandiose plans into which some of them had sunk substantial investments. Almost three years earlier, the same reporter had written an article for the *Chronicle* with a headline proclaiming that "Top Business Schools Seek to Ride a Bull Market in On-Line M.B.A.'s."[2] As this quick reversal showed, online education is no magic bullet. While it appeals to those studying business and other career-oriented fields, e-learning will take time to build and prosper, with its share of reversals along the way.

The online M.B.A. program offered by the School of Management of the State University of New York (SUNY) at Buffalo exemplified efforts that failed to fulfill rosy expectations. The university said in announcing the creation of the program in 2000 that it projected an enrollment of 1,000 students by 2002. The program had fewer than three dozen students when it closed in 2002. In actuality, it never amounted to more than a pilot effort, putting online only two of the courses needed for a degree. Little was done to tell potential students about the new online degree. A financial partner contributed less than one-third of the amount that the management school expected, and the dean who championed the idea left the school only a year after the rollout. SUNY Buffalo ended up with a fiscal folly on its hands. John Della Contrada, a public relations spokesman for the management school, said in 2002, after the program's demise, that the institution still was considering developing and offering M.B.A. courses online, but not enough courses to complete a degree without additional studies in a classroom.

If a substantial market eventually develops for online business courses, it could well be that it won't so much involve M.B.A. students as those who want continuing education, certificate-level, and even graduate-level work other than the master of business administration degree. Much the same pattern may unfold in the information technology field. Furthermore, in both business and information technology, universities expecting to build an online presence will probably face competition from corporate trainers and corporations themselves. As noted, Microsoft has already put its foot in this field. Thus, even though career-oriented education may fare best in the Internet environment, it will not be a walk in the park. The big-name universities that thought all they had to do was hang out their shingles and wait for the students to cluster around their computers have already been chastened.

HOW TWO UNIVERSITIES PURSUED WORKING ADULTS

Recognizing career-minded, working adults as a prime constituency for online learning, some colleges and universities carefully structured their approach to appeal to this market. The University of Phoenix had tailored its original classroom-based program in this way, and so it was simply a matter of more of the same when the institution put its program online. The University of Baltimore, an older institution with a more traditional history, took this path as a survival mechanism, when its former practices no longer paid dividends.

The University of Phoenix enjoys many distinctions. It was one of the first for-profit providers to get into academically oriented education when it offered such courses in 1976. It was one of the first for-profit entities to gain regional accreditation when it was recognized by the North Central Association of Schools and Colleges in 1978. It was one of the first educational institutions of any sort to put programs online when it did so in 1989. It grew so rapidly that it became the largest private university in the country with a total enrollment of 116,569 by 2002. The 37,569 online students lived in almost every state and many countries around the world. Though widely known for its online programs, the vast majority of Phoenix students attended classes at learning centers in 22 states, Puerto Rico, and Canada.

Traditional-age college students did not interest the University of Phoenix. The institution fashioned itself as a place for adult learners, particularly working adults seeking career-oriented studies. This focus, as mentioned earlier in the chapter, was the force behind the growth of the University of Phoenix Online, as the Internet portion of the institution was known. The university aimed a corporate training effort at Fortune 1000 companies, promoting online courses in such fields as business management, international business, e-business, information technology, project management, and marketing.

Phoenix operated on the basis that online students who enrolled in such programs as working adults with full-time jobs wanted more education to advance their careers, not to learn Shakespeare or to study ancient Greek civilization. The institution assumed that business travel and constraints on time made online learning attractive to adults who want to learn at hours and places convenient to them. Officials thought the kinds of students drawn to Phoenix did not want to study abstract theories; they sought to learn theory only to the extent that they could wed it to practice. In keeping with this approach, Phoenix hired mostly practitioners as instructors, people who were part of the workaday world and taught on the side. Such staffing also enabled the huge university to avoid building a faculty of full-time tenured professors over whom their control would be diminished and for whom the jobs would be permanent.

The University of Phoenix organized online courses with fewer than a dozen students in a class, encouraging them to move through a series of courses as a cohort of learners who could come to rely on each other and learn from each other through collaborations in which they linked up on the Internet. Classmates were divided into teams that pursued tasks together, working online in behalf of their joint learning, exchanging e-messages frequently each day. The interaction among team members ideally had the character of a team formed at the workplace to carry out a project for an employer. Such a team in an online course, for instance, might include a human resources person, an accountant, and an operations expert. The course would last five to six weeks and students would be online doing course work most days each week, according to Phoenix Online chief Digiovanni.

The web was a life preserver for the University of Baltimore (UB), an urban commuter institution where enrollments dwindled in the

1990s. The university's first online program was a master of business administration degree, offered as a companion to a campus-based program accredited by the American Association of Collegiate Schools of Business. The numbers tell the story. In the fall of 1999, the total M.B.A. enrollment was 538, with 522 in the regular classroom-based program and 16 in the new online program. By the fall of 2001, enrollment in the campus M.B.A. program had fallen to 365 but the online M.B.A. program had grown to 141 students, producing a total M.B.A. enrollment of 506 students and stabilizing the program. By going online, the University of Baltimore no longer had to rely on the willingness of students to commute to its urban locale. This change could be seen in the fact that by 2001, the online M.B.A. program drew 52 percent of its students from outside Maryland, while the on-campus program got only 27 percent of its students from outside the state. The experience at the University of Baltimore demonstrated how commuter institutions might use e-learning to change their enrollment profile without having to spend money to accommodate on-campus students.

Yet, even with its programs available on the world wide web, how is a lesser-known institution like the University of Baltimore to make prospective students aware of those programs? Marketing and cooperative arrangements with other institutions were the answer for UB. The university entered an agreement with Geolearning, a corporate trainer, to market UB's online credit programs to its noncredit corporate clients, and, together, Geolearning and the University of Baltimore planned to develop customized programs for specific corporate markets. Another arrangement, with Kentucky Virtual University, allowed Kentucky's students to apply through the Kentucky web site for admission to the UB online M.B.A. program. Those admitted paid Maryland resident tuition rates and had access to the services and virtual library of Kentucky Virtual University.

Venturing even farther afield, UB looked for educational marketers abroad who could line up enrollments for the Baltimore online program. One of the first such arrangements was struck with Mezon.com, an online organization that promoted academic programs to students in Turkey. Less concrete were the gains that the University of Baltimore hoped to reap from the increasing attention that its online programs got in the media. Officials were particularly gratified when *U.S. News & World Report* included UB on its October 2001 list of the best online graduate programs in business. "In such a new field of higher education, this kind of recognition may spell the difference between success and failure," said Ronald Legon, provost of the university.

THE CONTINUING EDUCATION OF TEACHERS

Purveyors of online learning see elementary and secondary schoolteachers as constituting one of their biggest potential markets. The numbers are huge. About one of every ten undergraduates prepares to teach, and public and private elementary and secondary schools employ some 3.5 million teachers. Not only do these positions turn over with regularity, but there are also shortages of candidates in some subject areas and in certain geographic locations. The demand for postbaccalaureate professional development by educators already working in schools is inexhaustible. State regulations and collective bargaining contracts mandate that teachers engage in continued learning, so-called in-service education, once they are on the job. School boards often link salary increases to such demands and spend more than 1 percent of their budgets on costs associated with professional development.

Given this huge potential, teacher-training institutions have wondered how to pitch online courses to this market. Teachers College, Columbia University, the largest graduate school of education in the United States, created a separate arm to explore the possibilities. Called TC Innovations, this venture in 2001 examined the possibilities in both for-profit and not-for-profit operations in the continuing education market for teachers. Teachers College financed TC Innovations with an initial infusion of $2.5 million and hoped to supplement this sum with money from foundations, businesses, and government. The college named Peter W. Cookson Jr., one of its administrators, as president of the offshoot. He developed a business plan that involved marketing courses in professional development to school superintendents around the country who would have their teachers enroll. Tentatively, each course would be taught in person in the teachers' home district, following a curriculum disseminated by TC Innovations. Another portion of the course would be an online component that the company would create with the aid of faculty at Teachers College and TC Innovations' own staff.

Leading teacher-training institutions like Teachers College could end up competing fiercely through online programs for enrollments from across the country. The best-known institutions now have the opportunity to attach their well-known names, what the business world calls "branding," to courses that they can offer in all parts of the United States and even abroad. Teachers College, Columbia University, after all, is not the only institution that could put a distinguished name on an online course. Graduate schools of education are found at Harvard, Stanford, Berkeley, and other prestigious institutions that might associate their names with online continuing education for teachers. The marriage of career education and online learning in this manner, carried forward by brand-name colleges and universities, might suddenly lead to a national market for a product that formerly seemed largely place-bound. For-profit providers recognized such possibilities long before the traditional institutions and now compete with them for the enrollments of such students.

Colleges and universities have long depended on undergraduate and graduate enrollments in teacher education, as well as continuing education and certificate courses for teachers, as low-overhead vehicles for bolstering enrollments and lining coffers. Now these institutions are uneasy with the competition introduced by online learning, which respects no geographic boundaries. They are also concerned with the propensity of profit-seeking businesses to enter this field, which already has more than enough competition. A white paper prepared for the American Association of Colleges of Teacher Education (AACTE) in 2001 estimated that more than 650 for-profit, degree-granting institutions and more than 2,000 virtual companies and universities were offering education courses. The paper recommended that AACTE take the following actions:

- create and establish policy guidelines and program characteristics to assist members in establishing innovative partnerships with nontraditional partners, including for-profit companies;

- develop membership guidelines that reflect the changing nature of those organizations that provide teacher education programs;
- establish collaborative partnerships with appropriate for-profit and educational foundations that are focused on providing high-quality teacher education and continuing education programs;
- develop policy and standards to judge the quality of for-profit education providers.[3]

Mounting interest among teacher educators looking to assure places for their institutions in the evolving market for professional development and graduate study prompted AACTE to hold a special, day-long institute, "Exploring the Education Industry," prior to its annual meeting in 2002. Teacher educators from more than 70 institutions went to New York City the day before the annual sessions to attend this institute. Gathering in a classroom building at City College of the City University, on the western edge of Harlem, they heard educators and business people describe the partnerships they had formed. It was a program of the sort that would have been unthinkable just a few years earlier, when business was anathema to the educators who still believed that they owned exclusive rights to the future of teacher education. "The old model may be ending," said Allen Glenn of the University of Washington in his opening remarks. "We're now in a neutral zone and we're not sure where it's going." He was the former dean of the university's College of Education and a former president of AACTE, as well as the author the previous year's white paper on for-profit providers in teacher education.

Teacher educators listened reverentially at the one-day institute as speakers from such commercial enterprises as Connected University, Sylvan Online, and the University of Phoenix described their for-profit businesses. Connected University went so far as to offer educators a place in the future by joining hands in partnerships with the for-profit company. Connected University, a part of Classroom Connection—which a few months earlier had become a part of Harcourt General, which in July 2001 had been bought by Reed Elsevier—sold workshops, professional development and continuing education courses, and graduate degree courses, all online. Scott Noon, a vice president of the

Classroom Connection, mentioned several times how distasteful it would be if his company had to obtain accreditation for what it does. Instead, it worked through such partners as Pepperdine University, Adams State College in Massachusetts, California State University at Bakersfield, Fordham University, Plymouth State College in New Hampshire, and Texas Tech University. These institutions approved Connected University's offerings, received a portion of the revenues, and awarded credits under the auspices of their accreditations.

Plymouth State, for example, reaped hundreds of enrollments in on-line courses in its graduate program as a result of its link to Classroom Connection's Connected University, which promoted the courses and registered the students. Students selected the courses on Connected University's web site and designated the partner college or university through which they wanted to earn the credit. Most students, generally teachers working in schools, took the courses for the continuing education units required to ascend the salary schedule.

According to Plymouth State, about 10 percent of the enrollees that it attracted through Connected University, continued into its master's degree programs. Connected University had revenue agreements with Plymouth State and other partner colleges and universities to share the registration and tuition fees. "I expect the marketing this year to really increase this," said Dennise M. Bartelo, associate vice president for graduate studies and continuing education at Plymouth State. Interestingly, the first seven online courses that these students had to take toward their master's degrees at Plymouth State originated through Connected University, which contracted with professors at colleges and universities around the country, especially in the California State University system, to create them. However, only the name of the institution granting the academic credit appeared on the student's academic transcript, not Connected University or the university that created the courses.

Rio Salado College, a campus in the Maricopa Community College District in Arizona, was among the first to offer online learning to students preparing to become teachers. In 1998, Arizona's State Education Department tried to address a teacher shortage by changing its regulations so that four-year institutions no longer had a monopoly over teacher education for undergraduates, thus opening the way for community colleges to enter the field. Rio Salado established a teacher education program to enroll students who already had their bachelor's degrees. As a community college, it could not credential students as teachers, but it could award them certificates of completion that would enable them to seek licenses from the State Education Department.

The program at Rio Salado began in 2001, with the course work online. Students could complete each course at their own pace within a 13-week period, as long as all the online work was done by the end of the period. Students were allowed to enroll in as many courses at once as they wished. Recognizing that experience with elementary or secondary school students in real classrooms was necessary for these future teachers, a portion of the program was real rather than virtual. A practicum of 10 to 25 hours in a classroom under the supervision of a mentor teacher was required. Each practicum had three parts: observations of the class by the student following a specific protocol; one-on-one tutoring of youngsters; and actually teaching the class. After completing a practicum, the student had to perform nine weeks of student teaching.

Should the Market Decide the Future?

Want to learn about Alexander the Great? Want to gain a deeper understanding of the mass media? The Global Education Network (GEN) thought it had a course for you. It didn't matter where you lived. This for-profit company, founded in 1999 by a Williams College humanities professor and an investment banker, dedicated itself from the outset to producing high-quality online courses in the humanities, arts, and sciences to offer to the greatest number of people at a reasonable price. Alexander Parker, an American with a British accent he acquired growing up in England, was its chief operating officer. He claimed that GEN spent up to $1 million to create a single course. The company rented a suite of offices in a high rise next door to Carnegie Hall, hired a bunch of techies, and set out to build web courses fashioned from classroom-based courses taught by leading professors. By the beginning of 2002, after piloting the first two of its liberal arts courses, the company had started building four more—in chemistry, Shakespeare, calculus, and art appreciation.

A big question was whether online students would want the kinds of courses that Global Education Network provided. E-learning's early days indicated, as noted, that the greatest demand was for courses with an occupational bent. Proponents of the liberal arts argue that their courses provide insights and historical context, teach critical thinking, improve speaking and writing, make one conversant with the human experience, and equip one with more than a few useful skills. In other words, the humanities, arts, and social sciences educate people, which ought to be an advantage in the job market. This may not be the kind of education, though, for which students turn to online learning. Even GEN realized this. The company sought to build a market by encouraging less-prestigious educational institutions to use the courses as a way of upgrading their liberal arts curriculums with offerings that originated with professors at elite institutions. The first three institutions enlisted by GEN were Bunker Hill Community College, Berkshire Community College, and Massachusetts College of Liberal Arts, all in Massachusetts.

It is one thing to say that online courses can legitimately respond to market demands and quite another to agree that this market orientation should be the sum and substance of online learning. The early response indicates that students and providers believe that web-based instruction can effectively convey occupationally oriented instruction. One cannot determine from this experience, though, whether all occupational training will benefit. "Everyone seemed to grasp the idea that you could do business courses online, understanding that they are mainly reading, research, and writing," said officials at Art Institute, a chain of proprietary schools with an online division. "It required some new thinking, however, to determine how to teach design online and yet, we found that design education followed a similar progression as business courses, though aimed at the right brain." Art Institute Online ended up striving to build its approach on the techniques the institute had used for decades in its classroom-based courses.

Online learning very likely could subsist almost entirely on a diet of such occupational courses. Accountants, teachers, health personnel, business and commercial workers—both in undergraduate and continuing education—could provide a wealth of ready and willing cyber learners. Jack M. Wilson, chief executive officer of UmassOnline, a part of the University of Massachusetts, went so far in 2002 as to predict that online programs will displace most professional graduate programs in business, computer science, engineering, nursing, and education.[4] There is nothing wrong with students pursuing education, on-campus or on-line, for its instrumental value. The earnings and periodic recertification of many people depend on their acquiring knowledge and skills related to specific jobs. Furthermore, even without a rich offering of the humanities and liberal arts online, students could still take such courses, if they chose, on campus and even through private reading and personal self-improvement.

Yet, at this juncture—still the genesis of online learning—one might harbor the hope that this newest style of formal education will not eschew the humanities and the liberal arts, which have so much to say to everyone, regardless of their career circumstances. What a pity it would be if online learning did not reach beyond those interested solely in career advancement. A full and comprehensive education requires more than learning how to perform the specifics of one's job well.

Nevertheless, Columbia University's Fathom, the Global Education Network, United States Open University, and others have found less-fertile ground for education that is not vocationally oriented. Fathom's fortunes took an interesting turn in 2002, when the weak appeal of its more intellectual courses caused it to announce that it would add corporate training to its offerings. This was a clear departure from its original intentions and just one more sign of where online learning's strongest appeal lies. On the other hand, campus-based education does not treat the humanities and the liberal arts with full respect either. Left to their own decisions, baccalaureate candidates on many campuses would not bother with courses in, say, philosophy, history, music, and the visual and performing arts. The departments housing these courses have in many instances been transformed into little more than service units, letting students fill out general education requirements.

Some critics of cyber education consider it just as well that the humanities and the liberal arts have not found succor in e-learning. They regard the web as a wrong and possibly perverted place to study Machi-avelli's *The Prince,* or the Platonic dialogues, or the Federalist Papers, or the technique of Rembrandt. This can be done only in person, in the company of scholars, they say. This attitude smacks of snobbery; it is much too soon to shut the book on e-learning as a source of education in the humanities and the liberal arts.

But it might not be too early in the short history of online courses to consider whether to spend public funds at some point to support provision of courses in the humanities and the liberal arts. Some people argued in the early days of television that the medium was too vital to yield all programming to market forces. And, so, they ensured the birth and sustenance of public television. Perhaps similar ventures might serve the humanities and the liberal arts on the web, which one could say is also too important to abandon its educational possibilities to careerism.

CHAPTER 9

BUT IS IT LEGITIMATE?

Regarding technology, John Merrow, the eminent broadcast journalist who specializes in the coverage of education, wrote: "[I]t creates the opportunity for cheating—widespread dishonesty in an unparalleled way. Most people know how easy it is now for a student to download something from somewhere else and say: 'This is my work.' In fact, 77 percent of high school students say they now use the Internet to research school assignments."[1] Two college incidents support Merrow's observation. Northwestern University, a prestigious, highly selective institution in Chicago's leafy Evanston suburb, faced a scandal in 2001 in which a professor suspected 14 undergraduates in a philosophy course of submitting papers that contained materials plagiarized from the Internet. Moreover, a physics professor at the University of Virginia, who developed a computer program to detect plagiarism by comparing students' papers, found 122 suspect papers out of 1,850 submitted over a three-year period.[2] And this happened at an institution with an honors code.

Plagiarism is a longstanding problem that technology exacerbates. A generation ago, scandals arose as entrepreneurs who wrote term papers for students went public by advertising their services. Now, students of all ages surf the Internet for material that they can electronically paste into work to which they sign their own names. Though it would not end the practice, it would help if instructors did more to teach students the elements of research and deepen their understanding of the differences between citing someone else's work and appropriating it as one's own. Information Literacy and Research Methods, a one-credit, required course for students working toward degrees at the University of Maryland University College (UMUC), represented one institution's response to these problems. With an expanding online enrollment, UMUC led the way with this course that included an effort to help students recognize plagiarism. Those who teach bear the responsibility of protecting educational integrity. It is incumbent upon them, whether their courses are offered in classrooms or in cyber space, to ferret out dishonesty.

For example, in one online program an instructor who suspected plagiarism confronted the student. He said that he "sat down with the student virtually," by e-mail, in other words, and told him that if it happened again the student would be dropped from the program. The instructor said that in the average large lecture classroom course he would have been far less likely to have identified the plagiarism because he wouldn't have been as familiar with the student's work as he was, seeing it regularly in the online discussions.

Such situations as these caused the *New York Times* to observe: "At a time when Internet literacy seems in inverse proportion to age, a new generation of students is faced with an old temptation made easier than ever: taking the work of others and passing it off as one's own. In this era of cut and paste, hundreds of sites offer essays and research papers on topics as abstruse and challenging as Shakespeare's 'Troilus and Cressida' and Sartre's 'Being and Nothingness,' some at no charge. And e-mail has made it simpler for students to borrow from one another's work."[3] There is no doubt that the Internet and the technology of which it is part have made cheating easier. Anonymity helps shield unethical behavior. Someone else may write a paper that a student submits as his own; the student may plagiarize the work of others from the Internet. Instead of doing the assigned reading or sifting through research findings, students may take shortcuts on the Internet, bypassing experiences that are supposed to lead to learning.

In none of these instances, though, are students necessarily enrolled in online courses. These are students in traditional classrooms who use technology in a questionable manner. The point here is that it doesn't take online learning to induce technological chicanery. But mention these problems in the context of a discussion of online education, and chances are that they tarnish the image of this instructional approach. Researchers found in questioning students that plagiarism from online sources was essentially no greater than plagiarism from books, articles, and other printed sources. They also found that any growth in plagiarism using Internet sources had not necessarily led to an overall increase in plagiarism, just shifting the source away from printed material. Furthermore, plagiarism of all kinds may not be as widespread as some suspect. While half of the students in one study thought that their peers often or very frequently plagiarized, only 8 percent said that they themselves plagiarized often or very frequently.[4]

If students find it more difficult to break the rules in courses that meet face-to-face, some may merely devise more ingenious methods to cheat in those classroom-based courses. Students may download material from the Internet when they prepare papers out of class. They may seek shortcuts when they haven't read the book or completed an assignment. They may slip each other answers on tests and look on each other's papers. "There is more cause for concern about academic integrity in the average freshman or sophomore lecture hall than there is online," said Wallace Pond, chief academic officer of Education America's online campus, a for-profit, postsecondary cyber institution. "There are lots of lecture hall courses where a student might not interact with a professor at all and the final grade is based on two exams and a paper. An environment of that sort may engender poor decision making by students who turn to such activities as plagiarism."

Pond, who previously taught in classrooms, said that he disagreed with the assumption that campus-based programs provide the standard for academic integrity. While he conceded the possibility of cheating in online courses, just as in classroom-based courses, he said nonetheless: "In a well-taught online course with an involved professor and 25 students, it would be very difficult for a student to put bits and pieces of someone else's work into his work. Everything, every word, in an online course is archived. The professor can go back and review all of the student's work."

This, according to Pond, means that it is possible for an online instructor to see what the student was thinking and saying throughout
the course—in e-mail, in threaded discussions, chat rooms—and to
recognize whether the tenor of the archival record is consistent with
work that the student turns in online or with outcomes of monitored
tests. "You don't have this in a lecture hall, in face-to-face teaching,
where the words go up in the ether," Pond said. He tried to illustrate
his point, recalling his experience in 1998 when he taught online for
the first time. It was a linguistics course for schoolteachers of students
from non-English-speaking backgrounds, which enrolled 11 students
and lasted for 12 weeks. During that period, by his count of the archive
for the course, he catalogued 765 individual communications online
with the students as a group and individually. It was relatively easy to
preserve the entire record when almost all contact took place online.
He could conveniently consult the archive to look back on students'
comments and observe how the online work of students fit with their
performance and with the papers they turned in, as well as with the results of the tests they took.

Similarly, Vincent Piturro of the University of Colorado at Denver,
who taught a hybrid composition course in which students met twice a
week for 75-minute sessions and did the rest of the work online, said
that he ran spot checks of the work that students produced in the two
settings, in person and online. "If the work was of *very* different quality," he said, "it would raise a red flag. It's never happened so far."

Whatever the actual incidence of plagiarism today, disreputable behavior plagued distance learning long before the onset of online education, beginning with correspondence courses in the nineteenth century
and continuing right into the first decade of the twenty-first century.
Athletes who enrolled in correspondence courses that they took to preserve their eligibility for varsity sports have been among the worst of-
fenders. And they didn't need computers to cheat. In 1994, the National
Collegiate Athletic Association (NCAA) set off emergency alarms
when it appeared that dozens of athletes in two-year colleges obtained
tainted academic credits through correspondence courses. In 1995, the
FBI collected evidence of academic fraud by athletes from five universities who took correspondence courses offered by an obscure religious

college in Texas. In 1996, the NCAA rejected a proposal that would have barred colleges from counting credits earned in correspondence courses on the transcripts of athletes transferring from two-year colleges to four-year colleges.[5]

HOLDING ONLINE LEARNING TO A HIGHER STANDARD

The question at this juncture is: Why hold online learning to a higher standard than other kinds of distance education or, for that matter, than traditional classroom education? Students who take all of their courses in person are seduced by the same temptations as those who pursue courses from afar. Students of the 1940s and 1950s, for instance, had their Classics comic books that provided the story line for many a book report. Then came CliffsNotes for those who did not want to read books. The absence of honor codes on the vast majority of campuses reflects the problem that institutions of higher education face in trying to keep students honest. Among the few universities with such codes are Princeton, the University of Virginia, and the military academies. But students at other colleges and universities, not to mention public elementary and secondary schools, are seldom asked to take oaths not to cheat and to report those whom they know to cheat.

One of the strongest attacks in this young century on traditional institutions for their alleged lack of academic integrity was leveled by Harold J. Noah and Max A. Eckstein in their book *Fraud and Education: The Worm in the Apple*. They charged that those involved in education are no less subject to lapses of integrity than people in business, government, professional sports, and the law. "Trust in the integrity of the educational process is eroded," they wrote, "as teachers, principals, and administrators, pressured to produce good test results, resort to unethical conduct and as confidence in the authority of academic credentials is weakened by the proliferation of fake diplomas."[6] The authors described example after example of fraud, cheating, and professional misconduct in higher education. And their observations are devoted to brick-and-mortar schools and colleges.

Some of the suspicion arises out of e-learning's invisibility. An anonymous person who had been offering legal advice that many sought on the Internet revealed himself in 2001 to be a teenager with no more experience in the law than he had gained in any other sphere of life during his tender years. Critics are concerned that what may appear to be a proper academic course online may actually lack quality control. They seem to think that flesh-and-blood teachers with students they see in seats in classrooms can more readily exact accountability. How? While technology and the Internet probably abet cheating, most of the resulting dishonesty occurs in courses that meet in traditional classrooms, where enrollments remain overwhelmingly concentrated. This hardly amounts to an indictment of online learning.

Another part of the concern over online education has to do with the growing number of providers who seek financial profit, a goal that seems unsavory to those who think the words "profit" and "education" should never accompany each other. Yet, the Education Commission of the States in its report on for-profit, degree-granting institutions offered an observation that took some exception to these reservations: "As both businesses and schools, they need to meet the quality standards of both industry and academe, and may be even more sensitive to quality control than traditional institutions."[7]

One could also raise quality questions about many of the ways that colleges and universities have deviated during the last 25 to 30 years from accepted practice in face-to-face classes. So-called weekend colleges and other time-shortened programs spread across the country as institutions sought to boost enrollments by making programs more convenient for working adults. Seton Hall University in New Jersey, for instance, has what it calls a fast track to an Ed.D. degree in educational administration. Candidates were told in 2002 that they could complete the degree in 10 weekends and two four-week summer sessions over a two-year period that wouldn't interfere with their career responsibilities. One could easily find many more such truncated degree programs. Are such innovations any more or less legitimate than online education? Given the prevalence of such offerings, one must wonder about critics who object to the availability of online degree programs merely because they exist.

In the search for students, many institutions cast their nets widely, well removed from the infrastructure that supposedly reinforces classroom courses, and they have done so for years. No one bothered to call it distance education when students convened in classrooms away from the home campus, perhaps even in another state. In some instances, these outreach activities took place at modest, stripped-down facilities, providing little more than a motel room in which students could meet with an instructor for a class. Often there were no libraries or student amenities. Instructors, in some cases, were not available to meet with students outside the classroom itself.

EVALUATING ONLINE LEARNING

One of the most common questions about online learning is whether it is better than education in the classroom, implying that being as good is not enough. The question is not easily answered and a large body of research that might speak to the issue is only now starting to emerge. Much of the evidence is composed of anecdotal findings that tend to be unpersuasive either way. There are, however, some parameters that may be applied in evaluating online learning, and one need not be an expert to take this measure. Two of the most obvious yardsticks have to do with course design and the interactivity of the course.

One can readily see whether an online course amounts to more than an extended lecture plopped on the web. At the other end of this spectrum, one can recognize what John Black, a professor at Teachers College, Columbia University, calls "a syllabus on steroids design," bells and whistles that capture attention but add little academic substance to a course. The happy medium in design reflects itself in a course that takes advantage of technology to deepen education, making it more memorable and providing learning experiences beyond those apt to be possible without the Internet. Interactivity, another main consideration in course evaluation, should use technology to connect students in meaningful ways to the instructor and to each other. "Ideally," Black said, "instructors throw out discussion topics, students respond, and there are responses to the responses." Moreover, instructors interact with students promptly and do not make them wait interminably.

Evaluations of M.B.A. courses at the University of Baltimore showed an intriguing split in students' attitudes toward the course materials and toward the instructors. The materials used in online courses got higher ratings than those used in classroom-based courses. This was true even in comparisons of materials used by the same instructor in online and classroom-based versions. The opposite was true in regard to the students' evaluation of the instructors. Students gave higher marks to instructors who taught face-to-face, including those who taught the same course in both formats. In other words, students in classroom-based courses ended up thinking more highly of the instructor than students who encountered the same instructor in the same course online.

Faculty members, of course, are evaluated by their employers as well as by their students. Ronald Legon, provost of the University of Baltimore, felt that the potential for documenting the quality of faculty instruction was greater in online courses than in classroom-based courses. He explained: "At most, traditional universities require occasional visits of senior faculty to the classrooms of faculty whose performance is being evaluated. There has always been divided opinion about the value and propriety of these visits. Critics argue that they are intrusions on the privileged communication that goes on between professors and their students, and that such occasional visits do not provide an adequate basis to judge the effectiveness of a teacher over the course of a semester. Even supporters of such visits concede that the presence of an observer alters the classroom experience, so that what the observer sees is not typical. The online classroom avoids many of these problems."

As Wallace Pond and Vincent Piturro did, Legon pointed to the extensive record of communication between instructor and students that exists for online courses, citing lecture materials, documents, threaded discussions, chats, e-messages, graded assignments, and other course artifacts that are electronically archived. "This body of evidence inarguably allows a much more comprehensive understanding of the learning process," he said. Yet, the degree to which instructors—from either an online course or a classroom-based course—wish to make such material available to institutions for the purpose of evaluating them is altogether another matter: issues of confidentiality and academic freedom come into play.

National Technological University (NTU) made an interesting comparison when the same course was offered in a classroom and at a distance—in some cases by CD-ROM and in other instances, online. NTU students consistently got higher grades than their counterparts who took the courses in the classrooms of leading universities where the classes were recorded or transmitted for use by NTU. Typically, these were engineering, scientific, and technical courses at the postbaccalaureate level. Patrick Partridge, NTU's vice president for marketing, speculated that his institution's students did better than those on campuses because they were older, more motivated, and better focused, even though they had full-time jobs and families. They were, on average, 39 years old and almost all had gotten their undergraduate degrees the old-fashioned way, in classrooms. In fact, a survey that Partridge conducted of NTU students found that only 7 percent thought that distance learning was not as effective as classroom learning. Sixty-two percent felt the experience was about the same as in a classroom, and 31 percent deemed distance learning more effective than the classroom.

Gary E. Miller, executive director of World Campus at Penn State, maintained that standards in online courses and in-person courses were essentially the same. Overwhelmingly, those who taught courses online at Penn State had taught the same courses in classrooms and had then worked with others to adapt the courses to e-learning. Presumably, the same course with identical content and the same professor resulted in the same teaching and learning.

Does the medium matter in evaluation? If some feature of learning online retards progress and diminishes educational attainment, then surely this is a pernicious method of education that holds back learning. But the same question could be asked about classroom lectures, hands-on experiments in science laboratories, internships, studying in groups, listening to an audiotape, or any other way that people seek to acquire knowledge. There are certainly some people for whom the medium matters and for whom online learning has a negative effect. Just as surely, though, others thrive in a virtual setting. Probably nothing inherent in learning pursued via computer necessarily makes it deleterious for large numbers of students. This presumes that the institution does not cut corners in course design, instruction and facilitation, and technical and academic support for online learners.

Higher education until now has not spent all that much time evaluating classroom courses and making them more learner-friendly for students. Probably the main inroads in this connection have been the student evaluations, mentioned in chapter 5, that have been omnipresent at colleges and universities since the 1960s. This was the result of pressure from students, not because institutions or their faculty members cared a lot about how students regarded the courses. These evaluations, flawed as they may be, show that faculty members working in classrooms range from the highly effective to the highly ineffective. Wouldn't the same be true of instructors in any medium?

The University of Phoenix, with more than 10 years of online experience, developed a systematic approach to measure and evaluate both classroom and online learning. The university's institutional research division sought to determine the effectiveness of its academic offerings and the academic achievement of its students. Its Adult Learning Outcome Assessment Project consisted of these components:

- an assessment of cognitive achievement to measure the competence that students develop in their professional disciplines;
- a professional and educational values assessment, given at entrance and at graduation, to measure the value a student puts on newly acquired knowledge and skills;
- a communications skills inventory, also given at entrance and at graduation, to measure growth in communications skills and abilities;
- portfolio assessments to provide actual examples of students' work in addition to information accumulated through tests and surveys;
- a critical thinking assessment to measure students' problem-solving abilities;
- validation through such national tests as the Graduate Management Admissions Test, given to random groups of students, to provide external backup to Phoenix's own cognitive and critical skills assessments.

In addition to this battery of assessments, the University of Phoenix tried to maintain quality control through its Academic Quality Management System. For this purpose, it used surveys administered to students upon entering the institution, separate end-of-course surveys given to students and faculty, surveys given to students when they completed their programs, alumni surveys, employer surveys, and other instruments. The University of Phoenix found that the institution's online students performed about as well as its classroom-based students in both the pre-testing and the post-testing.

SPECIAL PROBLEMS IN ASSESSING ONLINE STUDENTS

Elinor Grusin of the University of Memphis usually gave take-home exams to the graduate students in her classroom-based communications law course, so it did not concern her to give the same kind of tests to students in the online version of the course. She presented students with a hypothetical libel case and asked them to answer certain questions regarding the case: was this person defamed? is the figure a public figure or a private person? what test of fault must he or she meet? Students had to write a seven-page paper with citations from the law to make their points. The hypothetical case came from Grusin's head, so it required students to do original work to complete the take-home exam whether students took the course in person or online.

Schoolteacher Arna Clark, a 40-year-old online student at Western Governors University with ample experience of her own giving tests, said: "It's been strange to get straight-A grades in my recommended online university course work yet barely pass the WGU competency exams. I read the online resources available on the WGU web site, took appropriate courses, and consolidated my notes into outlines for intense study. Then I prayed a lot and ate several pints of Ben & Jerry's ice cream, chocolate." On the other hand, Clark maintained that some of what passed for rigor in the competency examinations actually may have been accounted for by faulty test construction. She found some questions ambiguous and thought that answers other than the ones deemed correct were equally valid. That, of course, could be a problem in both classroom and online learning.

Proctors and Other Assessment Devices

Teachers at the online University of Missouri High School usually marked students' lessons in one of two ways. If the student was asked to respond to multiple-choice questions, a computer generated a report on the answers and gave the report to the student. If the assignment called for actual writing, as in English or a foreign language course, an instructor provided written comments to the student online. This statewide high school, associated with the university's land-grant outreach, relied on an old approach to give credentials for a new approach. It required two proctored examinations in most online courses. Proctors were usually staff members at the student's regular high school, but they might also be librarians in the community, members of the clergy, or county extension agents—as long as proctors were not relatives of the student. One requirement for passing a course was a combined average of 60 on the two examinations. The high school said it had not devised an alternative to this approach, as all the other online possibilities it had considered for examinations did not seem sufficiently secure.

The United States Open University in its brief existence tended to use fairly standard ways to assess students, mostly quizzes, short papers, and projects of a week or so, sometimes requiring group work. Students were called upon to write a great deal in their courses, more in keeping with the tradition in Britain than in the United States, and these writing samples, too, provided evidence of students' progress. A proctor, perhaps someone who worked at a nearby community college or at a neighborhood library, supervised each student's final exam at the end of the course. This idea of continual feedback flowing between student and instructor—a process facilitated by the Internet—should mean that a conscientious teacher always has a fix on how well the student grasps the lessons. In turn, regular responses from instructors should keep students aware of what they still need to learn.

When it began, the Florida Virtual School had its students sit for examinations in the presence of proctors, who might teach in the regular

schools in which the students took most of their courses, or of parents
for those who were schooled at home. But this practice quickly became
impractical: as the school grew, arranging for every exam throughout the
school term to be proctored proved an insurmountable burden. Later,
only the final exam in a course was taken—over the computer—in the
presence of a proctor. "Do we know that the person monitoring the student is not helping him?" asked Julie Young of the Florida Virtual
School. "Of course not." Alexander Parker, chief operating officer of the
Global Education Network, expressed similar sentiments. "There's a
point at which we can't prove that someone is doing the work short of
putting electrodes on their heads and measuring what we find from
that," he said sarcastically to the question of whether an online student
or someone else takes the test.

Yet, the question of who is taking the tests and doing the work that
students submit as their own continues to plague online providers. It is
incumbent on schools and colleges to do all they can to guarantee the
integrity of the process. Invisibility remains one of the enterprise's most
troubling features. The growth and acceptance of online education depends on providers' assuring the legitimacy of academic outcomes.

Florida Virtual School said that it had ways of checking up on students. Throughout the year, it expected teachers to administer brief oral
quizzes during their telephone conversations with students. The questions, ideally embedded in conversations, were random and somewhat
different for each student in the course. Young said that the object was
to get to the heart of what students were learning. Based on their understanding of individual students, teachers supposedly knew without
even seeing scores on final exams what students were getting out of their
courses.

There was, however, another indication of how well students taking
courses in Florida Virtual School did. Those in the Advanced Placement (AP) courses sponsored by the College Board took the AP examinations, and their scores were reasonably good by most standards. This
test—the same whether students attended a virtual school or an actual
school, in Florida or in California—has a scoring range from 1, the lowest, to 5, the highest. Many colleges award advanced standing to students who achieve scores of 4 and 5. More than half of the students who

took their tests as an outgrowth of courses at Florida Virtual School scored 4's and 5's. Of course, this was a self-selected group, making it difficult to compare with the general school population.

Assessment as an Ongoing Process

The irony of the concern about how best to assess students in online courses to prevent dishonesty is that it comes when online testing of students in classroom-based courses is proliferating. Educational Testing Service and other major companies increasingly put their products online, seeing this as a way to make more money. The very critics who raise questions about the security of online assessment associated with online learning seem not to notice that the process is essentially the same for test takers who have never studied online. Those who worry about e-learning students' cheating in these assessments should have no less reason to think that anyone taking a test online may act dishonestly. Furthermore, classroom teachers give take-home tests and open-book tests that test takers also may exploit. Careful test design and diligent monitoring reduce dishonesty, but cheating occurs whether students take tests in person or online. There will always be test takers who give in to dishonesty, and online assessment makes it that much easier for them. This is surely one of the weaknesses of courses on the Internet, so much so that the University of Maryland University College required its online students to appear in person for monitored final examinations.

The online format with its continuing discussions through bulletin boards lends itself to a kind of ongoing assessment of students. In Sheila Seifert's writing courses at the University of Colorado at Denver, students had to respond to questions each week as part of the ongoing assessment. She asked them to identify one thing weekly that they had learned from the lesson and to write to her about it; she also asked students to write about aspects of the learning that continued to confuse them. These questions were answered in a discussion that was available for all members of the class to see. On a private basis, Seifert asked each student to write about the important idea presented in the readings that week and to send responses only to her through her e-mail. Seifert also administered online tests, not unlike those given in classrooms, calling for both short answers and extended responses. She graded such tests just as if they were taken in a classroom.

Gary Saunders, an accounting professor at Marshall University in West Virginia, worried about the security of online assessments. He said that "while Internet courses are here to stay, we have to work hard to make sure we have a level of control" over settings for exams. He wanted to ensure that the student and not a surrogate takes the test and that no cheating occurs. He preferred to have video cameras and microphones in rooms in which students took tests for online courses so that a monitor at the home campus could see what students did and hear what they said to each other during the tests. Saunders was not comfortable with the practice of some institutions of simply letting the online student find a proctor and leaving it up to the proctor to vouch for the security in place during the assessment.

Saunders had not taught an online course, but he had done research to see what colleagues in business schools around the country thought of such courses. He and Rick Weible, a faculty colleague at Marshall University, found in 1999 that 36 percent of the chairs of accounting departments and 46 percent of deans of business schools approved of online courses. When the survey was repeated in 2001, approval of online courses had increased. Saunders conceded that he resisted when his university pushed for an online degree in accounting. He thought the institution was hurrying and that it should prepare more slowly and carefully. "I don't have a problem with students not coming to class," he said, "but it's better to get in the controls over assessment so you're ready when it does happen."

Pointing to the troubling questions about human uniqueness that are raised by e-learning, the newsletter of the Institute for Advanced Studies in Culture observed, "The distinguishing qualities of the human person have been denoted by the natural and the real over and against the artificial and the virtual."[8] The specter of this concern inevitably haunts e-learning, which undoubtedly strikes some as inauthentic, an illegitimate combination of the human and the artificial. Even more, it can appear to lack the sensate, to be utterly without the social dimension that many believe underlies the growth of the mind.

The idea of separating education from traditional classrooms and, moreover, making it dependent on technology offends some people. They see this as a dehumanizing process that eliminates face-to-face interaction and advances the day when people will subjugate themselves to machines. One hardly has to be a Luddite to harbor such concerns. Almost every adult raised in the United States recalls school as a social kind of place where relationships were as important as the learning. Moreover, many remember individual teachers for their personal role in giving meaning to the pursuit of knowledge. Ballpoint pens, protractors and, for a few students, slide rules were the only gadgetry—outside home economics and industrial arts shops—that mediated the experience before calculators and, then, computers arrived in classrooms.

Yet, another concern lurks among those who challenge the legitimacy of e-learning. They worry that at its root lies a ruse, that the learning is not genuine nor subject to verification. People who can't be seen can't be trusted—be they the students or the providers, according to this line of thought. Something of the honor system underpins online learning; wherever and whenever such an arrangement exists, critics suspect, someone waits for the chance to exploit it. It is no accident that so few schools, colleges, and universities in the United States have embraced honor codes. Who is to say that some online programs do not feed junk to those who enroll and award them meaningless academic credits and even worthless degrees? Who is to say that some online students don't do as little possible, that they don't cheat their way through assignments and examinations?

This is the cynics' view of online learning and it may ring true in some instances. Such problems also exist, though, in classroom-based education where students and teachers can reach out and touch each other. The nation's brick-and-mortar high schools confer tens of thousands of diplomas annually on youngsters who have been wholly unequipped to prosper in postsecondary education or in any meaningful job. Colleges and universities give credit and degrees to students who have taken some courses in classrooms that produced hardly an iota of learning in major fields of study that command no respect in the academy itself. Online learning may inflict no more harm upon the Republic than a lot of what passes as official classroom education. Courses are already online, regardless of what objectors and detractors say about it. Perhaps the best action may be to give e-learning a chance, recognizing that, like all infants, it will take some flops, and to wait and see what emerges. In the meanwhile, brick-and-mortar institutions can learn from it, shamelessly borrow from it, and co-opt its best features.

CHAPTER 10

CONTROLLING THE PROCESS

A new reality that eliminates geographic restraints on the formal distribution of knowledge is stretching regulations that were written for an industry in which the purveyors were tied to certain locales. Yet, some educators from traditional programs seem to resent efforts to yank regulation into the cyber age, evincing hostility toward measures that would allow institutions to follow approaches different from prevailing practice. Education at all levels often seeks to preempt change by squeezing out innovation. Then, unsurprisingly, educational initiatives fail because they are not actually implemented. An inclination to change is clearly not one of education's virtues. Educators tend to find comfort and reassurance in the familiar and feel less threatened by what they already know. There are few rewards in schools and universities for those who take risks.

Opposition of this sort slows the advance of online education. Trying to hold back e-learning, though, will be futile. No one today can imagine banks, hospitals, airlines, law offices, research laboratories, and much of society without computers and the attendant technology. Online learning represents but one manifestation of the imperative for education to respond to the consumer orientation that impels so much of society today. Traditionally operated schools and colleges with their monopolies on the delivery system have only in recent years started to acknowledge market demands. Convenience ranks high for students even if educational institutions are slow to embrace it.

Many of the laws and regulations affecting education will have to change to accommodate the possibilities made possible in teaching and learning online. Students who spend little or no time in school or on campus confound the rationalizations that underlie many existing policies. Online courses demand new ways to deal with funding formulas, attendance and time requirements for courses, residency rules, eligibility for financial aid, the mandated size of library collections, standards for academic credit, student-teacher ratios, and pay scales. The straight jacket that constrains education is particularly restrictive on new technology. Regulations that govern eligibility for the federal government's student aid program exemplify the restrictions.

For its part, Congress has been under some pressure to loosen restrictions on online education since it recognized e-learning as a legitimate way of delivering education in the 1996 amendments to the Higher Education Act, which was originally enacted in 1965. Congress opened the door to remedying the regulatory situation at the federal level by authorizing distance education demonstration programs, starting in 1998, allowing a pilot group of 111 institutions to obtain waivers from certain regulations restricting aid to students in distance courses. Some viewed this measure as a way to determine whether officials should change statutes and regulations in recognition of the flexibility of distance education.

In 2001, a report on the demonstration program worried that restrictive provisions of Title IV of the Higher Education Act might limit the ability of institutions to exploit technology to enrich instruction. It was quick to add, though, that Congress should balance regulatory change against the risk of opening new avenues to the abuse of federal funds.[1] These developments made it likely that by the time this book is published Congress might have changed some of the regulations that worked to the disadvantage of distance learning. In fact, the Council for Higher Education Accreditation, the umbrella group of the accreditation agencies, issued a report in May 2002, in conjunction with the American Council on Education, asserting that Congress could relax the regulations with confidence as the accrediting agencies had reached the point that they could assess quality in online education.[2]

Federal regulations still in place as of the summer of 2002 required institutions offering instruction on other than a "standard" semester or quarter basis to demonstrate that students had at least 12 hours a week of instruction to enable them to qualify for federal student aid. Yet, a prescribed number of contact hours for a course may be inappropriate when students work online at their own pace, advancing perhaps at a rate different from students who go to a classroom for each session. What relationship does an arbitrary "12-hour rule" have to educational quality? This restriction arose from a desire by Congress in the early 1990s to protect students from abuses perpetrated by some institutions.

The U.S. Department of Education moved in the summer of 2002 to replace the 12-hour rule with a requirement that programs provide at least one day's worth of instruction a week. The new regulation, proposed for implementation by 2003, would almost surely make it easier for distance education students to qualify for federal assistance. Critics who thought the 12-hour rule was too liberal worried, though, that a 1-day rule would be equally subject to abuse by students whose degree of engagement in distance programs was difficult to gauge.

The so-called 50 percent rule declared that institutions that offered more than half of their courses via telecommunications could not participate in the federal student aid programs. In this case, Congress gave with one hand, authorizing some learning by technology, but took away with the other hand, not authorizing too much of it. Government should protect students and safeguard the distribution of money derived from tax revenues. But regulations that try to differentiate between charlatans and legitimate providers must not so limit possibilities as to freeze the delivery of education under a formula tailored to the circumstances of another century. Otherwise, any regulatory regime renders a disservice to bona fide online learning and the students it serves.

Michael B. Goldstein, head of the educational institution practice for a Washington, D.C., law firm, worried that too much of the regulation affecting online learning was intended simply "to protect those already under the tent." In other words, regulation that hinders newcomers should have a firmer basis than restraining competition. Better reasons for having gatekeepers, according to Goldstein, are to protect the learner, the integrity of the academic credential, and those who rely on academic credentials (presumably, employers and the public). The situation grows even more complicated when one moves below the federal level to the states, which have 50 different approaches to regulating education. Goldstein said that the states have primary responsibility for regulating education and that they have accepted the role with a vengeance. He cited a survey of the regulation of e-learning that found an increasing number of states have promulgated specific policies affecting technology-mediated learning at the postsecondary level. Twenty-three states required authorization of online programs that originated in other states.

THE ROLE OF ACCREDITATION

Accreditation, as the gold standard of education, symbolizes the effort to uphold standards and ensure the quality of degrees. Colleges and universities, and high schools too, voluntarily submit to accreditation. The process is one of the most important functions of education and one of the most arcane. Reviewers work beyond public view, and the details of their findings, as well as self-studies of the institutions, are seldom publicized. Though the public knows little about the process or the specifics of its outcome, people are vaguely reassured to know of an institution's accreditation. The more obscure the institution, the more important that it have accreditation to win public acceptance.

On the other hand, there are so many accrediting organizations—at least 80 of them—that almost any provider, from an electronics school to Yale University, can find one or another agency to put its stamp of approval on the institution or on one of its programs. One group, the Accrediting Commission of Career Schools and Colleges of Technology, even gave its imprimatur in 2001 to the Astrological Institute, a postsecondary school in Arizona that taught students to write horoscopes and give advice about the future. The government relies on accrediting groups to serve as the arbiters for eligibility for federal student aid. Online learning, though, introduced uncertainties into the process of self-regulation that higher education had used for decades. As the report in May 2002 noted, online courses have forced Washington to deal anew with questions involving program length, credit hours vs. clock hours, and measurement of students' financial need.[3]

Applying the Right Criteria

Consistency in the accreditation process will make it easier to address the issues raised by the advent of online learning, a fact that leading accrediting agencies recognize and are trying to address. One complication has to do with the fact that some accrediting organizations have greater prestige than others. Preeminent in this hierarchy are the eight regional accrediting groups that, together, encompass the geography of the entire United States: Middle States Association of Colleges and Schools; New England Association of Schools and Colleges Commission on Institutions of Higher Education; New England Association of Schools and Colleges Commission on Technical and Career Institutions; North Central Association of Colleges and Schools; Northwest Association of Schools, Colleges, and Universities; Southern Association of Colleges and Schools; Western Association of Schools and Colleges Accrediting Commission for Community and Junior Colleges; and Western Association of Schools and Colleges Accrediting Commission for Senior Colleges and Universities.

Traditional colleges and universities, and many high schools as well, are accredited by one of these regional groups. In addition, specialized accrediting associations endorse more than 17,000 programs and departments within these colleges and universities, for instance, their dental schools or physical therapy programs. In some cases, competing groups jostle for the right (and the dues revenues) to carry out specialized and professional accreditation. Finally, national accrediting groups of varying repute put their imprimaturs on trade and proprietary schools and many nontraditional educational institutions.

Under the mainstream accrediting process, a school, college, university, or program undergoes an intense self-study, and then a team of visitors sees for themselves how actual practices comport with the institution's vision of itself. Some critics of online education want to judge e-learning by criteria different from those applied to on-campus education. They think that perhaps unique, exacting standards of quality should apply to online education. Others say that existing standards deal adequately with the new issues that online education raises. They regard e-learning as just another system of delivery that may or may not have peculiarities of its own. "What is important," Sandra Elman of the Northwest Association of Schools, Colleges, and Universities said of the accreditation process for online learning, "is that it not be any more rigorous or any less rigorous. You want a level of consistency and equity in dealing with a new dimension of instruction. It should not be held to a higher standard." Elman said that her association tried to assure that teams evaluating institutions with online programs always included someone with experience in that field.

Accrediting agencies potentially face many questions as they scrutinize online learning. They should look for differences in content and quality between courses offered in classrooms and over the Internet and see whether institutions hold students in classrooms and online to identical standards. They have to determine the extent to which the design elements of courses count as factors that promote or inhibit learning. They may ask whether a facilitator who oversees an online course but has little role in developing the content should meet the same criteria as a professor whose content is the substance of a classroom course. They should decide how much regard to give to the amount and quality of electronic interaction in online courses and how much to consider the quality of the technical support that students receive. The Report of the Web-Based Education Commission to the President and the Congress of the United States recommended these six proposals for accreditors to consider in connection with online courses:

1. Determine whether new accreditation review standards and practices are needed and develop these tools where appropriate.
2. Provide assistance to institutions, programs, and new providers to develop internal quality review procedures for web-based learning.
3. Explore whether and how the regional accrediting agencies should expand beyond their traditional focus on nonprofit institutions to include more for-profit institutions.
4. Develop an improved capacity for course accreditation to accompany institutional and programmatic accreditation.

5. Strengthen coordination among accreditors to respond to web-based learning with agreed-upon standards.
6. Create partnerships for review of web-based learning where appropriate with other external quality reviewers.[4]

The eight regional accrediting commissions, responding to the particularities of online learning, developed guidelines on best practices in distance education. Though not official evaluation standards, the guidelines answered critics who said that regional accreditors did not show enough concern about the changes introduced by online learning. An earlier paper drafted by the Western Cooperative for Educational Telecommunications formed the basis for the guidelines. The eight regional commissions emphasized that, in spirit, the guidelines reflected such traditional values of accreditation as those holding that learning is dynamic and interactive, regardless of the setting in which it occurs; instructional programs leading to degrees having integrity are organized around substantive and coherent curricula; and institutions are responsible for the education provided in their name. The guidelines proposed that accreditors raise these questions in pursuit of best practices in online learning:

- Is the staffing structure appropriate (and fully qualified) to support the programs now operational and envisioned in the near term?
- Is there a clear and integral relationship between those responsible for electronically offered programs and the mainstream academic structure?
- By what process was the program developed? Were academically qualified persons responsible for curricular decisions?
- What provisions for instructor-student and student-student interaction are included in the program/course design and the course syllabus? How is appropriate interaction assured?
- If not all appropriate resources are routinely available at a distance, what arrangements has the institution made to provide them to distant students?
- How does the institution review the effectiveness of its distance education programs to assure alignment with institutional priorities and educational objectives?[5]

Sorting out Accreditation Issues

Many providers of online courses operate on the Internet under the aegis of the accreditation awarded to regular campus-based programs. The process and expectations of accreditation may have to change in the face of what online learning makes possible. For example, as Wallace Pond pointed out, a professor in Malaysia who reaches students who are mostly in Asia may teach an e-course that Britain's Open University developed. Pond, chief academic officer of Education America's online campus, wondered how accreditation will alter itself to deal with these new circumstances. When it comes to accreditation, online learning muddies waters that were already cloudy. Observers disagree, for instance, over whether an accredited institution offering courses in a traditional manner needs to get separate accreditation when it adds online courses. Do online courses constitute a different kind of education for the institution? Does this step alter the institution's mission? Or, are the online courses simply another way of delivering what the institution was already offering, marking no substantial change in the institution's mission?

The head of the commission that oversees accreditation in one region of the United States said that his agency's tendency has been to overlook online courses until an institution offers enough of them to allow a student to obtain a degree, thereby creating a program that seems beyond the authorization of the prior accreditation of classroom-based education. There is also the question of whether an institution exceeds its accredited purpose if it puts a program online that it already offers in classrooms. The North Central Association of Colleges and Schools, which accredited the University of Phoenix in 1978, has watched as that institution has gradually added online courses. "Each comprehensive visit since 1990 wrestled with whether they had shifted the nature of the institution with more and more online," said Stephen D. Crow, executive director of North Central's Higher Learning Commission. The verdict so far has been that these were not new programs, just a matter of putting the existing classroom-based program in an electronic format while retaining the mentoring and the work groups that are at the heart of Phoenix's courses.

Growing numbers of for-profit businesses like the Apollo Group, Inc., which owns the University of Phoenix, seek accreditation for their courses. Curiously, in a country where it has been acceptable to make money out of every activity from healing the cancerous to banishing weeds from lawns, suspicion remains for those who seek financial gain from making people smarter and better able to earn a living. In any event, the for-profit educational entrepreneurs, who first offered traditional forms of postsecondary education in classrooms, increasingly invest in online learning. Once, it was *verboten* for a regional accrediting agency to give its approval to commercial enterprises, but the University of Phoenix and a few others cracked this barrier when they got their regular courses accredited. Now more commercial providers expect to win accreditation for their online offerings. Jones International University was the first totally online, for-profit institution to win accreditation when North Central Association gave it that recognition in 1999 for a five-year period, after which the university's status will be reviewed.

There are yet other activities, not simply having to do with whether a degree is involved, that accrediting officials say may raise a red flag. Accreditors would take note if, for example, some small residential liberal arts college that has shunned career education suddenly started offering online business courses. Or if a college serving a small local area suddenly used e-learning to reach across the country for students. Officials may wonder whether such an institution has veered too far from the mission for which it was accredited. On the other hand, it might not cause a stir among accreditors if some public university committed to serving a far-flung population in a vast, underpopulated western state started enrolling online students in a corner of the state that lacks the critical mass for a campus.

Yet another issue in the accreditation of e-learning revolves around the extent to which a college or university retains responsibility for a course given online. Accrediting agencies do not want institutions renting out their names for others to use for educational purposes. Accrediting groups tend to want to know that whatever an institution offers under its name represents the efforts of its faculty and benefits from the same kind of quality control as that invested in an on-campus classroom course. Some colleges and universities that have separated their online programs from their classroom-based programs, both for-profit and not-for-profit, could encounter intense questioning the next time the institution faces periodic accreditation review. Such questions, too, may arise in connection with online courses largely designed by people not on the regular faculty. Sometimes schools, colleges, and universities buy these courses from commercial providers or from platform companies. As matters now stand, the question is not so much whether such courses are as good or better than those produced by regular faculty, but whether the courses actually bear the imprint of the institution. One wonders whether the institutional affiliation of the person who developed a course should be more important than the quality of the course.

REGULATION ISSUES

Online learning causes some degree of consternation because of the ease with which it crosses geographic boundaries. In 2001, the commissioner of higher education in Texas fined an online institution that he said lacked authority to grant degrees in the state. This particular institution, calling itself the Center of University Graduate Studies Graduate College, seemed of dubious merit—it didn't require candidates for doctorates to hold prior degrees. The authenticity of the education aside, the Texas case focused on issues that could just as readily have arisen if a highly regarded, accredited college or university from another state offered online courses outside its own state.

Almost every state has a statewide coordinating or governing board for higher education. The regulatory power of the board varies from state to state as does the amount of interest that the boards have shown in overseeing online learning that crosses their borders. These boards have tended to leave concerns about online learning to accrediting bodies. It represented a tacit endorsement of a free market in online higher education when governors in 19 western states banded together to form the Western Governors University. Also, such multistate consortiums as the Southern Regional Education Board and the Western Interstate Commission for Higher Education have lined up behind efforts to enroll students in courses delivered from outside their own states.

Wrestling with New Issues

The North Central Association of Colleges and Schools, the regional accreditation organization that first showed itself most receptive to online learning, set up a Technology and Digital Learning Focus Group during 2002 to wrestle with some of the main issues raised by this new delivery system. North Central asked the group to study and make recommendations on such issues as the tendency of online learning to involve more and more adjunct faculty and to use e-courses that institutions purchased from others. In its charge to the group, North Central also questioned what such practices will mean for accreditation in light of the existing policy of assuming that the faculty should be responsible for the instructional program. North Central asked the group to recommend how accreditation standards could encourage, if not require, the right balance among technology-enhanced instruction, faculty creation of a learning environment, and student learning. In addition, North Central wanted the group to think about e-learning's implications for academic libraries, which hitherto accreditors have evaluated, in part, by counting volumes. A main question for the group to weigh in this regard was whether accreditation should concern itself more in the digital age with access to information and with student capabilities for getting that information in new kinds of online libraries.

The arrival of e-learning closely followed the nation's move toward deregulation generally that was advanced by the Reagan administration in the 1980s. Beginning with correspondence courses, continuing with telecourses, and culminating in online learning, one question revolves around whether states have authority to regulate interstate commerce, a power that the U.S. Constitution reserves for the federal government. Unlike the freight carried by trucks or trains that roll across state lines, distance learning wafts from state to state in an ethereal manner, but one that officials could nonetheless classify as interstate commerce. Thus, questions of authority for the regulation of online learning remain unsettled. Attorney Michael B. Goldstein, for one, believes these issues must be addressed and resolved. "Elsewise," he said, "they will most assuredly limit the growth of technology-mediated learning and, more importantly, severely restrict the access of learners to the best and most diverse learning opportunities."[6]

All of these factors mean that the delivery of education, long a staid and predictable endeavor, is topsy-turvy with threats of change, in classrooms and online. For-profit institutions seek regional accreditation and take on the appearance of nonprofit institutions. Traditional universities try to make money from online learning entities that they have set up as separate enterprises, which look very much like your garden-variety for-profit businesses. Commercial companies award certificates for career studies that resemble what community colleges used to offer exclusively. Some educational institutions take an approach that amounts to renting out their names and their accreditations, becoming virtual franchises—in classrooms as well as online—for delivering education organized by other institutions. Sometimes online learning figures in all this; sometimes it doesn't.

Fears of competition as much as concern over quality spur arguments against out-of-state providers of education. There is an element of protectionism that resembles the opposition that American steel makers, rice producers, beet growers, and garment manufacturers have mounted against the import of foreign products. Perhaps this is in keeping with some of the change wrought by online education that James Mingle, former head of the State Higher Education Executive Officers organization, said, "is turning education into a commodity." But Mingle thought that efforts to promote protectionism in higher education were fading by the beginning of the twenty-first century. "There is still an undertone of protectionism in some states, particularly those with a strong independent sector," he said, "but it is greatly diminished. I think the current attitude is pretty much 'don't ask, don't tell.' States realize that much of their statutory authority is unenforceable or not worth enforcing. Not until a big major scandal on the level of the proprietary school defaults of the '80s will we see any change."

Defining Quality

Courses offered online vary greatly not only in quality but in the degree to which they are scrutinized by the institutions that offer them. Caveat emptor reigns, as perhaps it does in the classroom. Gary Natriello, a professor at Teachers College, Columbia University, who led a group of graduate students in the evaluation of online courses for Columbia's for-profit Fathom company, thought that one of the main problems was that good evaluation consumes so much time. He said that thorough evaluations would cost more than many providers would be willing to pay. Given the labor intensiveness of the process, Fathom seemed to back off from its original intention of rigorously evaluating each and every course made available at its site. Ultimately, to speed up the evaluation process and make it affordable in Fathom's case, Natriello's group produced an unpublished list of criteria for evaluating online courses. The evaluation protocol considered quality factors in several categories related to the institution, course, instructor, students, and support services.

Institutional quality included accreditation status; commitment to creating online courses on a par with classroom courses; and a review and approval process for online courses that involves regular faculty of the institution. Course design encompassed articulating learning goals and assessment opportunities to students; alignment of learning goals with the delivery system; content sufficient to meet the learning goals and appropriate to the online environment; interaction between instructor and students; and appropriate assessment techniques. Instructor quality tallied regular faculty members assigned to online courses; instructors with the highest degree in the field relevant to the course; and the experience of the instructor in online learning. Student support criteria concerned access to 24/7 technology assistance, to library, laboratories, and other resources, and to student services. Student characteristics looked at relevant information on admission to the course; relevant published advisories from the course instructor; and whether course enrollment was limited to 20 or fewer students.

The Southern Regional Education Board (SREB), a consortium of institutions of higher education in the southeast, put forward what it called Principles of Good Practice for virtual learning at its member colleges and universities. To uphold standards for degree or certificate programs offered online for credit, SREB said that members should ensure that the program or course offered electronically is provided by or through an institution accredited by a nationally recognized accrediting body and authorized to operate in the state where the program or course originates; and that member institutions offering programs or for-credit courses are responsible for satisfying all in-state approval and accreditation requirements before students are enrolled. In addition, they said, academic standards for all programs or courses offered electronically are to be the same as those for other courses or programs delivered at the originating member institution. They placed the onus on the member institution to review educational programs and courses it provides electronically and to ensure continued compliance with these principles.[7]

Officials of SREB said they were uncertain of the effects of the Principles of Good Practice, which the organization promulgated for the 2000–01 academic year. They believed, though, that a three-step process they established to undergird the principles helped promote good practice. First, an institution must evaluate a proposed online course against the principles themselves; second, the state in which the institution is located must endorse the course with particular emphasis on how well the proposal provides for related student services; and third, after the first two steps, SREB measures the proposed course according to a template it has developed for itself.

Dealing with K through 12 Cyber Schools

Regulation of online learning is no less of an issue at the elementary and secondary levels. Aside from the quality of the learning, much of the concern about these schools centers on matters of funding and accountability. Even many of the critics of online education at the precollegiate level grant that perhaps cyber learning has a role to play serving students in rural areas and youngsters whose schools do not offer some of the courses from which they would benefit, for example, Advanced Placement courses. Critics generally do not accept the notion, though, of pupils in elementary and secondary schools taking their entire programs online. They think that such an approach counteracts the purposes of public education, a contention that the final chapter of this book discusses. They worry that usually only adults have sufficient motivation to study online. They fear that someone other than the enrolled student—

the parent?—will be at the computer doing the work when it most counts. They see cyber schools as a financial threat to brick-and-mortar schools. They do not think that public authorities exact sufficient accountability from cyber schools. Finally, one must question the advisability of letting several cyber schools operate within a single state as occurred in Pennsylvania. For now, the Florida approach seems more solid and responsible with one virtual school, under state auspices, for the entire state.

Ohio and Pennsylvania provide ideal cases for examining these issues. In both states, cyber education gained a foothold by flying under the radar, using laws that authorized charter schools to establish themselves. Litigation in both states called the legality of cyber schools into question. A suit in Ohio united plaintiffs who frequently do not find areas of agreement—a teachers' union, a school boards' association, a labor union, and a parents' organization. They maintained that state law authorized charter schools only in big cities and locales with students at risk, provisions that they said cyber charter schools violated by accepting students regardless of place of residence. In Pennsylvania, the state school board association similarly challenged the law that it said authorized charter schools to serve individual school districts, not the entire state, as the cyber charter schools ended up doing.

The Ohio Department of Education developed standards in 2002 that it hoped would address the growing controversy. Still in draft form in the summer of 2002, the standards for cyber schools dealt with purposes, governance, improvement planning, student and stakeholder focus, staff and faculty focus, and education programs. In most regards, the standards hardly differed from those that would be demanded of a brick-and-mortar school. Among the proposals were requirements for cyber schools to design and implement communication processes that ensure that students, parents, and sending schools understand policies and procedures related to admission, enrollment, and student contact; monitor the effectiveness of the learning process to ensure that technology promotes, rather than interferes with, student performance and achievement; gather data to measure progress on goals and use the results to rapidly respond to areas in need of improvement, changing needs, or opportunities for innovation; and provide curricula that include clear, rigorous, and coherent academic content standards that align with and meet or exceed Ohio's academic content and performance standards.

THE FACULTY CONNECTION

No discussion of quality standards for online learning can be complete without consideration of the ways in which the process affects the role of teachers and their relationship to students. Those who teach want to know how online learning impacts their workload. Institutions must devise methods of determining these effects and of taking cognizance of them in faculty assignments. Online education puts new questions about intellectual property rights into play. What may have been clear about course ownership in a classroom enters a foggy realm when elements of courses reside on the web. Fiscal issues involving faculty thread their way through many of these new areas of concern. Educational institutions should address these matters with candor and openness.

The faculty's limited knowledge about online learning stems simply from the fact that they have spent their careers teaching in classrooms with students sitting in front of them, not instructing students whom they never see by way of a technology with which many of them still feel uncomfortable. Institutions are often in a quandary as they move into e-learning, not wanting to cede authority to people unfamiliar with a process they may not even trust. Officials of institutions realize, however, that they play a dangerous game if they try to exclude faculty from matters linked to teaching and learning. At the same time, faculty senates and other such bodies are notorious for their protracted decision making. The deliberative process of the typical faculty senate seems unwieldy for thrashing out issues concerning a controversial, new delivery system for education. Institutions sometimes want to move quickly to respond to market forces and keep some of their actions confidential as they strive to head off the gathering competition in online learning. This may involve keeping the inner circle small and not necessarily consulting a restive faculty. The seeds of conflict can be found here.

Placing online operations somewhat outside their usual purview may make it easier to deal with a suspicious and disgruntled faculty. Faculty members such as those at Temple University, where a profit-making scheme died, for example, raised critical questions about online learning. Reactions of this sort by faculty have complicated attempts by some institutions of higher education to incorporate virtual learning into their mission. Faculty worry about how online learning will affect the institution's reputation, but their concerns do not stop there. They fear they may be asked to do more work without adequate remuneration. They pose questions about quality control. They wonder about job protection. And, probably, rightly so. Online learning eventually could lessen the need for traditionally prepared Ph.D.s with their relatively low teaching loads and built-in time for research and writing. More academic positions in the future could involve less prestige, lower pay, and little paid time for reflection and scholarly activities. Such is the trend as part-time, nontenure appointments proliferate in classroom-based education; online learning could exacerbate the situation.

Extra Work

Institutions base faculty workloads largely on the number of class hours assigned to a person. If an instructor teaches three courses, each worth three credit hours, then the person's workload is calculated as nine hours. Simple enough. For each of those hours, the faculty member devotes a certain amount of time to office hours, class preparations, and marking students' assignments and examinations. On top of this, faculty may give time to departmental and university-wide activities. But what happens when a faculty member puts together and oversees a virtual course, with its 24/7 demands? How much work does this require? How much time should the institution allot for such tasks? The answers to these questions are still sorting themselves out and, in the meantime, faculty do not wish to be overloaded with work that no one has properly anticipated. Institutions still struggle to determine whether the work involved in teaching an online course equals a course taught in person, or whether an altogether different formula should apply.

Given its short history, there is precious little information about what online learning means to faculty workloads. One of the first major studies of the topic was released by the U.S. Department of Education in

2002, based on statistics gathered in fall 1998 from instructional faculty and staff at two-year and four-year colleges and universities across the country. The 6 percent of the instructional force who taught at least one distance education course had, on average, at least one more course to teach than their colleagues who were not involved in distance education. Furthermore, they apparently received little extra pay for carrying a heavier load.[8] Faculty members in the journalism department at the University of Memphis, for instance, first took on e-learning as a kind of overload. They were expected to carry their regular classroom teaching load and teach any online courses on top of that schedule. They were paid extra, but it amounted to only $68 a week, according to Elinor Grusin, one of the faculty members. Finally, the faculty refused to accept online courses on an overload basis. The University of Memphis then incorporated online courses into the regular teaching load.

Another aspect of the workload has to do with contact time with students. Some faculty members at four-year colleges and universities are accustomed to concentrating all of their class meetings into no more than three days a week. The rest of their time is free for research, writing, and the previously mentioned activities related to courses. In e-learning, though, students expect quick responses to their e-mails and to contributions to discussions that they post on electronic bulletin boards. Those who take seriously the responsibility of teaching online cannot think of their assignments as involving only two or three days a week of actually running the courses. They must interact with and respond daily to students who submit questions and comments via e-mail, bulletin boards, and chat rooms. The medium itself creates an expectation of immediate interaction. Each online course can take on a life of its own and readily expand into a 24/7 proposition.

Contact time with students does, in fact, grow, according to the report from the U.S. Department of Education just cited. It found that those teaching distance education courses had slightly more office hours and more contact with students, including a more extensive exchange of e-messages with students, than colleagues who did not teach such courses. This expanded contact with students, in part, probably arose from carrying a heavier total student load than those not involved in distance education courses. Also, as mentioned, e-mail communication with students almost certainly is more extensive in the absence of face-to-face contact. The report essentially lumped all kinds of distance education together, including correspondence and telecourses with online education, and so the findings do not apply strictly to online learning.

According to the report, those teaching distance education courses "appeared to interact with students or be available to them more" than their colleagues who taught only face-to-face classes. Thus, the bad news for those teaching distance education courses: they spend more time dealing with students out of class. The good news for those teaching distance education courses: they spend more time dealing with students out of class. The report offered this summary of the situation: "[D]espite carrying larger teaching loads, faculty who taught any distance classes were just as likely, and in some cases more likely, to indicate that they were very satisfied with their workload compared with faculty teaching only traditional classes."[9]

INTELLECTUAL PROPERTY RIGHTS

A course put on the web, unlike one taught on campus, has a huge potential audience, opening an opportunity for reaching far more students than can fit into a conventional classroom. No one seemed to care who owned the course material when courses reached relatively few students. Professors who sought larger audiences wrote articles and books that were issued under copyrights that assured them of ownership and royalties, if any. Exercising ownership rights over work put online is far more complex, making the issue a subject of contention that has spread beyond academia. In a landmark case in 2001, a court held after a protracted battle that freelance contributors to the *New York Times* and other publications were due royalties when their work was put on the web. Most professors want no less consideration from their colleges and universities.

The American Association of University Professors agrees with faculty members who want to retain ownership of work used for online instruction. The organization said that prevailing academic practice has been to treat the faculty member as the copyright owner of works created independently and at the faculty member's own initiative for traditional academic purposes. The statement continued: "This practice has been followed for the most part, regardless of the physical medium in which these 'traditional academic works' appear; that is, whether on paper or in audiovisual or electronic form . . . this practice should therefore ordinarily apply to the development of courseware for distance education."[10]

The American Council on Education (ACE), an umbrella group of colleges and universities, said that ownership of electronic courses could be evaluated along a continuum that depended on whether faculty created courses on their own initiative (owned by the faculty member), under a contract with the institution (owned by the institution), or as some combination of the two (owned by both the faculty member and the institution). The organization recommended a six-step process for colleges and universities to follow to clarify questions involving intellectual property. The main directives to institutions by ACE were:

1. Clarify the definition of intellectual property and the circumstances under which the institution will assume the costs of protecting intellectual property.
2. Define inventor and author rights, including rights of revision and adaptation, reproduction, display, and the most important, ownership.
3. Identify when and how the institution can use intellectual property generated by faculty whether it is via ownership or licenses, exclusive, nonexclusive, for internal and noncommercial purposes only, and what temporal or employment-related limitations exist.
4. Clarify how faculty will be compensated for the development and preparation of distance learning courses and how the parties will share in any royalties generated by the courses.
5. Identify who will administer the institution's intellectual property policies and what will be the initial dispute mechanism.
6. Clarify when the inventor or author can use the institution's names and logos when commercializing a work.[11]

The other side of this issue has to do with protecting not just the intellectual property of faculty who put their material online, but material that others have produced and that faculty appropriate for use in their online courses. The federal government codified a system of copyright laws, as long ago as the eighteenth century, to protect intellectual property. Copyright law can protect—when registered with the federal government—all sorts of creative works from plays to musical compositions to books to lectures and materials that a professor produces for a college course. One would hardly know it, though, from the way some instructors shamelessly borrow other people's materials in their online courses. This seems to be an extension of the widespread flaunting of copyright laws as faculty photocopy multiple copies of others' articles and books for use in their classroom courses without bothering to get permission, or, God forbid, pay royalties.

At a meeting of online instructors at an institution that shall remain nameless, an instructor who had videotaped advertisements from television programs to use for teaching purposes in her course said, in response to questions from other instructors, that she didn't know—and probably had not considered—the legal implications of putting this material on the web. "I guess it's something we have to find out about," she offered weakly. Yet, copyright protection gives owners rights over reproduction and distribution of their work. The law also allows for "fair use" of the work of others, producing an ambiguous kind of permission that has been repeatedly redefined by numerous court cases. The new age of information technology has already led to tortuous interpretations of copyright law, and the situation can only become more confusing as online learning spreads. A bill stalled in Congress in 2002 would have helped online learning by giving it some of the copyright exemptions that courses taught in classrooms receive. It probably would have made legal just such a use as the instructor was making of the advertisements from television programs.

CHAPTER 11

IN SCHOOL, ON CAMPUS

If nothing else, the availability of online learning may force schools and colleges to reflect on their missions and on how they discharge their responsibilities. Physical plants worth tens of millions of dollars depend on students continuing to come to campus for their programs. A virtual institution of learning, largely devoid of brick and mortar, has no such capital investment. The threat posed by online learning may lead traditional schools and colleges to make themselves over in ways more friendly to students and more closely aligned with students' actual needs, in and out of classrooms.

If, as is almost certain, most people prefer learning in classrooms with other students, then it is incumbent upon institutions with investments in campus structures to make the student experience as valuable and rewarding as it ought to be. This means revisiting such issues as the time and place of learning, learning outcomes, and cost effectiveness. When Sylvan Learning Systems signaled its intent to expand its presence in online learning, an educator with ties to traditional colleges and universities told the *Chronicle of Higher Education* that the action "will help us all become more responsive to the marketplace, and that's a healthy thing."[1]

THE TIME AND PLACE OF LEARNING

Distance education's most distinguishing feature is the ability it gives students to learn at their own pace at a place of their choosing. Not having to be in a classroom for a specified length of time at regular intervals means that a student may move through the material as quickly or as slowly—within reason—as he or she chooses or is able. When Dan Haerle, a professor of music at the University of North Texas, wanted a way to let some of his students advance faster through the first semester of his Jazz Fundamentals course, he put the course online. The precipitating problem, he said, was that increasingly, proportionately more students with stronger backgrounds arrived on campus than in previous years, and they grew bored during the 15-week classroom-based course that dealt with scales, chords, and aspects of theory.

The result of their being able to pace themselves online was that some students completed the work in as few as two weeks, and many others finished in fewer than the 15 weeks allotted for the classroom-based course. Moreover, for some the opportunity to pursue the course online meant that they could put off the work sometimes if they found it necessary, just as long as they were done at the end of the requisite 15 weeks. Haerle continued to teach the second semester of the course, which he said was more complex and required more time, in the classroom. In praising online learning for making it possible for his students to pace themselves, Haerle nonetheless saw limitations and did not think that the online approach lent itself to many other courses that music majors had to take at North Texas. The software that he found available did not let students click notes onto a staff, and he had to improvise a solution for the Jazz Fundamentals course. He also worried about bandwidth and its ability to convey the quality of sound that he wanted. He was glad to solve the pacing problem for this one course, but, he said, "some things are better off in the classroom."

When instructors move their courses to the Internet to facilitate pacing, they usually stipulate a length of time by which students must complete various phases of the work. Some people wonder about how much time a student should get to finish online assignments. Whether the course is offered in person or online, an institution has to decide whether to set parameters and if there is a period beyond which it will no longer accept a student's work. It may be in the interests of neither the student nor the institution for studies to drag on interminably. Moreover, there seems to be a consensus that online courses best serve the interests of students when they contain deadlines that keep students involved in the work.

A review of the federally sponsored Virtual High School, for instance, found that "timelines and deadlines must be clear and must be enforced . . . with explicit consequences if they are not met." Researchers said that students needed to have completion dates specified to keep them from falling behind or losing track of their work.[2] Students in postsecondary online courses undoubtedly have the same need. Michael Lambert, who was executive director of the Distance Education and Training Council, said that, from all he could gather, the more structure there was in an online course, the higher the completion rate. He said that students need deadlines to keep them on task.

Yet, carried out reasonably, there is room in most online courses for students to vary their paces more than in classroom-based courses. Students in the Core Composition I course that Vincent Piturro taught at the University of Colorado at Denver, partially in a classroom and partially online, received time limits by which to complete the online portion of their work each stage of the way. They had to contribute to a threaded discussion by a specified time and then got a second deadline by which to respond to the online comments of classmates. Piturro said that the deadline ensured that discussion was spaced out to allow enough time for reactions by all students and for him to evaluate those comments. If, for example, he assigned a question at a class session on a Tuesday, all members of the class had to register their responses online by Friday. Then, by Sunday, he expected them to comment online on the responses of other students. This gave Piturro enough time to evaluate the online exchanges and to discuss his findings in the Tuesday class.

Online learning causes more frequent questioning of the need for precise requirements for seat time. It underscores the challenge to the rigid structure of the traditional system of semesters and quarters that dictates the length of courses and the speed with which students may advance. Courses that unfold along a traditional academic trajectory will come under increasing pressure, following the example of online learning, to give students more leeway to select their own pace. Colleges and universities may loosen some course requirements for on-campus students in coming years. Often technology will lead these assaults on the strictures of time, as at Virginia Tech's Math Emporium, where many students in the university's mathematics courses were able to use online sessions to supplement their class meetings and set their own pace for learning.

Until the 1960s, the norm for most students pursuing a bachelor's degree was to enter college directly out of high school and spend four years at a single institution. Transferring from one college to another in those days represented a kind of failure, as did taking longer than four years to complete a baccalaureate. The foundations of this pattern were shaken by the student upheavals of the 1960s. Now, many students earn academic credits at more than one institution on their way to graduation, with more than half those who get bachelor's degrees taking more than four years to do so. The trend toward a longer period to complete a degree troubles some state lawmakers who would like to push students through state colleges and universities faster, reducing enrollments and holding down legislative allocations for higher education.

Most students enrolled in online courses today are also on-campus learners who take an online course or two in addition to campus classes. At the University of Central Florida, for example, 70 percent of the online students also took classroom-based courses. At the University of Colorado at Denver—a commuter institution filled with working students, many of whom are parents—four out of five of the students in online courses also took courses in person. Students try to take courses at times most convenient to them—sometimes on campus, sometimes online.

Some online courses at the University of Colorado at Denver involved internships, and others, hands-on, in-person experiences, possibly involving short periods of residency at the home campus. Furthermore, this arrangement could include live videoconferences, audiotapes, and perhaps some correspondence. Increasingly, faculty members combine several delivery systems within a single course, and students carry a mix of courses in their schedules, ranging from those fully online to those taught entirely in classrooms. This approach reflects a world in which attendance exclusively in a traditional classroom is no longer *de rigueur*. Time requirements also have to change to allow students to vary the speed of their journey through formal education.

A NEW EMPHASIS ON LEARNING OUTCOMES

If being counted present and serving time matter less, then something else—learning outcomes—has become more important. Until recently, outcomes tended to pertain to such factors as progress toward degrees, graduation rates, and passing levels on licensing examinations. These are important signs of success in education, but they are only proxies for actual learning. Accrediting organizations showed signs in the late 1990s of moving toward a new understanding of outcomes, one that is inherent in many programs of online learning. Questions of outcomes in this case tend to revolve around what students learned in a particular course. Online education may speed up this process if only because advocates of e-learning feel compelled to prove the merit of the approach. The very meaning of outcomes changes in the parts of the cyber world that stress learning goals in each course.

The paucity of knowledge about learning outcomes in the classrooms of colleges and universities was underscored in "Measuring Up 2000," a report that contained state-by-state report cards on the condition of higher education across the country. The states got letter grades in six categories—preparation, participation, affordability, completion, benefits, and learning. Interestingly, every state got an "I" for incomplete in learning. The National Center for Public Policy and Higher Education, sponsor of the report, said that it could not award grades for learning because the individual states, and the institutions themselves, knew so little about what students actually learned in their courses.[3]

Skeptics of e-learning insist that it could not possibly produce the results that students attain in regular classrooms, a curious assertion in light of the lack of knowledge about exactly what they learn in regular classrooms. The evidence on this issue is mixed and authorities will not know more until online learning grows and researchers develop some good models for comparing the two approaches. Interest in finding out about the effectiveness of online learning might also produce a closer look at the learning outcomes in traditional classrooms, where proceedings have been largely off-limits to concerned policymakers. To those who speak of the classroom as "sacred space," Clint Brooks, distance learning coordinator at North West Arkansas Community College, posed this challenge: "Is the overcrowded lecture hall part of this sacred space? . . . How about the classrooms understaffed by minimally trained graduate students doing their best to deliver curriculum (I was one)? . . . If we are to critically evaluate technology in education, we must first acknowledge the need to critically evaluate education . . ."[4] It is time to concentrate on mastery of content and not worry about the delivery system by which that mastery is achieved.

One of the classroom-centered institutions that has focused its efforts most in this direction, Alverno College in Milwaukee, won wide attention for its ability-based curriculum. Students at Alverno received no grades but earned degrees by demonstrating competence in eight categories—analysis, problem solving, communication, social interaction, valuing in decision making, effective citizenship, developing a global perspective, and aesthetic responsiveness. To show their competencies, they applied what they learned in regular courses not only through tests but by internships with accessors from outside the college, team projects, and online digital portfolios, which the college began using in 1999 to replace paper portfolios. Each of Alverno's 67 major fields of study had its own criteria by which students demonstrated competency in the eight areas.

Excelsior College, based in Albany, New York, operated on a philosophy of "what a person knows is more important than where and how that knowledge was acquired."[5] In keeping with that idea, the institution let students demonstrate their knowledge in assessments that focused on outcomes, not the process by which the candidate gained the knowledge. Students at Excelsior typically were about 40 years old, with lots of life experience and academic credits that they had earned over time at several colleges and universities. Excelsior let them pull together their experiences and previous credits, as well as new learning, to obtain degrees; assessments documented previous learning and the newly gained knowledge. The institution granted 5,000 degrees a year, almost evenly divided between the associate's and bachelor's levels. Excelsior was founded in 1971 as a program of the New York State Board of Regents and in 1998 became an independent college.

Students could visit Excelsior's web page to download Examination Content Guides for the tests that they would take. The college also had study guides on the web to accompany some of the content guides; a study guide summarized the materials that students needed to master and provided sample questions. Students prepared for the examinations at their own pace. In addition, Excelsior offered its Electronic Peer Network online to help students organize themselves into study groups that used electronic chat rooms, so that they could confer as they prepared for examinations. Students went online or used a telephone for virtual library services to help them get information they needed to prepare for exams. The college contracted with the Johns Hopkins University in Baltimore to dedicate a position to a librarian who worked with Excelsior students. Other than in a few special circumstances, Excelsior offered no courses, classroom-based or online, to students pursuing undergraduate degrees. Nothing precluded students from taking courses at other institutions if they thought that such courses would help them garner useful knowledge for an Excelsior examination. For its three graduate degree programs, though, Excelsior offered online courses. At this level too, examinations tied to outcomes counted most, not the time spent in the courses.

Excelsior's performance criteria for students to earn a bachelor of science degree in general business illustrated the institution's outcomes-based approach. Each student had to: demonstrate a fundamental knowledge of business administration; apply quantitative fundamentals to problem solving in the business world; demonstrate basic knowledge of the principles of macroeconomics, microeconomics, and statistics; demonstrate effective oral and written communication; demonstrate understanding of culture, human behavior, and the relationship between business and society; demonstrate a working knowledge of computer usage with business disciplines; demonstrate advanced-level knowledge in one or more business subject areas; and demonstrate the ability to integrate the knowledge and skills necessary in the business world.[6]

A similar focus on learning outcomes was exemplified at Western Governors University (WGU), which operated online. Students could earn degrees from WGU based mostly on the results of a series of examinations through which they demonstrated competencies. How students obtained competencies did not matter to WGU. Some students followed programs of independent study before taking the examinations, which comprised objective tests, essay tests, and performance tasks. At the outset, WGU used competency tests developed by others, including the College Level Examination Program of the College Board, but the university sought eventually to develop competency examinations of its own design.

WGU students took online courses from other universities to prepare for the competency tests. The university offered no courses of its own, instead serving students through its web portal that steered them to the online courses of the various collaborating universities. Presumably, students could then learn what they needed in order to pass the competency tests. The online courses identified by Western Governors were mapped to conform with the competency requirements so that students would know that they received proper preparation for the tests. It was also possible for students to submit transcripts from courses and get equivalent credits toward satisfying competency requirements. Officials of the institution said that they were not altogether comfortable with translating academic credits into competencies, but conceded the necessity to do so because the rest of the academic world organizes itself around credits.

Nineteen states and institutions of higher education in those states collaborated to form WGU. The university offered programs in three areas—business, information technology, and teacher education—leading to degrees at the associate's, bachelor's, and master's levels. Fewer than a dozen full-time mentors worked for Western Governors University, guiding and coaching students as they prepared for competency examinations. Though they taught no actual courses, the mentors had the usual credentials and qualifications of college faculty. Each mentor took responsibility for about 100 students at the undergraduate level and about 75 students at the graduate level.

Whether at Western Governors University or elsewhere, online learning and the ability it gives students to pace themselves represents one more challenge to the lock-step character of education. One of the most important reasons that classroom courses last for a prescribed length of time is the need to measure learning. Presumably, a student who goes to a class two or three days a week for 15 weeks learns more than a peer who attends a similar class two or three days a week for 9 weeks. This presumption, of course, is faulty, but it has been a cornerstone of educational organization for decades. Now, online learning, possibly linked to the demonstration of competencies, as Alverno, Excelsior, and WGU required, may be a way to break through education's time barrier.

Another institution, Art Institute Online, the e-learning arm of the chain of 24 postsecondary schools located in cities around the country, had specific education outcomes defined for all its courses. It said that the outcomes were identical to those for the on-ground versions of the courses. The institution charged each course-creation team—consisting of an instructional designer, a subject matter expert, and a media designer—with creating an online course to produce the outcomes listed on a syllabus. The school's curriculum development staff checked for compliance with the stated outcomes. Art Institute Online standardized its courses in an effort to ensure that all students, regardless of instructor, advanced toward the same learning outcomes. This kind of approach, while perhaps more apt to lead to the fulfillment of goals, engenders controversy on the many traditional campuses where even a whisper of standardization would foment a faculty uprising.

The effort by the Accreditation Board for Engineering and Technology (ABET) to identify instructional objectives in laboratory courses represented yet another example of how online learning has affected in-person education. Growing interest in having ABET evaluate online offerings led to questions about how schools might assess the portions of their programs involving online laboratories. The board discovered, in reflecting on the learning that occurs in online laboratories, that it had not in any systematic way accumulated learning objectives for the work that students did in the laboratory sections of their classroom-based courses. Thus, ABET asked educational institutions to write down and agree upon instructional objectives for labs so that the organization could then apply those goals in evaluating online courses. "The onset of online delivery really motivated this study," said George D. Peterson, executive director of ABET.

A report on the future of e-learning for adults by the National Governors Association predicted that online education would produce increased reliance on new means of assessing and certifying learning results that emphasize skills and knowledge rather than on courses taken or hours earned. The 2001 report urged policymakers to work toward the implementation of new measures and methods of assessment that would take cognizance of this new stress on learning outcomes. "Traditional institution-based approaches to assessment and certification are not well suited to an e-learning world," said the report from the Commission on Technology and Adult Learning.[7]

Those same institution-based approaches to assessment make it difficult to determine just how much the emphasis in online education on learning outcomes can affect elementary and secondary education. The emergence of e-learning coincides with the promotion of the standards movement. It remains to be seen how friendly the examinations to measure standards in precollegiate education will be to the online courses increasingly available to younger students. On the one hand, it is altogether possible that the outcomes orientation of e-learning will lend itself to the standards movement, which increasingly stresses accountability. On the other hand, abundant testing of pupils, grade by grade, and the kinds of examinations that most states and localities use for these purposes are not apt to align with the sort of performance standards toward which e-learning has often aspired.

COST EFFECTIVENESS

While developing a course for online instruction may be more expensive than creating a classroom course, e-learning in the long run might enhance productivity and contribute to cost efficiencies. David Leonard of Georgia's Mercer College, who developed and taught graduate-level online courses, predicted that schools that charge too much tuition may experience decreased enrollments as the realization spreads that education need not be restricted in time and place.[8] Furthermore, e-learning may lead to savings on the construction and maintenance of buildings that will never have to be built for students who seldom, if ever, enter classrooms. Cyber libraries, which already number resident students among their users, will be even more useful to students who pursue their education entirely online. It is not that libraries in the information age will be without cost, but expenses for acquisitions, journal subscriptions, and storage may be less, and institutions may be able to get along with less space for their libraries. As mentioned elsewhere in this book, new costs will mount for online information services and the accompanying hardware and software.

A background paper prepared for the Washington State Higher Education Coordinating Board asked whether the anticipated savings in online learning were illusory. It asserted that while distance education may relieve institutions of certain expenditures on behalf of students who don't use the campus, the easier access provided to courses could lead to the matriculation of students who wouldn't otherwise enroll, causing institutions to spend money on instructors and a virtual support structure for those students. The paper went on to assert that savings may be less than expected because campuses devote only 20 percent of their facility space to instruction and instructional support. From the institutional perspective, according to the paper, distance education is an add-on or a complement to brick and mortar, not a substitute.[9]

Education generally is bound to feel the influence of the corporate model of the University of Phoenix and other for-profit providers in practices and policies in the nonprofit sector. Even with its emphasis on the bottom line, Phoenix discovered that online courses, done properly, cost more than in-person education. For one thing, the university said that its average online course had fewer than a dozen students as compared with at least 15 in a classroom course. Presumably, Phoenix, like other institutions, also found it more expensive to develop a course for delivery online than for a classroom. The extra expense was apparently worth the effort for the University of Phoenix, where enrollment growth in online learning substantially outstripped increases in classroom-based education in recent years.

The University of Nebraska at Lincoln, which offered more than 200 courses by computer, video, and other distance systems by the middle of 2002, estimated that it could get the average online course up and running for $10,000, according to Arnold Bateman, assistant vice chancellor. He said that the basic cost could rise to $25,000 if the course required a considerable amount of animation. The university had been giving faculty members grants of about $12,000 each to develop these distance courses, an amount that it cut to $10,000 when the budget tightened. Furthermore, the fiscal constraints meant that Nebraska had to reduce the number of grants it made. In part, costs varied according to the expense of technical design for the course. Bateman said that Nebraska simply could not consider spending the $100,000 to $500,000 that some institutions lavished on an individual online course. "We have quality and we don't need glitzy courses," he said. The university offered 15 graduate degrees through online learning, television, and other electronic forms of distance education. Sixty-five percent of the participating students lived in Nebraska, according to a survey by the university, which also found that 67 percent of them were women and almost one out of five was over the age of 50.

All indications are that no one can be certain whether in the long run online learning will prove more or less cost effective than current practices. Much of online education still resides in the great unknown. It may cost more, it may cost less, it may cost about the same. And it may not be worth the hassle if the institution turns to online courses only to save money. Done on the cheap, e-learning can provide economies, but if that is the main reason for moving in this direction, the process will discredit itself and prove as fleeting as last year's campus fad. E-learning's raison d'être must be the soundness of the educational approach and the need for the alternative that it represents. It should enhance teaching and learning, not distract from the process. Institutions should properly explore how it can be carried out well and economically. The million-dollar courses that have attracted attention are almost certainly unnecessary. On the other hand, it seems not worth going online if the courses lack sufficient investment to take advantage of at least some of the possibilities of the web environment. That is the rock and the hard place between which e-learning resides.

By the end of this decade, it will be abundantly clear how much it costs to produce good courses online.

Controversies Surrounding Cost Effectiveness

Some critics of online learning have seized on its connection to possible fiscal savings to condemn the phenomenon, as if making higher education more financially viable were a malevolent goal. The American Federation of Teachers, for instance, in its report "Virtual Revolution: Trends in the Expansion of Distance Education," spoke of the approach being "built on corporate ideas about consumer focus, product standardization, tight personnel control, and cost effectiveness" as "contrary to the traditional model of higher education decision-making."[10] Why should higher education be immune to efficiencies? Why is it necessarily bad to care about gaining control over expenditures in an industry in which costs in most years have outpaced the rate of inflation?

This is not to say that everything proposed and being carried out in the name of e-learning is sacrosanct or even desirable. Online education should not be license to dilute quality in either content or instruction. But educational institutions, no less than other sectors of society, share an obligation to search for ways to pursue their missions more efficiently and with greater financial accountability while not compromising on central tenets. Online learning holds some promise in this regard, though it is by no means a panacea, and it may end up costing more and be more difficult to carry out than some observers think. Higher education is headed inexorably toward more cost control than it has exerted in the past, and the influence of e-learning can hasten the process by heightening the pressure for fiscal reform.

Standardization makes it easier and cheaper to staff courses, which become less dependent on the content expertise of the person assigned to the course. It also assures that prescribed material gets taught and that an instructor does not omit something on a whim. For-profit educational institutions have been most inclined to march down the path to standardization. These institutions set off in this direction prior to the advent of online learning and more recently have taken advantage of the web to further the process. Even the disputed push toward standardization of courses that sometimes accompanies online learning may lead to increased questioning about the benefits that accrue to students on the same campus when the content and quality of a particular course vary according to who is the instructor. Standardization is anathema to the academic profession. The idea of a uniform curriculum for each course, taught in a more or less uniform manner, mightily offends faculty who, as a group, are accustomed to deciding what to teach and how to teach it, regardless of the course title.

Controversy swirls about the classroom whenever concerns turn to cost control, whether or not the issue is standardization. As long as jobs appear to be at stake, any attempt to tamper with the traditional configuration of the classroom stirs disputes. Until now, it has been impossible to imagine mass education based on a classroom of one. Imagine having to pay an instructor to teach the same lesson over and over again, separately, to 25 students, who otherwise could gather together. With technology, though, the prospect of a classroom of one raises possibilities for all sorts of different staffing patterns.

Pursuing Partnerships

Another aspect of cost effectiveness has to do with wasteful competition and duplication throughout education, emblematic of the failure of institutions to do more to work together for the common good. David Szatmary, a vice provost who headed the online efforts at the University of Washington, was convinced that partnerships were crucial to the expansion of such programs. "To craft really high-quality distance learning," said Szatmary, "is an expensive proposition that calls for both content and technical expertise. To do it right, there has to be a confluence of expertise in both of these areas." He envisioned partnerships of all kinds—with other research universities, with other kinds of four-year institutions of higher education, with community colleges, with high schools, with governmental agencies, and with private businesses. Szatmary felt that the university could best leverage money and expertise needed for developing content and appropriate technology through collaborations that tapped into the expertise and resources of more than one institution.

To that end, the University of Washington provided leadership in a consortium of 34 leading research universities in R1edu, a project offering free connections to searchable data bases for those involved in online learning. The university was also part of a consortium of 20 institutions sharing content on a research television and webcasting channel called the ResearchChannel that provided content in basic and applied research using webcast, cable, and direct broadcast satellite to reach scientific and public audiences. In still another partnership, the University of Washington banded with three other research institutions—Wisconsin, Penn State, and Berkeley—in an alliance to develop, license, market, and deliver online education. The university joined a partnership with Hong Kong University of Science and Technology and several community colleges in Washington State to offer distance learning programs in South China.

Partnerships figured strongly in most aspects of the university's growing online program. The University of Washington worked with the Public Broadcasting System, Pearson/Prentice-Hall, and the World Organization of Webmasters to develop four Internet-related certificate programs for information technology professionals under a $1.4 grant from the Learning Anywhere Anytime Partnership (LAAP) of the U.S. Department of Education. It made partners of the governor's office, three private industry councils, and three community colleges to design an online version of a modular degree in computing and software systems under a $1.5 million grant form the U.S. Department of Labor.

The University of Washington's efforts were not limited to higher education. The institution collaborated with the governor's office to create a pilot project for Virtual UW in the High Schools, starting in the fall of 2001 with a geology course made available to eight rural high schools. The state's office of public instruction awarded the university $50,000 to deliver an online version of Project REAL (Realizing the Essential Academic Learnings) to 40 elementary and secondary teachers on the Olympic peninsula. Project REAL helped teachers align their curriculum with the state's Essential Academic Learning Requirements. The National Institutes of Health awarded the University of Washington $200,000 to develop, implement, and evaluate a three-course certificate program about brain research in education, designed primarily for teachers in elementary and secondary schools in rural areas.

Among traditional institutions of higher education, the University of Washington emerged early as a leader in online education, in a state where many higher education institutions, including Washington State University, saw the Internet as figuring prominently in their future. At first confounded by a controversy that surrounded a governor's master plan for expanding higher education through online programs, the University of Washington gradually gained its footing as the conflict subsided. The university built its capacity for e-learning, and by the summer of 2001 it offered 24 certificate programs and 11 degree programs online. There were almost 10,000 course enrollments in 306 distance education courses, mostly online but also including some in streaming video. By 2001, the university employed 20 skilled instructional designers who worked with content experts to create more than 50 new courses a year in an online program that officials said was self-supporting.

Another institution, the ill-fated U.S. Open University, also saw partnerships as a vehicle to attract students. The approach was based on identifying "rising research universities" that were concentrating resources on developing new doctoral programs. These institutions, preoccupied with the costs of the doctoral programs, would presumably not have money for online courses and would look to the Open University to fill that gap for them. United States Open University entered such partnerships with Indiana State University to offer a joint online bachelor's degree in business administration, and with the University of Maryland-Baltimore County for a joint master's degree in information science. But partnerships were not enough to save U.S. Open University.

Columbia University's for-profit company, Fathom, also sought synergy through partnerships. Columbia settled on a consortium approach rather than flying solo presumably because that arrangement provided more online intellectual property than the university could make available on its own. Fathom also had an eye toward creating a global presence on the Internet, which it did by including in the consortium some non-American institutions. Putting a number of providers under one banner also seemed to promise that its educational approaches were more varied and might appeal to a wider range of interests and learning styles.

Partnerships and consortiums predate computers, but they have seldom fulfilled their promise in education. Collaborations on behalf of e-learning by Fathom, the University of Washington, and others contrast with the previous practice of every institution going it alone, a tendency that has held back the academic world in the past. The country is replete with needless program and degree duplication. Only when they are in the most dire straits do educational institutions eliminate programs that they maintain for reasons of prestige despite sparse enrollments. The new interest in partnerships sparked by online learning may spill over into regular programs. That would be good for all of education.

CHAPTER 12

SERVING THOSE LEAST SERVED

Think about the single mother working as a bookkeeper at a corporate headquarters outside Chicago who would like to pursue an M.B.A. but cannot spare time from a schedule that demands that she race home from the office each afternoon. Or the three young sons of a husband and wife in Texas who move from place to place for jobs harvesting fields and orchards, causing the boys to miss and interrupt their education. Or the severely disabled youngster in Cincinnati, confined to a wheelchair and needing constant nursing, whose parents would love to see her receive a high-quality education without enduring the ordeal of traveling to and from a school each day. Or the very able seniors in a rural high school in Alabama who could thrive in an advanced calculus course if only it were available to them in their remote locale, where there are few students to take calculus and no one to teach it. These are just a few examples of the underserved students whose education could be enhanced by online learning.

The more students differ from the traditional norm, the less responsive schools and colleges and universities tend to be to the needs of those students. The advent of online learning has the potential to enhance service to nontraditional and underserved students by compelling traditional institutions to pay more attention to these groups, whether or not they enroll in online education.

SERVING NONTRADITIONAL AND SPECIAL NEEDS STUDENTS

One of the largest such groups—students past traditional college-going age who commute to classes that they take on a part-time basis—could find e-learning particularly suited to their circumstances. Jobs and family obligations make attendance in regularly scheduled classes on campus an ordeal for many of them. Adult students don't have to look far to find the motivation to sit down at a computer and take a course at a time and place of their choosing. Some adults, like the almost two million who are incarcerated, may have no other direction in which to turn.

Educational institutions have tried for years, with varying degrees of success, to adapt themselves to the needs of the employed. Part-time students, most of whom work, have been the fastest growing sector of the enrollment for decades. Course schedules, especially at community colleges, have been cut, sliced, and shredded to fit offerings into early morning hours, evening hours, and weekends that have little appeal to traditional students. Online learning, with its flexibility, could have great appeal to such students. If courses on the web draw a sizable following, it will be because those who enroll in them prefer to decide when and where to pursue their studies. Students who work must squeeze their campus-based studies into the scarce hours before and after their jobs, often chasing across town to do so.

The provision of opportunity was central to the mission that brought Kentucky Virtual University (KVU) into existence in 1997 as part of the state's postsecondary education reform act. The legislation set a goal of increasing the number of Kentuckians with post–high school skills and, correspondingly, raising the state's average per capita income. KVU offered no courses and awarded no degrees but used its online capacities to facilitate the enrollment of nontraditional students, lending support in registration, academic advising, tutoring, library access, and technology backup to cope with online problems. "Our job is to help change the culture," said Daniel A. Rabuzzi, chief executive officer of Kentucky Virtual University. "We are not just a passive broker of existing material. We have money to loan for the development of online courses." KVU wanted to ensure that place, time, and economic circumstances did not preclude adults from gaining the education and job skills that would change their economic situation.

How attractive will adult, part-time students in Kentucky and elsewhere find the proposition of setting their own hours for course taking by having the power to switch on the computer at will and avoid a journey to campus? KVU and other institutions offering online learning hope to discover the answer to this question; it remains to be seen how prospective students will react. Providers of online learning could be disappointed with the response. It may turn out that part-time students don't really want different treatment, that they prefer to sit in classrooms with peers and to take courses on campus just like everyone else—even if it means stretching their time to the breaking point.

The attraction of online education and its impact on regular programs may affect many beyond part-time adult students. In elementary and secondary schools, for instance, e-learning could meet the needs of the children of migrant workers, disabled students, pregnant teenagers, and youngsters living in rural areas and inner-city neighborhoods that lack complete educational resources or staff within their schools. Disruptions plague the education of children in migrant families, for instance, as they move from place to place, following the vicissitudes of the agricultural cycle. E-learning could inject continuity into the education of such youngsters. The University of Texas at Austin has shown what schools and universities, working together in classrooms and online, can do for these peripatetic youngsters. The Migrant Student Program, operated by the university's Continuing and Extended Education division, offered high school credits for students not able to remain in one location for their schooling. The courses conformed to the diploma requirements of the state of Texas. Students earned credits through correspondence, CD-ROMs, an online course, and—to the extent possible—in regular classrooms.

The goal was to help migrant students get their diplomas. Using a $70,000 grant from Microsoft Corporation to experiment with the role that online courses might play, the program offered a course called Math Models. The university spent some of the money to provide youngsters with laptop computers and modems to enable them to download studies from the web wherever their families relocated for a succession of jobs at farms and factories. It was not an unmitigated success; some laptops were lost or damaged, or were used to visit web sites that educators deemed inappropriate. But the lessons learned from the experiment led to some changes. The program opted to have computers kept at schools and at other accessible buildings, where the equipment was safer and the youngsters could be supervised. Also, this meant that the program no longer had to pay for expensive Internet connections from remote sites. Another major change involved making a version of the course available on CD-ROM, with an optional Internet connection to reach links that embellished the course. In 2002, officials of the Migrant Student Program said they were still fine tuning their approach; they acknowledged the need for greater technical support for students who pursued courses online and the need to do more to involve parents in the program so that they would reinforce it.

When it comes to technology, other issues impede the educational progress of girls of all social classes. A report sponsored by the American Association of University Women showed that the use of computers by girls diminishes as they move through the grades. By secondary school, they are far less inclined to be technologically active than they were in elementary schools. One might expect such findings to indicate a lack of inclination by females to enroll in online courses once they reach the postsecondary level, but this is not necessarily the case. A number of online programs that track participation by gender found that females were in the majority, a rather surprising statistic in light of some of the other figures. Teenagers who drop out of high school for a variety of reasons—work, pregnancy, the need to take care of children or other family members—and might not otherwise continue their education could benefit from online courses.

Then, there are students who live in inner-city neighborhoods so besieged by crime that travel between school and home is a threatening ordeal. Online learning could be part of a response to this sad state of affairs. The chance to stay at home and attend virtual classes might provide some relief. As it is, crime, violence, and drug dealing have forced school systems in some urban locales to consider holding classes in community rooms at housing projects so that children would not have to venture onto unsafe streets. Elsewhere, secure routes to and from school have been designated and patrolled by citizen volunteers to protect children. Online learning could be yet an additional response to this egregious situation.

Some schools cannot provide all of the courses that students need. The state legislature established West Virginia Virtual School (WVVS) in 2000 because the small, widely scattered schools that rural students attend simply could not offer the variety and depth of courses needed to enrich their education. The situation was exacerbated by the impoverished state's dwindling population, a phenomenon that robbed the public schools of both fiscal support and sufficient numbers of teachers. "The state wanted to assure the equitable access to education that all students do not necessarily have face to face," said Donna Miller, coordinator of West Virginia Virtual School.

The state could not afford immediately to create or deliver its own online courses, so WVVS was set up as a broker to arrange for making courses available to students in West Virginia. The Southern Regional Education Board facilitated a partnership with Florida Virtual School to provide online courses for West Virginia students, 468 of whom were enrolled in the courses by the second year, 2001–02. In 2002, with adoption of a new regulation mandating that all of West Virginia's middle schools offer foreign language courses, WVVS again arranged for Florida Virtual School to provide the courses online to schools that have neither the teachers nor the numbers of students in individual schools to offer the courses in classrooms.

Students with disabilities are another underserved group for whom online learning holds potential advantages. Students at the Model School for the Deaf at Washington, D.C., as well as deaf children at other schools around the country participated in the courses of the federal government's Virtual High School. "It put our students on a more level playing field with students at other schools that participated," said Joyce Barrett, who coordinated the use of technology for the Model School, part of Gaullaudet University. The Model School simply had too small an enrollment to give the courses in its classrooms, and it turned to the Virtual High School. "Because it involved reading and writing, our students could interact with hearing students in regular classrooms without having to be in those classrooms with interpreters. It gave them exposure to different kinds of kids in different places," Barrett said. She added that some students at the Model School who rely on American Sign Language were at a disadvantage in e-learning, but that, on the other hand, having to read and write to keep up in online courses helped build those skills for them.

Students with various disabilities might benefit from online education. Schools could use e-learning in some instances to comply with federal law requiring them to accommodate disabled youngsters, especially in dealing with the least mobile of them. The ability that online learning confers on students to set their own pace for learning is just one of many advantages. The technology that makes e-learning possible offers various accommodations for the disabled. Voice recognition software, for instance, can assist dyslexic students, who comprise perhaps 30 to 40 percent of all students classified as disabled. Special keyboards can ease the physical process of writing so that students may concentrate on the ideas they are trying to develop and be less concerned about physical manipulations. Usually, students who need them use these keyboards in classrooms, but they can readily be adapted to online education, providing one more tool by which e-learning can benefit such students.

David Rose and Anne Meyer, writers on special education, maintained that the biggest potential benefit that educational technology offers the disabled will be to change the nature of learning. This will happen eventually, they said, with multiple means of representation on computers. Going beyond such assisting tools as special keyboards, computers will present information in various ways that are accessible to students regardless of a host of disabling conditions. It will occur, too, they said, with multiple means of expression that will allow students of varying disabilities to interact and respond to the material in ways most suitable to their needs. Finally, they said, multiple means of engagement can be individualized to appeal to students with, say, attention deficit disorder or Asperger's Syndrome. "The particular benefit for students with disabilities," they said, "is that the new technologies will, by necessity, recognize both the reality and the virtue of diversity. The technologies of the future will be more, not less, diverse, and they will engage many kinds of learners."[1]

Adapted to online learning, technology holds endless possibilities for individualizing education for all students. Another educator, Denzil Edge, who spent almost three decades as a professor of special education at the University of Louisville, thought that online learning already could accommodate disabled students by taking advantage of existing technologies if only institutions ensured that courses complied with provisions of the Americans with Disabilities Act. Edge, who became chief executive officer of Spalding University Online in 2001, said: "I don't know of any program that can't be done online for people with disabilities if the program attends to the accessibility issues." He said that he meant this statement to include the visually and hearing impaired.

Intellectually gifted students, another group with special needs, have received notoriously poor treatment in elementary and secondary schools. Online learning with its self-paced characteristics could make such children less dependent on regular classrooms to advance through material. Whether they seek enrichment or acceleration, intellectually gifted students could find online learning to their liking. Competition from online learning might force elementary and secondary schools to fashion fresh approaches in classrooms to the challenges of gifted education, an area they have typically neglected in the past.

There is also the possibility, yet to be thoroughly explored, of online learning enhancing remedial education, which for all the $150 billion that has been spent on it through the federal government's Title I program since it began in 1965 has often yielded disappointing results. Perhaps students for whom classroom settings have been so relentlessly unproductive might find online learning a way to finally gain dominion over what has been frustration heaped upon frustration. Granted, this idea is a long shot, but part of the lack of progress of some struggling students has stemmed from their feeling that they lack any power over their own learning. Online courses might offer a breakthrough, a way to put them in control for the first time. Online learning in the security of their own homes, shielded from peers who scoff at academics, could offer an opportunity that other measures have seemed unable to provide.

THE IMPACT OF THE DIGITAL DIVIDE

Access has been a dominant concern in both K through 12 and higher education during the last half century. The grip of school segregation started to loosen with the 1954 decision in *Brown v. Board of Education.* Thoughts turned to making a higher quality of schooling available to black children in elementary and secondary schools. Then, in the late 1960s, especially after the assassination of the Rev. Martin Luther King Jr., colleges and universities examined their admissions policies and vowed to increase minority enrollments. Reverberations of these attempts to widen access to education still echo through the corridors of educational institutions, both precollegiate and college level, in debates over desegregation efforts and affirmative action policies. Even as skirmishes over access continue on these old fronts, a new battleground may open as efforts to provide access to online learning gather momentum. The College Board was so aware of access in online learning as an emerging issue that it devoted an entire report to the subject—"The Virtual University & Education Opportunity: Issues of Equity and Access for the Next Generation"—and pleaded that policymakers put access "at the core of system design."[2]

Unfortunately, e-learning could turn out to be just one more manifestation of the digital divide. The technology and knowledge that one needs for comfort with online learning are not distributed evenly across the economic spectrum. In 2000, for instance, computers were in the homes of 77 percent of white non-Hispanics, 72 percent of Asian Americans, 43 percent of blacks, and 37 percent of Hispanics. Eighty-seven percent of households with incomes of $75,000 or more had computers, and 79 percent of these households had at least one person who used the Internet at home. Only 28 percent of households with incomes of less than $25,000 had computers, and just 19 percent in this income range had someone who used the Internet.[3] People without computers and without access to the Internet do not participate in online learning, at least not from their homes. Can education offer the same opportunities to all sectors of the population if access to and knowledge of information technology are distributed unequally?

The disparities appear in schools as well as in homes. By and large, low-income and minority students have fewer computers in their classrooms than youngsters from affluent backgrounds. Furthermore, the computers in the classrooms of the poor also are more often out-of-date and less apt to figure prominently in the instructional program.[4] Studies have found that the more poor children in a school, the fewer computers, the less they are used, and the less likely that they are linked to the Internet. A curious remedy may somewhat alleviate this situation. Microsoft offered in 2001, in response to a class-action suit alleging that it overcharged customers, to install reconditioned computers and software in more than 12,500 schools in low-income neighborhoods around the country. Critics dismissed the offer as a public relations stunt, and a federal district judge in 2002 did not accept it, saying he found flaws in the proposal. The court left the door open to a revised offer. Whatever one thought of the offer, it highlighted a deep-seated problem, one that society will have to overcome to bridge the digital gap.

The digital gap stretches beyond the schooling of low-income and minority groups and almost surely will have an impact on their employment prospects. Young people who do not acquire ease and comfort with technology as students are apt to shy away from or never be hired into jobs requiring extensive use of technology. They may also be disinclined as adults to engage in online learning. Judging by the statistics, much the same is true of students who grow up in rural areas and children of immigrants. While cultural influences may figure in some of these situations, poverty, by and large, drives the largest wedge between the haves and the have-nots when it comes to technology. The disparities manifest themselves in the infrastructure essential to e-learning. The country needs to install and continually renew a system of interconnection with the capacity to carry the enormous volume of traffic that will surge down the information highway by the end of the decade. It will require large sums to install all of the broadband connections to keep technology from lagging for want of capacity.

"I believe that whether or not students are learning on campus, or learning off campus, or learning in a combination of campus classroom work and online work, what we need to do is to strive to eliminate the disparities," said Bernard Gifford. Head of the InterActive Media Study

Group at the University of California at Berkeley, Gifford spoke of using technology to increase educational opportunities for students not well served in conventional classroom settings. He endorsed "location-independent, web-based, computer-mediated" instruction in higher education as part of the mission of educating and retaining students. He used the term "location-independent" instead of distance learning, he said, to stress that "the quality of instruction is not diminished as a function of location."[5]

Most discussions of the digital gap focus on the availability of hardware and access to the Internet, but teachers and pedagogy also are important factors. Not only do teachers use technology less in educating poor children, but they use it differently. Lessons taught to low-achieving, poor children tend to be less sophisticated and do not take full advantage of the range of technological possibilities. While poor children drill on the computer, higher-achieving students have more chances to work with data bases, spreadsheets, and graphics, for example.[6] The different roles that technology plays in the instruction of poor children and advantaged children is a function not only of the equipment, but of the fact that teachers who work in schools with concentrations of low-achieving youngsters are less likely to receive training that enables them to infuse their students' lessons with sophisticated uses of technology. Schools in general have been notoriously lax in providing teachers with professional development in technological applications.

The schools with the greatest funding needs tend to give teachers the least help in this regard. Given their experiences with such teachers, students from modest backgrounds may end up neither prepared for nor receptive to online learning. Government bears much of the responsibility for wiping out such disparities, but the fiscal year 2003 budget proposals by the Bush administration contained disappointments for those who hoped that two of the programs aimed at closing the digital divide would prosper. No more funds were proposed for these two efforts, the Community Technologies Centers (CTC) Program in the Department of Education and the Technologies Opportunities Program (TOP) of the Department of Commerce.

The racial impact of the digital divide could be seen on the campuses of the nation's historically black colleges and universities, which lagged badly behind historically white institutions. The United Negro College Fund (UNCF) tried to help close this gap with its Technology Enhancement Capital Campaign, which had raised $94 million by the middle of 2002. Recognition of the need for this campaign came in the late1990s, after UNCF got a $42 million grant from the Lily Endowment and was able to distribute about $1 million to each of its member institutions for faculty salaries, scholarships, and physical plant improvements. In administering the grant, UNCF discovered that one-third of the needs that absorbed the money were related to technology, underscoring the extent to which these colleges and universities were bereft of hardware, software, and technological know-how.

Based on a survey it conducted, UNCF found that students at its 39 member institutions, as compared with those at predominantly white colleges and universities, were less likely to own computers, to have any place on campus to plug in the computers that they owned, and—even if all of the students were given computers—the institutions did not have the network capacity to accommodate the computing. These schools had much to do before most of them could even begin thinking about offering any substantial body of online courses. Even faculty members at UNCF colleges and universities had less access to computers than their counterparts around the country. The institutions used money from the enhancement campaign to purchase thousands of desktop and laptop computers, servers, and printers, as well as for wiring and technical upgrades. Other money would have to be spent on training faculty to take advantage of technology, a crucial step if UNCF institutions are to originate their own online courses. The Digital Learning Lab at Howard University offered a companion program in this regard, launching Project Archimedes in 2001 to help faculty, staff, and students at historically black colleges and universities learn to use digital technologies.

The digital divide is real enough, but not everyone agrees that spotlighting it will necessarily help those who seem most disadvantaged in terms of their access and use of technology. Some prefer to see fewer mentions of this topic lest it lead schools, colleges, and employers to stereotype minorities, women, and the poor as technologically disadvantaged and to expect less of them. Furthermore, critics evince concern that minorities, women, and the poor—hearing continually that they are on the deficit side of the digital gap—will shy away from computers and technology, cutting themselves off from certain courses as students and from certain jobs as adults. It would follow that they would be less attuned to online education than other candidates for such courses. "As well-meaning as it is as a policy initiative," Said Henry Jenkins, director of comparative media studies at Massachusetts Institute of Technology, focusing on the digital divide "can be marginalizing and patronizing in its own terms."[7]

BUILDING A SEAMLESS SYSTEM

Online learning, both through entire courses and in web-related class-room courses, can help break the monopoly that has made precollegiate education dependent on the largesse of higher education. Colleges and universities no longer hold all the power when it comes to building seamless connections. The courses and the knowledge they convey are available to everyone, courtesy of the Internet. Even the greatest academic libraries are accessible to high school students who may live in the most forlorn inner-city neighborhoods or the most remote rural areas. The door has now opened for elementary and secondary school pupils and teachers to initiate and carry out more of their work, with or without the assistance and blessing of colleges and universities, in building seamless connections between secondary schools and higher learning.

A process of learning that employs technology to free itself from strictures of time and place raises fresh questions about the restraints that sustain the separateness of high school- and college-level studies. The education establishment has honored the notion of a seamless system of learning, but schools and institutions of higher education have not consistently followed through on implementing programs that embody this philosophy. High schools do not always smooth the way for students who would gain from spending part of the school day in college courses. Now, if institutions themselves do not cooperate to let students advance their studies, youngsters can turn to online courses and take matters into their own hands. E-learning makes students less subject to institutional whims and empowers them to act on their own to take the courses they want, without regard for whether they enroll in high school or college courses. Online education might close some of the fissures that separate the two educational sectors, and even the threat of this happening could hasten change in removing some seams from the system.

Kentucky Virtual University saw itself playing a role in the state's P-16 Initiative. KVU set out to fashion the specifics of this role in consultation with Kentucky Virtual High School (a separate entity), the Kentucky Community and Technical College System, the Department for Adult Education and Literacy (relating to GED candidates), and the Kentucky Higher Education Assistance Authority (the student loan agency). Good intentions of this sort have not always been enough to take the bumps out of what ought to be a smoother system from prekindergarten through college. The difficulties of trying to close the gap between schools and colleges are persistent. Institutions at the secondary and higher education levels have developed largely independent of each other despite their ostensibly symbiotic nature; the administrative and governing apparatuses of schools and colleges are entirely separate. Furthermore, problems and failures have tended to plague attempts to bring about more cooperation between the two sectors. High school personnel tend to regard college-level people who say they are "coming to help" as natives regard colonizers. At institutions of higher education, a faculty reward system built on achieving success at research and publication accords scant recognition to work done in or for public schools. Community colleges, not as worried about prestige issues, have been by far the most active sector of higher education in this regard.

The school reform movement across the country gives growing attention to improvements that have a K through 16 orientation as a way to underscore the need for seeing the education system as a single entity, but some experts question whether this effort, on its own, will amount to more than lip service. "Although there are a number of K-16 projects in many states, little effort has been made to coordinate reform systemically across the educational levels in order to improve academic opportunities and the chances of success throughout students' entire educational lives," wrote Stanford University's Michael Kirst and Andrea Venezia.[8]

The problem has historic dimensions. The Ford Foundation, during the $30 million Comprehensive School Improvement Program that it funded in locales throughout the country between 1960 and 1970, had hoped to aid schools by getting colleges and universities to work more closely with them. Ford tried to get traditionally black colleges and predominantly white universities to collaborate with the schools. The results were deemed largely unproductive. Working together often meant little more than school districts spending Ford Foundation money to pay college professors to go to schools to offer advice.

An evaluation of the program found that "school administrators tended to limit strictly the role of university consultants" and universities "often boasted of strong and improving 'town-gown' relations, when in fact they did not exist."[9] The report went on to say: "Seldom did the power of the university as an institution function as a force for improvement of educational quality in elementary and secondary schools. The university was not seen by any of the parties as an instrument of educational reform for the nation's schools. Hence, while university faculty members worked in schools and with teachers, they functioned as part-timers . . . who . . . could not become involved in the nitty-gritty, and did not carry with them the university's expressed commitment."[10] It was not until the 1990s, under enormous pressure, that colleges and universities finally conceded that the fact that they educated all of those teaching in the nation's elementary and secondary schools indicated that perhaps higher education had a reciprocal stake in addressing the shortcomings of the schools.

If students waste the senior year of high school or at least do not use it as productively as they might, surely this shortcoming reflects on the structure of formal education and the lack of connections between high school and college. It is incumbent on school districts and nearby institutions of higher education to devise ways to bring college-level studies into the lives of youngsters while they are still enrolled in high school. The availability of college courses online could help bridge this gap. It might push brick-and-mortar institutions to take steps to integrate portions of the last year of high school and the first year of college for students who could gain the most from such collaboration. Students could use computers in the high school to pursue college-level work during part of the school day. Furthermore, high school teachers might tutor the students in the online college courses, building on relationships that they have already formed with those same students.

One of the most troubling and most problematic areas of the relationship between precollegiate education and higher education revolves around remedial education. It is the bane of both sectors, reflecting poorly on high schools that promote ill-prepared students and lowering the reputations of colleges and universities that find a considerable portion of their effort devoted to teaching high school–level subjects, sometimes without notable success. The upshot is that when about one-third of students arrive at postsecondary institutions unprepared for college-level work, only about one-half of those who enroll at a four-year college or university get a degree within six years.[11]

E-learning has the potential to introduce new approaches to deal with this gnawing problem. SMARTHINKING, Inc., a company that marketed its online tutoring service to educational institutions, represented the sort of approach that may embody the future of remedial education. By consigning much of remedial education to online courses, an institution could stop using its facilities and faculty time for remediation, which, critics assert, does not belong in higher education. A unit of state government or some third party might absorb the cost, and students of any age, at any institutional level or at no institution whatsoever, could pursue the tutoring they need without regard for whether it is the responsibility of high schools or institutions of higher education.

A hint of the possibilities was seen in the contract that SMARTHINKING made to tutor 700 students at five high schools in Massachusetts in math and writing through a pilot project in 2002. The students, eleventh graders in five school districts, had the previous year failed the state examinations required to receive diplomas. The state, looking for the best alternative that it could find to costly face-to-face tutoring, settled on SMARTHINKING's "real time" online tutoring by computer. Each student was tutored in math by entering a personal electronic chat room in which the person at the other end fired back immediate responses.

Paula Sack, a consultant to the Massachusetts Department of Education, said that the usually unmotivated students responded positively, excited by the idea of their tutoring coming through a computer and enjoying the instant gratification. This pilot project may be a harbinger of more such efforts as a result of the federal No Child Left Behind legislation for elementary and secondary schools enacted by Congress at the end of 2001. Following a plan laid down by President George W. Bush, failing students will be eligible for outside tutoring at public expense. Tutors will undoubtedly provide much of this assistance in person. Projects such as the one on which SMARTHINKING embarked in Massachusetts could proliferate, and other online solutions could figure in these efforts, too.

CHAPTER 13

REDEFINING THE EDUCATIONAL INSTITUTION

Futurists propounded a vision at the 1939–40 World's Fair in New York City in which technology triumphed over time and place, speeding passengers to their destinations, eliminating tedious housework, making it possible for Americans to enjoy leisure as never before. World War II delayed the fulfillment of this utopian vision, but the half century after the war produced jet travel, a new generation of time-saving household appliances, high-speed trains, and the computer. As the war in the Pacific neared its end, another aspect of this vision of the future appeared in the pages of the *Atlantic Monthly*. It was offered by Vannevar Bush, director of the U.S. government's Office of Scientific Research and Development. With stunning prescience, Bush, who would help create the National Science Foundation, wrote: "Consider a future device for individual use, which is a sort of mechanized private file and library . . . in which an individual stores all his books, records, and communications, and which is mechanized so that it may be consulted with exceeding speed . . . On the top are slanting translucent screens on which materials can be projected . . . Books of all sorts, pictures, current periodicals, newspapers, are thus obtained. . . ."[1]

Glimpses of the educational future at the dawn of the twenty-first century present a view filled with the kind of technological optimism that permeated the World's Fair and was encapsulated by Bush in his description of the computer yet to be born. E-learning is a central element in this emerging picture of the digital age. Meanwhile, most educational institutions are still groping their way into the world of cyber education, and it is too soon to predict the outcome of their efforts, which, collectively, amount to a large pilot project. Online learning remains a work in progress, a process riddled with questions. Even in its inchoate form, however, it gives promise of introducing fresh thinking into schools and colleges.

The form and organization of formal education have barely changed in the United States in a century. Primary schools achieved their current form in the nineteenth century and secondary schools took shape early in the twentieth century. The small liberal arts college of the mid-nineteenth century hardly differed from its counterpart of the early twenty-first century and doctoral institutions of the late nineteenth century bore many of the characteristics of today's counterparts. Essentially, the ways that teachers deliver instruction have remained the same through the decades, and even the calendar of the academic year has stayed steady in the influence it exerts over instructional possibilities. One can best appreciate the revolutionary nature of online learning against this backdrop, a tableau of constancy in which variations on time and place figure hardly at all.

It appears at this juncture that cyber learning may have a deep and lasting impact on higher education. Almost certainly, growing numbers of faculty will adapt web-based innovations to courses that meet primarily in classrooms. Fully online courses, representing a more fundamental challenge to the definition of higher education, face more formidable obstacles. A writer in the monthly report published by information technology guru Esther Dyson offered an observation in 2000 that remains no less salient today. He said: "[T]he Net has yet to change much of the process of education itself. Educational institutions, like large bricks-and-mortar enterprises, have established patterns of behavior that take time to evolve in response to new technology. Also, education has generally been removed from the Darwinian economic forces that drive efficiencies (and technology adoption) in the business world."[2]

The nature of the enterprise compels educators, and lay people as well, to confront old paradigms about learning. The organizational structure of an educational institution can hardly remain the same in virtual reality as it was in brick and mortar. The definition of the teacher's role is also up for grabs in cyber courses that use instructors in new ways, raising fundamental questions about what it takes to teach a course online and whether schools and colleges should organize their faculties in the future for online teaching as they have in the past for classroom courses. And what about the heart of the educational enterprise—the library? Does it make sense to adhere to formulas about size and function when the Internet opens untold collections across the country and around the world to students and their teachers? The academic library is changing as a result of technology, regardless of what becomes of online courses.

Institutions of higher education face the challenge of retaining their essence while embracing features of the new. Vartan Gregorian, president of the Carnegie Corporation of New York, said that the love affair with technology, while enriching teaching and making education more affordable and accessible, should not mean spurning practices and values that have taken the university eight centuries to acquire. He continued: "[I]t is the university that invented the computer, the Internet, distance learning and even the term management . . . The issue is whether they abdicate their inventions, their ideas, their roles and their possibilities to the outside world—or whether they shape their own future. Universities will survive provided they don't undermine themselves; for I believe that they are not so much at risk from external threats as they are from internal ones of our own making."[3]

WHAT IS AN EDUCATIONAL INSTITUTION?

It was once clear that an entity calling itself an institution of learning was supposed to have a campus, a library, a resident faculty, and classrooms where students attended courses. This is no longer the case. Online learning is redefining the concept of an educational institution. Such entities as Western Governors University, Michigan Virtual University,

National Technological University, and Kennedy-Western University are virtual institutions of higher education lacking almost all of the features shared by most other universities. The same is true of such cyber high schools as those in Missouri, West Virginia, Ohio, Pennsylvania, and Florida. A growing number of educational institutions in the future may need little more physical presence than an address on the Internet.

The Changing Structure

It will not be so easy to recognize an educational institution if it has no campus and its faculty and students are out of sight. Online learning should lead to a reappraisal of what defines a school, college, or university. How widespread will the stripped-down version of an educational institution become? What beyond the courses themselves will remain? Institutions are always changing and colleges and universities are overdue for some revisions. Older Americans can remember when a soda fountain and a counter that sold ice cream sundaes and milk shakes defined a drugstore. Try to buy a milk shake today at Rite Aid or CVS, which have replaced soda fountains with electric can openers, hair dryers, and a host of products seldom seen in the drugstores of yore.

It could be that online learning will prove to be a life line for some small, remote educational institutions that have had an increasingly difficult time attracting students. Many of the religious denominations that founded colleges in the nineteenth century purposely sought settings far removed from what they viewed as the temptations and sins of big cities. These sites became liabilities, though, by the second half of the twentieth century when commuting distance took on more importance for growing numbers of students who lived at home. When students don't have to travel to campuses and locale no longer matters, as happens with distance education, some of the institutions at out-of-the-way places may find new ways to compete. They could try to reinvent themselves in the cyber age. On the other hand, they will face new competition from bigger, wealthier institutions, including ones in the for-profit sector, who can more easily afford to incur the costs of online learning.

Businesses established to generate profits have shown that education can be no less a commodity than a pair of candlesticks or a carton of milk. Members of the public increasingly have demonstrated their willingness, both in physical settings and online, to trust their learning to businesses that sell education to them, sometimes using approaches that they developed for training their own employees. Wallace Pond of Education America's online division predicts "a free-for-all" in coming years as cyber learning fuels competition and providers battle for shares of the education market. This will occur on the ground as well.

As so often happens when change tries to push its way through the bulwarks of higher education, online learning will penetrate deepest at colleges and universities below the upper tier. Less prestigious institutions, under pressure to maintain enrollments, will prove most receptive to online learning and alter themselves most in response to it. If online education pervades such colleges and universities, it could ultimately weaken the power of academic departments, to both good and bad effect. E-learning lends itself to building bridges between and among disciplines by allowing those who design and teach courses to more readily break through the rigidities that the departmental structure imposes on the organization of knowledge. Interdisciplinary study more closely parallels the ways of the real world, but it could prove disruptive to an academic system that has long served the inclination of scholars to center discourse and discovery around ever narrower disciplinary topics.

Furthermore, online courses, with their inclination to use instructors as facilitators, mentors, and coaches, could lead to a devaluation of faculty research. Students would benefit enormously if higher education raised the prestige of teaching, but institutions must consider whether such a shift in mission would also lead to a diminution of research, and whether entities outside the academy would take up the slack. Admittedly extreme, this scenario is worth reflecting on, given that some aspects of traditional educational institutions, once lost, may prove difficult to reestablish.

Collaboration

In another change hastened by technology, education is becoming a more collaborative enterprise, sometimes blurring distinctions between individual institutions and the conglomerates that they join. A consortium representing a group of colleges and universities that offer online courses might just as well award the degree itself. The consortium approach to collaboration did not originate with e-learning, but the Internet offers new ways of spreading the concept. Consortiums existed in the past to pool academic resources and to allow students to enroll in courses in more than one institution, goals that were carried out in classrooms and are now being pursued in the ether. One of the most successful of such arrangements, for instance, was the Five Colleges Consortium in Massachusetts that allied the University of Massachusetts, Mount Holyoke, Amherst, Hampshire, and Smith.

Online learning allows such cooperation to flourish to an extent not possible when a student had actually to travel to the campuses of the participating colleges to take courses. The work of the Southern Regional Education Board (SREB) illustrates the new collaborative reality in which an educational institution may really be a group of colleges and universities. When SREB decided in the 1990s to assemble an Electronic Campus in the 16 southeastern states that it served, the organization vowed not to compete with the participating institutions and, therefore, not to grant certificates and degrees in its own name. Prospective students used SREB's home page to find the courses they wanted, and then the web directed them to the colleges and universities offering those courses. By 2001, some 250 certificate and degree programs were available online from institutions affiliated with SREB. It was entirely possible for a student not only to pursue programs online but to combine courses taken at several SREB institutions. The Electronic Campus was an offshoot of the Academic Common Market that already existed to allow students to take campus-based courses at various SREB colleges and universities.

At present, students on the Electronic Campus have to choose a home institution through which to accumulate their online credits. Eventually, though, it seems possible that some entity will evolve—as the Regents External Degree program did in the 1970s in New York State—to let students aggregate courses taken online at several institutions in order to earn a degree that might not bear the name of any of those individual colleges or universities. In fact, the Western Governors University has already started doing this. For several decades, such institutions as Thomas Edison College in New Jersey and Excelsior College in New York state have existed for just that purpose— to pull together credits that students earned at several institutions and to award them degrees.

Given a student's ability to accumulate credits from several colleges and universities without leaving home, there is now even greater reason to create online vehicles to amass academic credits in pursuit of a degree. The question of a student's institutional affiliation could grow less relevant with the ease of simultaneously enrolling in cyber courses at several institutions. Students, courtesy of online learning, increasingly will earn academic credits at two, three, four, and even more institutions on their way to degrees. Degrees may no longer always be the exclusive domain of individual institutions; they will, under this approach, reflect work that a student has done at several institutions. Education may have to adjust to an era in which learning is individual-based, not institution-based.

Educational institutions historically had an easy time identifying their students, almost as if they bore cattle brands. Students matriculated and took all their courses at that school, college, or university. There have always been exceptions: for instance, students who cross-registered at a neighboring college to find a course that was unavailable on their campus, or the small number of high school students who spent part of the day at a nearby community college to take one or two courses as part of an accelerated program. But few observers ever wondered about the home institution with which such students were affiliated.

Determining which students belong to which institutions will become more complicated as students take online courses at several institutions, thereby challenging traditional notions of affiliation. Furthermore, colleges and universities may have to address the question of state residency in new ways for students, wherever they may live, who don't come to campus for courses. This will be an important issue for state-related colleges and universities that usually charge higher tuitions to out-of-state students. Online learning makes such a policy questionable. "The physical locale of a student has become increasingly secondary," said Bruce Chaloux, director of the Electronic Campus of the Southern Regional Education Board. Such changes may also affect state-based financial aid.

SREB promoted the idea among its member institutions of not charging online students out-of-state tuition rates as long as they resided in one of the member states. The organization proposed a special tuition rate for out-of-state e-learners that fell in between the instate and out-of-state rates. But the economic reversals in 2001 prevented adoption of such a policy. Nonetheless, it may grow ever more difficult to justify differentiated rates of tuition. Penn State's World Campus, for example, charges the same tuition whether an online student lives in Aliquippa, Pennsylvania, Albuquerque, New Mexico, or Aberdeen, Scotland. "In the future," said education professors Nicholas C. Burbules and Thomas A. Callister, "many online courses will mix on-campus, off-campus, and international students."[4]

Army University Access Online (AUAO) illustrates as well as any institution how technology has altered the definition of a university. This university was principally an amalgam of software systems that functioned as an educational broker at an address on the Internet, eArmyU.com. AUAO had no faculty and offered no courses. It gave no academic credits and awarded no certificates or degrees. In just its first year of existence, 2001, however, it enrolled 12,000 students and expected to add another 22,000 in 2002, with a goal of 80,000 by 2005. Students designated one of the 23 participating schools as their home institution, the one in whose name a certificate or degree would eventually be awarded. Along the way, students pursuing one of the 89 certificate and degree programs might take courses at any of the institutions.

The programs ranged from a certificate in long-term care administration to an associate's degree in business administration, to bachelor's degrees in such majors as business administration and health care management, to master's degrees in such fields as computer information systems and English. The participating institutions included Anne Arundel Community College in Maryland, Kansas State University, Northwest Missouri State University, and Troy State University in Alabama. Central Texas College garnered the largest enrollment at the outset, perhaps reflecting its proximity to Fort Hood, where soldiers already were familiar with the institution. All of the participating institutions belonged to the Servicemembers Opportunity Colleges Army

Degree program, guaranteeing the transferability of credit among the institutions, as well as credit for prior learning and military experience.

For the Army, the goal was to bolster the recruitment and retention of soldiers, according to Andrew Fairbanks of PricewaterhouseCoopers, the contractor that assembled and integrated the entire system, working with the colleges and universities and hiring a host of subcontractors to perform various services in conjunction with the software platform. The Army saw a collateral advantage to its university, presuming that soldiers, as cyber students, would gain technological savvy that they could apply in military situations. Enrollees had to have at least three years' service remaining to enter Army University, and the Army hoped that some would find the prospect of a free degree sufficient reason to reenlist. So enthusiastic were the troops that when enrollment opened at midnight, January 1, 2001, at Georgia's Fort Benning, they were already in line to enroll.

Like Army University Access Online, Pennsylvania Virtual Community College Consortium (PaVCC) existed as a portal that steered students to its member institutions, the state's 15 community colleges. PaVCC gave the colleges a cohesion that they did not have as campus-based institutions in a state without system-wide governance of its community colleges. Students could choose from among 600 courses—as of 2002 only nine of the colleges had online or video courses to list with the virtual college—and select a home institution, from among the community colleges. For the most part, the courses required no attendance whatsoever on campus.

Students could earn enough credits for associate's degrees without ever leaving their homes, but the virtual college itself admitted no students and granted no degrees. Having identified a home institution, students could take online courses originating with any of the community colleges without submitting another application. PaVCC, in effect, became the vehicle by which the more than one-third of the state's population in locales beyond commuting distance of one of the 15 campuses could attend a community college. (Pennsylvania State University does, however, have 17 two-year campuses around the state, substituting for community colleges in those places.) As it turned out, PaVCC during its first three years drew about half of its enrollments from among students who already took courses at one of the 15 campus-based community colleges and wanted to add online courses to their schedules.

WHO IS A TEACHER?

Online learning alters the role not only of the institution but, potentially, of the teacher, as well. Paradoxically, such courses can both widen and narrow the role of teachers. Depending on the institution's policies, teachers may have a diminished role or a larger role. First of all and most obviously, instruction online requires different—or at least expanded—talents. The pedagogy is not the same as that used in the classroom. Teachers certainly adapt some aspects of face-to-face instruction to online courses, but they must learn new skills, too. Usually, for instance, a good online course takes advantage of such devices as electronic bulletin boards and chat rooms to raise the importance of discussion in the service of learning.

Rather than acting as the sage on the stage, as some glibly put it, someone who presides over an online course may assume more of the attributes of a facilitator, guide, mentor, or coach, helping students find their own way to knowledge. Such a transformation could spread into classrooms as some of those who facilitate online learning adapt that approach to their teaching on campus. Not all who teach for a living have developed proficiency in presiding over discussions and using them to advance learning. Online learning makes this omission glare, and teachers who do not alter their pedagogy in response run the risk of embarrassment. Discussions, albeit online, are vital to e-learning and cannot be avoided as they might be in some classrooms where lectures make up the entirety of instruction.

Shared Responsibility

Online learning can lead to a disaggregation of the traditional role of teachers. Instructors, as discussed in earlier chapters, sometimes must surrender authority over content or at least share some of their jurisdiction. That is true particularly if they teach courses designed for the web by someone else. Some other courses, if not wholly developed by others, may be so-called shells, containing the guts of the course and limiting the latitude of the instructor to improvise. In other cases, so-called content providers make available cartridges that an institution may inject into online courses, allowing the content provider to determine only part of the course material. It is entirely possible, when one group of people develops cyber courses and another group teaches them, that those who teach may have little or no role in determining the design and/or content. There are several reasons why the teacher may be left out of this process, including the strong possibility that the teacher lacks the technical skill to take full advantage of the virtual environment.

Beyond that, some institutions like the idea of standardizing courses so that the content remains the same no matter who teaches the courses. Standardization of content, with little room for the person leading the course to deviate, may help ensure that students achieve prescribed learning objectives. On the other hand, this approach requires less instructional expertise and opens the door to using instructors who are paid less and lack the academic credentials of the average faculty member. Someone who interacts with students online in a standardized course—and keep in mind not all online courses are standardized and some standardized courses are taught in classrooms, especially at career institutes—may be a facilitator, capable of leading threaded discussions but perhaps lacking a formidable curriculum vitae. In other words, institutions can, if they choose, more readily dispense with regular faculty in online courses. Some institutions may see this as a road to more control and to lower costs. Such an approach is anathema to many faculty members, accustomed as they are to reigning supreme over content and the way to present it.

The way that Jones International University created courses and organized its faculty illustrated various facets of some of these approaches. The university's methods related both to its being a totally online provider and to its for-profit status. Jones began operating in 1995 and in 1999 was the first fully online educational institution to receive accreditation, which was awarded by the North Central Association, one of the major regional groups. Jones did not offer a single course in a classroom. As one can imagine, the decision to accredit Jones International was fraught with controversy, earning a letter of protest from the American Association of University Professors. Jones by 2002 had 27 degree programs, mostly business related, at both the bachelor's and master's levels. Based in an office building in Englewood, Colorado, Jones International University did not need much space, employing only six full-time faculty members.

An academic advisory board of mainly outside consultants presided over each degree area at Jones International. Each board defined the curriculum for its degree area. Then, the university contracted with content experts to flesh out the courses. For this purpose, Jones said that it used faculty members from such major institutions as the University of Colorado, the University of Wisconsin, the University of North Carolina, and the University of Texas. Jones described its content experts on its web site as "world class teachers drawn from the world over." They received a fee, and Jones retained all rights to the content that they created for the courses, which apparently tended to reflect the content that these outside faculty members taught in courses at their own universities. Technology staff from Jones worked with the material from the content experts to organize it into the eight one-week modules that made up a course for online presentation. Jones said that its full-time design staff comprised five instructional designers, six web designers, and two multimedia designers.

Those who actually dealt with students and led online courses were an almost totally separate group. The content experts almost never taught the courses. The teaching faculty were part-timers who had knowledge of the content, had frequently taught somewhere else, and were often business practitioners. They worked on contract and some lived outside the United States, an arrangement eminently possible for a cyber university. Each of Jones's six full-time faculty members, in addition to teaching some of the courses, oversaw a certain number of the degree programs. The six full-timers also took responsibility for assessing teaching performance in those programs and for recruiting teaching faculty. Given the prescribed curriculum, the part-time faculty had limited latitude and steered the courses to meet prescribed outcomes. But even under such circumstances, these online instructors exercised judgment in facilitating the online discussions that were an essential part of the learning, and in marking and responding to the work that students submitted.

Jones listed the names of the content experts and their institutional affiliations at its web site, an apparent effort to bask in some reflected prestige. Conversations with several content experts confirmed that they generally had no further contact with Jones International after creating the course content and getting paid. Some of their courses continued in the curriculum and others were replaced. "I don't know what they're doing with it," Kathleen Allen, a faculty member at the University of Southern California, said of the material in the four graduate courses that she and a colleague had designed for Jones two years earlier. The courses were Fundamentals of Entrepreneurship, Feasibility Analysis of New Ventures, Developing Business and Marketing Plans for New Ventures, and Strategies for Emerging Ventures. Allen continued: "The experience was fine. I didn't announce all over the world that I was doing it. I do teach at USC, but I felt it wasn't competitive."

Elsewhere, the Global Education Network (GEN) also set out to take the classroom-based courses of distinguished professors at leading colleges and universities and adapt them for online courses that would be led by others. In pilot projects, the new online courses were offered to students at community colleges. The core of the online lectures and the main content were, in effect, what the professors had taught at their own colleges. Designers took apart and reassembled the content in modules suitable to the web, with technical features that incorporated the new medium of delivery. The instructors handled the electronic interaction with the students, monitored their participation, answered their questions, marked their electronically submitted papers, issued grades, and dealt generally with students' needs.

Some of online education's most severe critics consider virtual learning nothing more than a scheme to eliminate much of the teaching faculty. The American Association of University Professors, an organization that has academic freedom as a central concern, raised questions in one of its reports about the freedom of faculty members involved in online learning. Drawing on its classic 1940 Statement of Principles stating that "teachers are entitled to freedom in the classroom in discussing their subject," the report made the following observation:

The scope of that principle is relatively clear in the physical setting, where a "classroom" is bounded by walls, floor, and ceiling. But where the learning site may be a virtual space, the import of this principle is far less clear . . . Much of the course-related communication may occur through e-mail, either individually targeted or addressed to the class as a group. Under these conditions, the scope of the operative term 'classroom' must be enlarged to encompass electronic formats for those virtual spaces and areas where the communication inherent in the teaching and learning process may occur—web sites, home pages, bulletin boards, chat rooms, and e-mail lists that convey or share information and ideas within the contexts of a university class or course—as well as to the traditional physical classroom in which much teaching will continue to take place.[5]

From early indications, instructors in distance education and, presumably, online courses in particular, are somewhat different from their classroom-bound colleagues. Moreover, the differences give ammunition to critics who worry that e-learning may serve as a vehicle to diminish the professoriate. Instructors of online courses, as compared with those who do not teach such courses, are more likely to work at two-year colleges, lack doctorates, carry heavier course loads, spend more time on student contact out of class, keep slightly more office hours, not have a tenure track appointment, and work part time or without faculty standing.[6] Perhaps, though, these findings simply reflect disproportionately heavier involvement in online education by community colleges, where the statistics would pertain, as well, to those who teach in classrooms. This profile may well change in time as more faculty at four-year institutions dip into cyber waters.

Learning to Be a Different Sort of Teacher

The University of Colorado at Denver's Diana Wheat thinks she is the kind of teacher destined to find success and satisfaction in the virtual university, and she feels good about her achievements. Her highest degree is a master's in biology, and her academic rank is instructor in a world where a doctorate is a prerequisite for climbing the ladder to full professor. She was certified to teach high school biology, which she did for two years, and—still in her 30s—expects that she might never bother to pursue a doctorate, a step that seems unnecessary in order for her to thrive as an online instructor. She was already teaching an online section of an introductory biology course, demonstrating an ability to deal with instructional technology and to handle large groups of online students. Could this be the pattern of the future, a situation in which doctorates are rendered irrelevant for a portion of the academic teaching force? Online programs now refer to those who lead courses as facilitators and by other titles that do not resonate with the authority of professor. How different is this, though, from the situation in classrooms at colleges and universities around the country, where more than one-third of the course hours are taught by graduate students and adjunct faculty?

Whatever titles they have, instructors in online courses need training to learn how to use the software and how to interact with students electronically. Some concern has arisen across the country about institutions that act as if anyone with experience working in a classroom can automatically teach online. "Not all faculty are suited for the online environment, and academic institutions are making some serious mistakes when deciding who should teach," said online education authorities Rena M. Palloff and Keith Pratt. "Faculty who may be resistant to making the transition to the online classroom are being told that they have no choice and are being sent on to develop courses with little preparation or training in how to do so."[7] These may not be ideal teachers for online courses.

Faculty need professional development to help them understand and use technology, whether they want to put entire courses online or add web-based components to classroom courses. This is a bigger challenge, especially in higher education, than may seem apparent. The academy, as mentioned earlier in this book, has not valued pedagogy. It was only in the 1990s that centers to assist faculty in their teaching became widely established. And even with such efforts, many professors resisted efforts to get them to think more deeply about instructional strategies. The extent of the challenge looms large. It just may be, though, that the many faculty members who could not admit to deficiencies in classroom pedagogy may more readily concede their lack of expertise in the mysteries of online instruction. The ability to teach students in classrooms was taken for granted and shortcomings were not easily confessed. But this new-fangled technology—well, it's not such a big thing to acknowledge that you need help with it—so does the guy or gal in the office down the corridor. So does almost everyone.

There is a push at many institutions and nationally to retain full faculty authority over online courses. At places like Penn State and Central Florida, regular faculty members usually handle the course development and teaching. The universities assembled into the Asynchronous Learning Network by the Alfred P. Sloan Foundation committed themselves to use regular faculty throughout all phases of e-learning. Chances are that many schools, colleges, and universities will follow suit, so long as they can mount adequate technical support for faculty as they take on this new role. One obstacle to faculty involving themselves more extensively in learning the ins and outs of online courses has been the slowness with which the academy has recognized such tasks as worthy of consideration in evaluation procedures leading to promotion and tenure. Until work in e-learning counts for more, untenured faculty in traditional settings will have to take care not to divert too much of their energy in this direction.

WHAT IS A LIBRARY?

The Internet has had greater impact so far on libraries than on courses. It is easier and more efficient to digitize library collections and information retrieval than to deal with the machinations of designing courses for the web and putting them online. It is conceivable that by the end of the decade a virtual library will figure in the learning experience of almost all students even if they do not enroll in online courses. Many students in the 1990s started to take advantage of the convenience of the Internet to visit libraries on their own campuses as well as libraries across the country and around the world. Academic libraries are reconfiguring their budgets to accommodate this shift. The hulking piles filled with books that have been standard features of the campus landscape may no longer require the space that they have occupied in past years. Major research universities will be loath for the time being to take the chance of relying only on electronic documents, but some four-year colleges, two-year colleges, and high schools will sacrifice this reluctance for the sake of economies. Increasingly, undergraduates, continuing education students, and even some master's-level and professional school students will find that the virtual library suffices in their searches for information.

Kentucky Virtual Library predated Kentucky Virtual University, but it was incorporated into the younger KVU to underscore its central role in education in the state. The virtual library's data base had links to the state's municipal libraries and libraries in elementary and secondary schools, as well as to the state's college and university libraries. Kentucky Virtual Library, with its motto "Equal Access to Information," trained librarians around the state to use its data base and expected them, in turn, to train library users of all ages. Users searched KVU's 35 licensed data bases 600,000 times a month. The head of the virtual university regarded the virtual library as the linchpin of his institution.

Resources for Information Searches

Physical collections of journals and some other materials will be less essential at all but the major research universities when print has been digitized and students can pull up what they need with a flick of their fingers across a keyboard. There will also be less demand on space in libraries when students make fewer trips to retrieve books, to study, and to socialize. These changes will free up money that might have been spent on structures and certain collections for other purposes. Even staffing patterns could change when libraries have fewer journals and other reference sources to catalogue and retrieve. In an era when books as physical commodities stop circulating as much, libraries will save money that they might otherwise have spent to re-shelve materials and to replace lost and stolen books.

Information technology requires an infrastructure of its own, though, and the cost of electronic resources that make the virtual library possible may absorb much of the money that libraries may save on other purposes. Even reference services are changing to accommodate the shift.

Students and faculty can now communicate with some academic libraries by phone, e-mail, and even interactive software that allows for asynchronous online chats about a particular search. One decade's expenditures at the State University of New York at Buffalo illustrate the shifting priorities. In 1991–92, when SUNY Buffalo spent $4,104,424 on library materials, electronic resources accounted for $215,210 or 5.2 percent of the expenditures. By 2000–01, spending had reached $6,282,453, with $2,026,005 or 32.3 percent of it directed toward electronic resources.[8]

Librarians point out that they devote technology expenses such as those at Buffalo to more than merely accumulating a body of digitized materials. Libraries must update software regularly to allow users to manipulate and print out materials that were digitized at different times and, perhaps, use different software. They must spend resources to train students and faculty to make use of a treasure trove that would otherwise be inaccessible for lack of sufficient knowledge. Increasingly, libraries will have to maintain and even find ways to enhance reference services for distant users. The cost trend is clear—even if not a single user enters the library in person.

Georgia was among the leading states to use resources to best advantage by linking libraries and reducing duplication. The governor and the legislature authorized Georgia Library Learning Online, known as GALILEO, in 1994, with the support of distance learning as one of its main goals. Now, people throughout Georgia have access to all of the state's public libraries and libraries at schools, colleges, and universities. In 2002, efforts were underway, as part of GALILEO, to create a single catalogue for all the state's library collections, including the 6 million volumes in the university system. No one knew how many GALILEO users were online students, as they were included with others from the institutions they attended, but surely the achievements of GALILEO could help expand e-learning. Other consortiums similar to GALILEO exist throughout the country, operated by states and by regional groups of academic libraries, which together form the basis for what may someday become a national virtual library.

Access and availability are key elements in the virtual library. Online searches enable students to obtain information quickly and conveniently. This process involves much more than computerized card catalogues.

Anyone who has sought information through an Internet search has had the experience of entering a search term and getting inundated by thousands of hits. The Internet has created the largest depository of garbage masquerading as worthy facts that the world has ever known. No one vets the endless lists that a search term produces, and no scholarly juries determine what gets posted on the Internet. Everything and anything goes. Young, less-sophisticated students do not always realize that something does not necessarily have value just because it has been published electronically. For those who know the difference, inquiries through ordinary search engines produce staggering amounts of information that, like the town dump, mix the garbage with the pearls. Thus, libraries have to become arbiters and expediters.

What to do next? The contributions that the Online Computer Library Center and other library organizations have made toward pulling together vast amounts of materials from respected sources for searches looms as one of the most important functions of academic libraries. These libraries try to make searches more manageable by assembling the most pertinent information into new, more user-friendly data bases with search engines of their own. This is a function of the Online Computer Library Center, a membership organization that serves 41,000 libraries in 82 countries. It gathers sets of resources—full texts, indexes, and abstracts, for instance—under its own search engine. Someone looking for information enters a term and the search focuses more precisely than a search on Yahoo or even Google. The libraries at some major research universities perform much the same function for their users, using custom-made search engines to draw materials from many web sites and to reorganize the results in a manner that lends efficiency to academic searches.

Books in the Evolving Digital Library

The idea of electronic books has fascinated people since the beginning of the digital age. The prospect of gaining access to an entire book over the Internet seems to represent the fulfillment of a technology that some expected would render print and paper obsolete. There was even talk of major publishing houses releasing books strictly in electronic versions, saving the expense of printing and distribution. A marriage between e-learning and entire books conveyed over the Internet seemed natural in the technological order of things. And, in fact, several commercial companies arose during the 1990s to produce such books. Questia Media and netLibrary digitized tens of thousands of books and sought to sell access to them to academic libraries, which then, on a perstudent fee, would parcel out subscriptions to students. The idea was that students could avoid trips to the library, obtain access to books on a 24/7 basis, and the libraries could save money by buying and shelving fewer books. This approach lent itself particularly to those searching for references and citations in books. One can readily see how digitized books would fit into online learning for students scattered across a wide geographical area.

So far, this vision of a less expensive, more convenient future has played out in only the sketchiest terms. By 2002, netLibrary had failed and was absorbed by OCLC; Questia teetered and its survival was in question. Success proved elusive despite the fact that the two companies created huge data bases that users could bring up on the monitor screens of computers. In the final analysis, neither company was able to sell sufficient numbers of subscriptions to its services. Moreover, they could not shake free of the suspicion that they were plagiarism mills—cut, paste, and, presto, one has a term paper, footnotes and all. As pointed out earlier, this kind of cheating takes place without technology, which merely simplifies the process. For their part, libraries tend to see the digitizing of entire books, at least for now, as a frill of limited benefit. Few libraries would reduce their purchases and rely on electronic books, or even electronic journals, for fear that the companies offering the digitized versions could go out of business. There is not yet a basis to trust that, like a real volume on a real shelf, the digitized book will be available tomorrow if the company providing the service disappears.

Many publishers now produce digitized versions of books that they hold in abeyance as they publish and print the books on paper. Publishers want to be ready for the day when they reach agreements for the electronic distribution of these books. Universities, too, see the value of such endeavors. In 2002, the universities of the Big Ten conference and the University of Chicago set out to explore the possibility of producing electronic versions of books as they are published in print by their university presses. Then, the digital books would be shared online among the institutions. Many academic journals publish both paper and electronic versions, and a number of new journals publish only electronic versions. The Johns Hopkins University, receiving financial support from the National Endowment for the Humanities and the Mellon Foundation, launched Project Muse to make the 42 journals of the Johns Hopkins Press available electronically. In so doing, the university was able to create a data base that aided searches by cutting across the entire group of journals. James G. Neal, the Eisenhower Library director at Johns Hopkins who in 2001 became university librarian and vice president for information services at Columbia University, identified several barriers that he thought libraries will face in this decade as they remake themselves to serve virtual needs:

- technology—the need for bandwidth and computing capacity to keep pace with the changes;
- intellectual property—the need for revisions in the law to accommodate the advances that technology makes possible;
- learning styles—the need for more pedagogical information about the strengths and weaknesses of students when they pursue information and knowledge in a virtual environment.

There is, as mentioned, a debate over whether the ascension of the virtual library will mean a decline of the physical library. It is not so much a question of whether libraries and what they offer to researchers will remain essential—almost everyone agrees that role will continue—but whether the library will retain its vitality as a space for scholars to assemble. In part, the controversy revolves around whether students in the future will spend as much time in the library building (as opposed to the library web site) as their peers of former years. It is entirely possible that the nostalgia of older college graduates who recollect the late-nighters in the stacks will be shared by fewer and fewer students in the future. Certainly those whose course taking is predominantly via the web will be disinclined to go to the library. Not that publications on paper will vanish, but access via computer is just too convenient not to happen. For the scholar seeking a reference, wanting to cite a passage, hoping to find scaffolding for an argument, the ability to apply a computer search to a digitized book or journal offers too great an opportunity not to be exploited.

One hesitates, though, to predict that the physical structures that house libraries will disappear from campuses, if only because libraries will not readily dispose of the millions of books stored away in each of them. For some students, the advent of the virtual library has already meant fewer trips to the real library. Marshall Cook, in his final year at T.C. Williams High School in Fairfax County, Virginia, spoke of how he never went to the library anymore: "Now, in my senior year, I am taking far harder courses, such as Advanced Placement government, and writing long research papers. Even so, my library card lies unused in my wallet. All the reference materials I need lie at my fingertips on the Internet . . . Why waste time driving to the library when I can do it all at home while enjoying a slice of pizza and a Coke?"[9]

Even students who go in person to libraries in schools and on campuses may spend more time retrieving information on the library's computers than hunkering down in the stacks or thumbing through books and journals. Anthony Grafton, a historian at Princeton University, thought there had been a change and, with it, a lessening of sociability and some loss of civil conversation. He mused: "[W]hen I arrived at Princeton, the cramped metal carrels that line the library's stacks formed the cells in a vast, industrious hive. In September and October, carrel lights went on as seniors burrowed into the library to research and write their theses and graduate students prepared for general examinations. Only in June did the bulbs finally go out. Nowadays, the once-bright windows of these steel boxes, behind each of which two or more students pounded away on their portable typewriters, generally remain dark. Students do their writing—and, increasingly, their research—on computers."[10]

CHAPTER 14

ONLINE COURSES ACROSS THE GAMUT

Much of the talk about e-learning deals with online courses and campus courses, as if the distinction will forever prevail. The dichotomy will be far less clear by the end of the decade, when most courses will have online components and faculty who fail to use the Internet in their teaching will be as derelict as today's professor who omits a syllabus. Already, across the country, a multitude of hybrid courses has emerged, incorporating various features of the standard classroom and the web. All indications are that what some observers call a distributed or hybrid model will proliferate during this decade and more and more courses will combine various methods to deliver content. Students will work in the same course in person, online, and perhaps using CD-ROMs and videotape, as well.

This idea of combining approaches means that, despite the continual appearance of new instructional technologies, good teachers will not limit themselves to the latest iteration. Transportation technology provides an analogue. For most of human existence, people traveled on foot, the only locomotion available. Then, for a very long time, they rode or were pulled by animals. The low-tech bicycle and the high-tech train grew widespread in the nineteenth century, depending on whether a traveler had a short or a long journey. The automobile followed these innovations at the dawn of the twentieth century. Finally, farther into the twentieth century, passenger planes took to the skies. These innovations appeared in succession, yet none of them made previous modes of getting around obsolete. People today use them all, sometimes even on a single trip. So it will be with the delivery of instruction. Good teachers will draw on the method that seems most suited to the learning task.

The current situation and the future are best seen along a continuum. At one end is the classroom course in which a student does nothing online. At the other end is the purely online course that involves no work in a classroom. Strung along the continuum are courses that to a greater or lesser extent are mixtures of online work and classroom work. The place at the far end of the continuum occupied by the course given wholly online is new, the successor to the course offered by correspondence or television. A student today can enroll in enough such courses to complete a degree without ever setting foot on campus. This radical option serves the needs of some, but can hardly be expected to predominate. More likely, many students will eventually take a few such courses for the sake of convenience and to overcome scheduling difficulties.

Meanwhile, most of the rest of their courses will meet in classrooms. These courses will become more and more dependent on the infusion of technology for such activities as turning in papers, visiting web sites that elaborate on topics, exchanging e-messages with each other and with instructors, going to chat rooms related to the courses, and participating in threaded discussions that expand interaction beyond the fleeting contact of the typical classroom. Educational institutions and individual instructors throughout the United States are trying to determine how best to proceed into this uncharted territory. E-learning will serve students at every level, and students will be involved in online learning whether or not they enroll in courses taught entirely from a distance. With the web figuring in most courses, differences among courses are apt to revolve around the extent to which the course is situated online. This means that online learning, given the ubiquity it will attain, will transform the ways of teaching and learning. Technology will allow for more modeling, visualizing, simulating, interacting, collaborating, and analyzing than has usually been the case until now.

The Futures Project at Brown University, a major effort to gauge the Internet's effect on colleges and universities, filled one of its reports with examples from around the country of campus-based programs in a multitude of disciplines that took advantage of technology to embellish courses. The list included a biology laboratory, a course on *King Lear*, a math course, and a gravity simulation in a physics course. The report described the potential of technology as "a tool to enhance teaching and learning . . . that allows the process of learning to take place in more effective and compelling ways; in ways that, increasingly, will not be possible to accomplish without the use of technology."[1]

When Chris Dede, a professor of learning technologies at Harvard's Graduate School of Education, testified to a congressional committee, he tried to illustrate the potential of using technology to enrich courses by describing World View, a learning tool that was part of the Science-Ware curriculum developed by the University of Michigan's Center for Highly Interactive Computing in Education. To make his point, Dede presented members of Congress with a computer model of a creek somewhere in Michigan that let ninth-grade science students alter and account for the impact of weather, people, and other factors on the environment. Students could adjust the simulation by manipulating the variables. "By enabling sophisticated technologies that focus on guided learning-by-doing, collaborative learning and mentoring in virtual communities of practice, learning technologies empower teachers to inculcate deeper content and more complex skills in a wider range of students earlier in their intellectual development," Dede testified.[2]

This example is but one of a plethora of possibilities for a curriculum bristling with technology. It happened to be an example found at the secondary level, but the curriculums of elementary schools and institutions of higher education are no less affected. The implications are great not only for the curriculum, but also for the preparation of teachers and professors who must work with those curriculums and for the instructional policies of the schools and colleges that are hosts to such curriculums. The danger is that the technologies and the accompanying possibilities will outpace educational institutions and the people who work in them. If this happens, there will be a massive case of unfulfilled potential for assessment, accountability, and the management of time and place. Dede said: "Creating policy frameworks that foster the development of powerful learning technologies, the delineation of conditions for their successful implementation, and the preparation of teachers and schools for effective usage is crucial."[3]

The whole country will get a look at web-based courses at one university, Massachusetts Institute of Technology (MIT), as a result of that school's decision in 2001 to create web pages for almost all of its undergraduate and graduate courses and to post them online so that others can view them at no cost. MIT expected that its faculty, acting voluntarily through its OpenCourseWare (OCW) program, would put web pages for more than 500 courses online by the end of 2003. These web pages will be a resource freely available worldwide for noncommercial purposes. According to MIT, the pages will assist faculty at other colleges and universities in developing their own curriculums, serve as a model for faculty members across the country who want to create web-based resources for their classroom courses, and help individuals engage in self-directed study. The Andrew W. Mellon Foundation and the William and Flora Hewlett Foundation gave MIT a total of $11 million to launch OCW, and the university projected that it would spend between $7.5 and $10 million annually on the effort.

An MIT representative interviewed for this book said that the institution believed that copyright protection would guard against a for-profit entity's making unauthorized commercial use of the course materials. "By posting copyright notice and terms of use which address issues of permitted uses, attribution, and restrictions, along with a copyright infringement notification, we feel MIT will have established the legal precedent to take action if we discover unauthorized use of OCW materials," said Jon Paul Potts, communications manager for the courseware program.

These web pages, as valuable a resource as they may be, will not be the same as a good online course. They may include course outlines, reading lists, lecture notes, and assignments—all possible components of an online course. But the give-and-take of online discussions and chat rooms, the back-and-forth of e-messages, and the interactive design of the presentation provide the scaffolding of a true online course. Thus, what will probably emerge from OpenCourseWare will be vital content for courses, both in classrooms and online, but not full-blown online offerings. MIT said in a fact sheet about OCW that it did not regard the venture as a distance learning initiative.

Nationally, educational institutions now accord greater attention to computers and technology. Schools, colleges, and universities across the country are equipped for e-learning even if they deliver few entire courses online. They have spent hundreds of millions of dollars to acquire hardware and software and to wire classrooms, libraries, and student residences to accommodate computers. Almost every elementary and secondary school building in the country had computers with Internet access by the fall of 2000, and 77 percent of all public school classrooms had at least one computer with access to the Internet.[4] It is shortsighted to expect that this capacity will serve only to let students obtain online syllabi, send e-mails to each other, search occasionally for information on the web, and download music. More is in the offing and regular courses will make increasing use of this digital capacity. Some institutions require students to have computers and, even in the absence of such a mandate, many students arrive on campus bearing computers. In some instances, institutions give computers, and printers as well, to students. Students should be able to make good use of all this equipment.

A building that once housed a department store in Blacksburg, Virginia, provided another glimpse of the future. In a space where bolts of cloth were once sold by the yard, the only product now available was mathematics. Virginia Polytechnic Institute had reincarnated the store as its Math Emporium. Virginia Tech's math department used the facility to give new exposure to the college's courses and to the outcomes-based approach that technology enhances. The math department created 500 work stations around pods throughout the vast Math Emporium, just a few blocks from the main campus. Students in at least a dozen math courses pursued part or all of their course work at the site. Most studies were self-paced in what amounted to a personalized computer lab. Students used online materials to coach themselves and tutors walked the floor, like clerks in the former department store, to lend additional help when needed.

Two courses were taught entirely online, with the Math Emporium serving as the closest thing that students in those courses had to a classroom. One was Math 1015, a college-level algebra course in which life science majors—i.e., aspiring medical school applicants and those on related tracks—studied functions, experimentals, and logarithims. The other was Math 1114, in which engineering majors delved into Euclidean vectors, complex numbers, and topics in linear algebra. Typically, students in 10 other math courses still went to classrooms two days a week and spent the third day in the Math Emporium instead of in a classroom. Each time they came, the session started with an in-person lecture of 15 to 30 minutes on the material of the day. Then, they could either peel off and continue the work on computers at the Math Emporium or leave and work on a computer at home, a coffeehouse, or wherever they most liked to solve math problems. A course like Math 1114 cost Virginia Tech $300,000 to develop, so this was an expensive commitment to online learning.

RESPONSES TO WEB-BASED LEARNING

Fairleigh Dickinson University (FDU) in New Jersey was among the first campus-based educational institutions in the country to require students to take an online course when it mandated that all of its freshmen during the 2001–02 academic year enroll in a course entitled The Global Challenge. Twenty sections of the course were offered in the fall term and 20 sections in the spring term. Students examined such issues as the environment, health, armed conflict, and population from a world perspective. Starting with that class of freshmen, Fairleigh Dickinson planned to require all of its students to take at least one online course each academic year. The university expected to spend $12 million over five years to develop the courses and install the information technology infrastructure needed to support the online program. FDU signed up about two dozen scholars and others around the world to teach the courses. This group that the university called its global virtual faculty included such people as Nilufer Bharucha, a professor of English literature at the University of Mumbai in India; Cheng Ming Yu, head of the economics unit in the faculty of management at the Multimedia University in Malaysia; and Tomas Chuaqui, a political science professor at the Instituto de Ciencia Politica of the Pontificia Universidad Catolica de Chile. Other members of this global faculty were drawn from such countries as Hungary, Israel, Jamaica, Japan, and Korea.

Michael Sperling, associate provost at Fairleigh Dickinson, said the requirement had a twofold purpose: to provide students with courses that have a world view and to make the Internet a fundamental tool for learning. Some of the 100 online courses that FDU hoped eventually to offer through its global virtual faculty would be general requirements, and probably most of the rest would be specific to individual academic disciplines. In embarking on this global program through online education, FDU said that it wanted "to bring the world to the campus." It maintained that it was using e-learning as the latest step in what had long been an international orientation at Fairleigh Dickinson, which had programs in England and Israel and relationships with institutions in Spain and Turkey.

To Go or Not to Go . . . Online

Some colleges and universities have been slow to embrace online learning out of concern that it will alter the character of the institution. The continued reliance of Ohio University on correspondence and interactive video reflected the fact that the institution evinced no great effort to gear up to offer a full program of online courses. Ohio's Board of Regents in 1975 designated the university as the institution in the state primarily responsible for distance education, and in those days distance education meant correspondence courses. Nothing happened to alter that designation, and in 2002 the university had 4,000 correspondence course enrollments, leading to three separate associate's degrees and one bachelor's degree. Interactive video, begun in 1983, was the university's other large component of distance education.

Thus, Ohio University, situated in picturesque hills in the remote southeastern corner of Ohio, had only a small presence in the provision of courses totally online. "I believe this a conscious decision by the university," Thomas A. Shostak, dean of lifelong learning, said of the minimal incursion into online learning. "The university has a long tradition as a residential university with a beautiful campus. I think this is what it would like to maintain and that it is not interested in increasing its undergraduate presence in distance education." Shostak thought, however, that the state's Board of Regents had been lax in not revisiting what its designation of Ohio University as the state's primary institution for distance education meant in the twenty-first century, when it could be offering more online learning.

Wellesley College estimated in 2000 that 65 percent of its courses were enhanced by electronic information. About 165 of the college's courses had web sites and more than 250 courses maintained a presence on the institution's centralized system to provide support for e-mail, bulletin boards, and conferencing. Thirty-nine of 42 academic departments offered at least one conference via the Internet during the academic year, with an average of six such conferences per department. Some departments—art history, biology, chemistry, geology, and astronomy—made particularly extensive use of digital images stored on file servers. The Knapp Media and Technology Center in the Wellesley library and the Knapp Social Science Center in the renovated Pendleton classroom building had facilities for audio and video digitizing, editing, scanning, and videoconferencing. Wellesley had a video network, television studio, radio station with streaming audio, and other state-of-the-art multimedia facilities.

Here is a residential liberal arts college in which instructional technology has embedded itself in the mainstream, surely a harbinger for most institutions of higher education. While Wellesley did not offer online courses, it was investigating what, if anything, it ought to do in this regard. The college experimented with the possibility of going online, accepting funds from the Global Education Network to produce some trial courses and using the money to pay faculty for their time. Simultaneously, an advisory committee appointed by the college's president weighed the e-learning issues facing Wellesley. The committee tried to figure out how the college could balance itself on the technological edge without jeopardizing its financial vitality and examined the ramifications of simply holding to the path it was on. This response, not unlike that embraced by hundreds of colleges and universities, eventually will almost certainly lead to the incorporation of online features into almost all academic courses, even if those courses remain accessible only to on-campus students.

United States Open University, which perished by the middle of 2002 for lack of students, dipped cautiously into these very same waters, adhering to a distance learning model that included use of the Internet while relying on a delivery system as old as the Pony Express—the U.S. Post Office. Insiders at the Open University debated among themselves whether theirs was an online institution. "Students find out about us at our web site, reach us online, find the courses at the web site, and reach the faculty through e-mail," said Richard Jarvis, chancellor of the university, which was spun off from the 30-year-old British Open University. "They also can go to study guides, assignments, and discussions online, but we don't dump all of our material online." The university sent its books, videocassettes, and bulkier materials to students through the mail, and did not put them online for students to download. Students could pursue fewer than 10 percent of the courses entirely online and those tended to be information technology courses.

U.S. Open University began operating in the fall of 2000. By the summer of 2001, it had 500 course registrations involving some 300 individuals, and the institution was hoping to double its enrollment every semester, a goal that it found unattainable, though the test period may have been unreasonably short. Courses were offered at the graduate level and to upper-division undergraduates, juniors and seniors. The university took its nonprofit status seriously and did not seem interested in launching a for-profit arm, which was apparently anathema to its trustees. Jarvis said in an interview for this book that he had raised the question with his board of converting the institution into a for-profit entity so that it could seek money from investors. "We have well-funded competitors and I can't spend the money that they can," he said. "I asked the board whether I should get investors, but they were uncomfortable with the idea."

Less than a year after that interview, the university closed. University officials hoped that juniors and seniors would take all of their courses with the U.S. Open University. Officials conceded, though, that many students were probably "schedule shopping," taking a few courses with the institution, as well as courses with other universities, both on- and offline. Even though it no longer exists, the experience of U.S. Open University illustrates the pitfalls of online learning even for—and, perhaps, especially for—institutions that seek to offer high-quality liberal arts courses.

Is it an online course if the part sent through the mail is integral to the program? Courses at the U.S. Open University, like those at traditional British universities, required heavy reading loads. The institution found it simply more convenient to mail high-quality printed books to students than to expect them to print out an estimated 60 to 80 pages a night from the web. This would have been a cumbersome and tedious process that Jarvis doubted students would want to do. "I don't know if others will go our way," he said of the approach. "What we do is expensive and it's cheaper to just put lecture-based text on line." But that is not what U.S. Open University did. As a matter of fact, Sir John Daniel, former vice chancellor of Britain's Open University, said that the value of putting all courses in their entirety online was overrated and not the best way to carry out higher education. He conceded that students wanted to use the Internet to facilitate their education, but opined that it was to obtain services, access the library, and for computer conferencing. "Students aren't nearly as interested in using online technology to study course material," he said.[5] As it turned out, they weren't sufficiently interested in U.S. Open University in the form that it took either.

Hybrid Courses

The same commercial companies that sell colleges and universities the electronic platforms to incorporate features into courses that are entirely online also cater to the needs of courses with only a few aspects of e-learning. The heads of three of these companies, while fervently competitive with each other, agreed on at least one matter: 80 percent of the courses using these electronic platforms met in classrooms at least part of the time and employed technology to enlarge upon campus-based education. They said that only 20 percent of the courses using the platforms as of the end of 2001 were entirely online.

Matthew Pittinsky, chairman and cofounder of Blackboard, one of the companies, looking 10 and even 25 years into the future, sees online learning having its main effect in traditional, on-campus programs, not through courses offered exclusively on the Internet. "I don't believe there will be a dramatic restructuring of higher education or that lots of traditional institutions will go out of business," he said. "The biggest impact of the Internet will be on traditional programs." When students at Teachers College, Columbia University, were asked in a survey in 2001 about their "preferred mode of instructional delivery," 65 percent wanted campus-based courses, 6.4 percent wanted web-based courses, and 28.6 percent wanted a combination of the two.[6] Robert Tolsma, who oversaw online learning at the University of Colorado at Denver, said that on-campus courses increasingly used technology and employed web-based instruction as a supplement. Research for this book has shown that to be a national trend. It will become more and more difficult to distinguish between an online course and a campus-based course as fewer and fewer instructors teach courses entirely in a classroom with no regard for ways that the Internet can augment the courses. The blended course that combines the characteristics of online and campus-based learning will likely come to dominate instruction in higher education.

Diana Wheat taught just such a hybrid course at the University of Colorado at Denver: Basic Biology I for nonmajors, a course with large enrollments because it was required. The institution decided to experiment during the 2001–02 academic year, offering one section in the traditional manner—two 75-minute lectures a week and one two hour lab—and another section with the lectures and accompanying materials online and only the lab portion in person. Wheat taught both sections, each with an enrollment of more than 100 students. There was a web page for the students in each section, giving classroom-based students access to supplementary and enrichment materials. The university provided Wheat and her colleagues who taught such hybrid courses in other departments with six two-hour sessions to prepare them for the task. Instructors were taught how to incorporate graphics into their web materials, how to give quizzes online, how to run online discussion groups and, generally how to make their online presentations more interesting.

SPECIAL CONSIDERATIONS IN K THROUGH 12 EDUCATION

For the most part, online courses at the elementary and secondary levels have been more slapdash than in higher education. Less care and originality seem to go into the courses, and elementary and secondary providers apparently spend less money to develop and design online courses. On the other hand, the programs remain in their infancy and providers may have sacrificed quality to get online quickly. A look at course development for precollegiate education in several states gives a sense of the strengths and weaknesses of e-learning at this level.

The virtual high school serving the State of Missouri with online courses started in the late 1990s, building on a distance education program that was almost a century old. Distance education began in the state as an outreach effort by the University of Missouri, a land-grant institution charged with providing extension services to citizens. High school courses were seen as part of this extension philosophy, alongside agricultural programs that the university provided to the state's farmers. Thus, correspondence courses were for decades the essence of the accredited high school-level outreach by the University of Missouri's Center for Distance and Independent Study. Then, in recognition of the arrival of the computer age, in 1997 the program first offered online courses along with its correspondence courses, for those studying at the high school level. There were only 14 enrollments for online courses that initial year but enrollments by 2002 grew to 2,399. Very quickly, more students submitted lessons online than by correspondence, an option available to the enrollees in correspondence courses as well as those in the online program.

In Ohio, a charter school law was used to create cyber education. The Electronic Classroom of Tomorrow, known as eCOT, started under the auspices of the Lucas County Education Center, one of Ohio's countywide education service centers. The school was open to students throughout the state and said it had 3,000 course enrollments by 2002. The founders of the school, having watched the progress of virtual learning at the higher education level, reasoned that it was time to give the same approach a chance at the elementary and secondary levels. The majority of eCOT students were at the elementary level, very likely including substantial numbers of home schoolers. The state provided the school with $5,000 to pay for each youngster's education and the school was able to give every student a computer, a scanner, and a printer.

Florida Virtual School was established to serve public and nonpublic school students throughout the state with online learning. It began in 1996 as a collaboration between two rural counties with 77 course enrollments. It was officially converted into a high school for the whole state the next year and its course enrollment immediately jumped to 2,796. The course enrollment more than doubled to 5,900 for the 2000–01 school year and rose to more than 8,000 in 2001–02, reaching just about its capacity under the $6.5 million allotment that the school received from the state. There were more than 4,500 individual students taking one or more courses each. The school expected to offer 66 courses, almost all of its own creation, in 2002–03. The 70 teachers, all certified by the State of Florida, were a mix of full-timers and part-timers, whom the school referred to as adjuncts. Many held jobs in regular schools and worked on the side for the virtual school, a practice made possible by not having to meet with students in a classroom at a set time.

In spite of the advances by cyber schools in Florida and some other states, precollegiate education may respond less readily than higher education to the opportunities afforded by technology. The authors of one journal article pointed to two historical reasons for this slower pace. First, they cited the lag time that, they said, slows innovation in elementary and secondary schools. Second, they mentioned the structure and organization of schools, particularly high schools, with their sharply defined time schedules and departmental boundaries. More than that, these authors were dubious of technology itself, writing of defects and glitches that impede instruction. They found in the high schools studied that access to equipment and software seldom led to widespread teacher and student use of computers.[7]

Course-Taking Patterns

The courses that students took by correspondence and online from the University of Missouri High School generally supplemented those that they took in person at regular high schools. Students enrolled in a distance education course, for example, when their own high schools were too small to offer the courses, or when their schedules simply did not accommodate the courses, or when they wanted to add courses to their transcripts to graduate early. It was not even possible at first to use distance education to accumulate all of the courses needed for a diploma. That was scheduled to happen in 2002. The future of the University of Missouri High School as an online enterprise was uncertain. The online courses, alongside the correspondence courses, would continue to provide a supplemental option to students in regular high schools, as well as a place for adults who never completed high school to finish their work on diplomas. It remained to be seen, though, whether educators at brick-and-mortar schools would be as favorably disposed toward the virtual high school once it reached the potential to fully compete in the diploma-granting business.

Other factors, too, jeopardized the growth of online high school education in Missouri. Students had to pay out of pocket to take online courses, a requirement seemingly favored by school districts as a way to dissuade students from enrolling in the program. The school, not financially subsidized by tax monies, was supposed to support itself. Early on, before online learning was deemed a threat, home high schools were more willing to pay for students' online courses. After it demonstrated some appeal, however, the virtual high school was viewed as a competitor with regular high schools, an enterprise that might drain off enrollments and dollars. Previously, brick-and-mortar high schools cooperated with the University of Missouri High School by letting staff and faculty members help students with their work in online courses. It was one thing to lend such aid to a student who took a calculus course because his or her own high school did not offer it, but it became a different matter once students wanted to enroll in online courses that were the same as those given by their home high schools.

Many of Florida Virtual School's students were enrolled in regular schools and took only a course or two online, usually selecting courses because their home schools didn't offer them or because of schedule conflicts. At least half of the students took their courses on computers right in their home schools. The virtual school operated strictly at the high school level, enrolling middle school students only if they wanted to take high school courses to accelerate their education. In this way a middle school student could simultaneously earn middle school and high school credits. By 2002, the school considered adding middle school courses to its curriculum.

Home schoolers were an estimated 35 percent of the individuals taking courses in the Florida school, according to officials. Students could take all the courses they needed for diplomas through the virtual school's online offerings, but the school did not put its name on the diplomas, which had to be granted by brick-and-mortar high schools. This meant that a student who fulfilled the state diploma requirements by working online had to negotiate with a traditional high school to accept the credits and award the diploma. Furthermore, as Florida required candidates for diplomas to pass the statewide tests, online students had to arrange to take the examinations through brick-and-mortar schools. Predominant among the students who came close to taking all of their courses for a diploma through the Florida Virtual School were home schoolers, and they did not necessarily bother with diplomas: many of them simply sat for the SAT and hoped for the best. Partisans of traditional education tended to oppose the idea of enabling the virtual school to award diplomas, a step that would introduce new competition for students into Florida's education system.

The Federal Government's Virtual High School

One model of online learning that could guide programs at the elementary and secondary level—and did, in fact, in Kentucky, Michigan, Illinois, and some other states—was the federally sponsored Virtual High School (VHS), a five-year pilot project. The U.S. Department of Education started the school with a Technology Innovation Challenge Grant. By 2001, when the grant period ended, the Virtual High School had enrolled more than 2,000 students in 200 high schools in 26 states in 125 full-semester e-courses. Its students had to attend regular high schools, where they took almost all of their courses in person. Students' home high schools awarded academic credits for the online courses, and there was no provision for students to take all of their courses solely online. The federal government intended that the program enhance regular high schools, not replace them. Each school affiliated with the

Virtual High School was supposed to appoint a site coordinator whom VHS trained as the regular school's liaison for the program.

In most cases, students enrolled in VHS courses that were not available in their high schools' classroom-based programs, a feature that various evaluation reports lauded. VHS, in effect, allowed a high school to enrich and enlarge its curriculum offerings at a minimal cost. Schools could avoid having to hire additional teachers or build extra classrooms for new courses. (Apex Learning, a for-profit provider of online Advanced Placement courses, took a similar approach, advertising that it was creating classrooms, not replacing them.) During the 2000–01 academic year, the Virtual High School offered courses ranging from Advanced Placement in chemistry and statistics to microbiology, music composition, and southern writers. Drawing upon the enrollment of the entire VHS collaborative, a high school no longer had to worry about a lack of the critical mass for a particular course.

Almost half of the schools in the VHS collaboration had fewer than 800 students. A rural K through 12 school in Alabama, so small that it was on the verge of closing, rescued itself by joining VHS. A student in Texas whose schedule was so filled with Advanced Placement courses that she couldn't fit in a course required for graduation took the course through VHS. A teacher at a small rural high school in Ohio, who wanted to give a course on the Vietnam War but simply did not have enough students to do so in his own school, offered the course through VHS. What emerges from the experience of the Virtual High School is the idea that the current campaign to create smaller brick-and-mortar high schools could benefit from high-quality online courses to supplement a classroom-based curriculum reduced in size for lack of critical mass. Enrollment in a VHS course was limited to 20 students.

The Virtual High School, which depended on teachers in the participating real high schools to design and teach the courses, also demonstrated how professional development fits into the expansion of online learning. A vital component of the program was the training that regular high school faculty around the country received to qualify them as teachers of virtual courses. Teachers had to successfully complete a graduate-level, online professional development course given by VHS; they could take a 26-week course to design and prepare their own network-based course or a 15-week course to learn to teach an existing course designed by someone else. Officials of the Virtual High School said that they continually revised and fine tuned this training, based on the experience of faculty who actually taught the online courses. The school exercised quality control to the extent that not all of the courses that teachers designed through the program were deemed good enough to offer to students.

After the U.S. Department of Education's pilot project ended in 2001, the Virtual High School incorporated as a not-for-profit corporation so that it could continue to offer courses. No longer supported by federal funds that allowed it to operate at no cost to participating high schools, VHS set out to achieve self-sufficiency by charging the schools an annual membership fee of $6,000. The money was spent on administration, management, technology, and course monitoring. VHS styled itself as a cooperative, with its courses taught by teachers from member schools. By the fall of 2002, 150 schools were members of the VHS cooperative, which enrolled some 2,000 students in about 120 course sections.

ONLINE COURSES AND THE FUTURE

The National Association of State Boards of Education (NASBE) issued a report on e-learning near the end of 2001 that praised the process but, at the same time, urged caution upon schools as they venture forth into the cyber age. On the one hand, NASBE lauded e-learning as an innovation that should be implemented as soon as possible and called on schools to award credit for online courses. Yet, the organization also warned that special interests were lobbying state legislatures to move immediately ahead with hastily conceived e-learning initiatives. The best course of action, NASBE recommended, would be for state policymakers to seize the opportunity and take the lead to assure that e-learning spreads in ways that strengthen the public education system.[8] This report offered a window on the struggle now under way to determine who will control online learning and who will benefit from it.

Some observers mistakenly assume that the success of online courses revolves around the extent to which they are designed, taught, and resemble classroom courses. Why should it be so? The medium dictates new approaches even if the goal of substantial learning remains the same. Online courses introduce the possibility of new roles for faculty. The possible separation of content, design, and facilitation opens the door to differentiated staffing of online courses. Controversy envelops this aspect of online courses. At first blush, in the eyes of many within the academy, something is amiss if those in charge of courses do not resemble the teaching force in today's classrooms. Why do they assume that the future must be a rerun of the past? E-learning deserves a full chance and the ultimate measure of its impact should revolve around the quality of the learning, not who presides over that learning.

That is, indeed, the rub. It remains to be seen whether online learning will protect and promote quality and integrity in its courses. There is vast opportunity for the dishonest and the greedy to exploit this field. Cynics assume the worst, that online providers are positioned to become tomorrow's Enrons. The new and the different often face such derision. The best policy will be to let this experiment go forward, to see what it can contribute to learning. All the while, state regulators, accrediting organizations, Congress, education associations, and consumer groups should remain vigilant. They should judge e-learning by the outcomes, seeing whether the courses deliver what they promise—not condemning the courses because they are designed and taught in ways that challenge the status quo.

CHAPTER 15

EDUCATIONAL PURPOSES IN THE CYBER ERA

E mbedded in the issues raised by competition from online courses are questions about the benefits of face-to-face education and the meaning of the campus experience. Of what value is it for students to interact with each other in person, to participate in activities outside of classrooms, to attend concerts and events on campus, to take roles in campus governance? Schools and colleges pride themselves on the ways in which they say they shape the attitudes and character of students, supposedly equipping them for responsible citizenship, for life itself. What will happen then if students can get an education without having to go to the campus of a school or college? Will they end up as less than fully developed persons?

It is not as if those who participate in a classroom of one are necessarily hermits (though those of hermit persuasion may find this proposition attractive). Social interaction occurs in many settings besides those provided by schools and colleges. Younger students mingle with siblings, parents, and other adults, not to mention their contact with neighborhood playmates on playgrounds and at sites of after-school lessons and activities. Older and adult students spend time among spouses, children, and other relatives, as well as with friends and fellow workers. Added contact comes with those they encounter at the supermarket, at the gas station, at the post office, and in the coffee shop. Furthermore, the highly vaunted residential campus experience fully benefits only a small segment of students. Another segment of today's students are older: Many are parents and/or full-time members of the labor force, and they attend their institutions on a part-time basis. The impact of college on their character and social development is problematic, and one wonders if studying online instead of on campus makes much difference to some of them. The issues in K through12 education are somewhat different and will be discussed later in this chapter.

HISTORICALLY ASSUMED PURPOSES

A generation ago, doom-sayers predicted the demise of hundreds of colleges; it did not happen. It seems harder to kill a college, especially a state-supported one, than to move a cemetery. It would be foolhardy at this juncture to prognosticate once again on the future of small colleges, which have shown a great deal of resilience these last 25 years. In fact, occasionally new ones are founded. Soka University of America opened to students for the first time in 2001 on a magnificent $220-million campus in Aliso Viejo, California, with the appearance of a hilltop Tuscan village. One could safely predict, though, that the founding of new campus-based educational institutions will be infrequent as competition intensifies.

In part, the whole idea that educational institutions should shape the character of their students stems from the religious origins of most older colleges. It naturally followed that their founders had the same sort of concern for affecting the moral development of students in their colleges as they did for parishioners in their churches. Furthermore, in the earliest days of higher education, when the tone was set for the colleges of the future, students were closer in age to today's high school teenagers and institutions had that much more reason to care about shaping their character. Religious denominations have loosened or altogether dropped their ties to colleges and universities. *In loco parentis* has gone the way of sock hops and freshman beanies. The case for education having a responsibility for the spiritual and civic development of students, however compelling it may remain in the abstract, is far more difficult to make in the twenty-first century. If the campus experience no longer figures as prominently in character development—especially when nonresident students make up so much of the enrollment—online learning is hardly a main culprit in this undoing.

Thus, access to online learning raises fundamental questions about what schools and institutions of higher education should offer students beyond the courses themselves. When students come to campus for courses, especially as residents of college housing, the institution usually provides for their dining, health, counseling, social, and recreational needs. The college or university helps facilitate student publications, student government, and an array of varsity sports, as well as providing the arenas and stadiums to house those teams. The institution hires coaches, campus bus drivers, and security and maintenance personnel. It builds libraries, dormitories, performing arts centers, and student unions. Commuter institutions may truncate some of these services and facilities, but they usually provide acres of parking spaces.

Campus-based higher education, more than previously, will have to demonstrate that it truly offers a unique experience to students. Online learning poses some peril to the hegemony of campus-based education if some of the reasons for attending classes in person have less currency. The most marginal of small colleges could be pushed to the precipice if online enrollment surges. The Committee on the Changing Landscape of Higher Education at Boston University declared in a report that it "foresaw changes in instruction that would ultimately call the viability of residential colleges and universities into question . . . One outcome of the new technology is that an important new source of competition to residential college and university education is arising. So far, students attracted to distance-education programs have tended to come predominantly from age groups and segments of the public who form a very small segment of the residential college population. We expect that will change as distance education matures."[1]

In the future, educational institutions will have to provide more cogent arguments to persuade students to spend tuition dollars and pay for campus housing than the chance to watch football games and participate in weekend parties. For a long time, colleges and universities have gotten away with declaring that they play a special role in the development of young people, but not following through fully on that promise. The afore-mentioned committee on Boston University's future, after considering the threat of online learning, reaffirmed the institution's commitment to deliver a high quality residential experience for its students. The university was urged to "maintain and clearly enunciate its educational goals" as a way to assure its future.[2] As Frank Newman, director of the Futures Project at Brown University, observed: "This forces us to address our values."

What makes the campus experience distinctive? What, for example, makes a Harvard degree a Harvard degree? Is it just a name on paper that accounts for the prestige that the degree carries? Or, is it something that happens term after term on Harvard's ivied campus that contributes to the standing of the degree-holder? Such questions were at the heart of the deliberations of a faculty committee that in 2002 examined Harvard's residency requirement with an eye toward possibly allowing students to earn Harvard degrees online. An inquiry of this sort raises crucial questions about the goals of higher education. It forces a reappraisal of the extent to which the purposes of an institution are linked to regular attendance at classes on a college campus. In Harvard's case, students traditionally have had to spend at least one year in residence at the university in full-time study at the full tuition rate to earn a degree.

Harvard's president, Lawrence H. Summers, asked the ad hoc faculty committee to review the origin and history of the university's residency requirement and to consider the benefits and attributes of residence. Summers charged the committee with figuring out the reasons for the requirement. The committee was to accompany any suggestion for a policy change with suggestions for quality assurance. Could it be that the continuation of residency requirements, which obviously work to the disadvantage of online courses, has as much to do with a university's distrust of education that occurs out of sight as with the professed belief that the campus experience transforms students? Harvard, with more than 350 years of tradition, has been slow to embrace e-learning, offering no degrees entirely online. As of the summer of 2002, the university made available just 32 online courses for credit, mostly through its Extension School. Fully half the courses were in computer science.

Relaxing Harvard's minimum, one-year residency requirement would involve more than online learning. President Summers in forming the committee had in mind, perhaps to a greater extent, on-campus degree courses that follow nontraditional calendars. The university said that some of its schools had been discussing flexible midcareer programs, time-compressed programs, and interinstitutional programs, as well as online programs and hybrids, that would call for less than a year of residence. In this connection, Harvard's School of Public Health launched a master of science degree program designed specifically for physicians who want to qualify for leadership positions with health care organizations. The two-year program consisted of three-week summer sessions on campus, five four-day weekends a year on campus, and monthly teleconferences. Given the professional working status of the participating students, the program did not adhere to the university's residency requirement. This nonresidential master's program, created apparently in violation of Harvard's policy, received a one-year exemption from the rule, pending the outcome of the ad hoc committee's deliberations.

The outlines of what might emerge at Harvard, given a green light—especially at the postbaccalaureate level—could be seen in the activities of some of its ten schools and colleges. The Business School with its noncredit management programs for working executives seemed poised to create online or hybrid versions; the Medical School, through its Harvard Medical International division, already had forged a collaboration with Ireland's Royal College of Surgeons to put examination study material for surgical residents online; the Law School, through its Berkman Center for Internet and Society, had begun computer-mediated seminars on such topics as intellectual property and domain name dispute resolution; and the Kennedy School of Government was cooperating with the Otter Group to offer a noncredit executive education program in an interactive online format. A change in policy could clear the way to award Harvard credits and, possibly, degrees for some similar efforts.

ADJUSTING PURPOSES TO NEW REALITIES

Some students, especially older ones in career-oriented programs, don't want the amenities. They say they enroll for the courses alone and desire little else from an educational institution. Art Institute Online said that it found that their students were not interested in activities that did not directly support meeting their specific learning goals, which revolved around obtaining a job or a promotion in their chosen art-related field. "They are not antisocial," said an official of the school. So the question, in the age of cyber learning, becomes what to do about a student who almost never sets foot on campus. Colleges and universities predicate many of the activities fees that they charge on the assumption that students will need and use certain on-campus services and facilities. Should institutions charge online students fees that help subsidize services for resident students? Should there be an altogether different fee structure for online courses? Should resident students who take a portion of their schedules online receive a prorated reduction of charges? Should all students, classroom-based or otherwise, have more choice in whether they pay fees and in the purposes to which those fees are directed?

These are questions that institutions will increasingly face in coming years, along with having to reevaluate the role they should play in a student's life beyond the courses themselves. The *Chronicle of Higher Education* found that the university system of Georgia was experimenting with differentiated charges, the University of Wisconsin system had created a category called segregated fees that online students were not charged, and the University of Oregon waived some campus fees for some online students.[3] Some online students may conclude that they don't need the rest of the package and refuse to enroll in colleges and universities that won't adjust charges for them. Moreover, students may not consider the absence of such amenities as a mark of not caring about them. They may want educational institutions to show caring in other ways.

Kathy O'Neill, formerly on the faculty of Georgia State University, recalled a young woman whom the institution accepted into a graduate program only to see her back out at the last minute and enroll in a graduate program at the University of Phoenix, which would let her pursue courses online. The student felt that Phoenix, a for-profit, accredited university, not only had a quality program but that the university was concerned about her as an individual despite its lack of a football team or a health center. She appreciated the fact that the University of Phoenix kept in touch with her as she weighed her enrollment decision.

She liked what she considered the customer-oriented attitude of the university, which lacked most of the campus amenities of Georgia State. "I think this is very interesting since the excuse that traditional programs give for not using online instruction is that it is impersonal," said O'Neill, who left George State for a position at the Southern Regional Education Board. "This student thought the traditional university made her feel like a number and the online experience did not."

Online providers of education, particularly those pursuing profits, may teach traditional colleges and universities a lesson in how to treat students as customers in the best sense of the word. This word did not offend Ann Kirschner of Columbia University's Fathom, a for-profit company. "When you take someone's credit card, they are a customer," said Kirschner, referring to those who visited her company's web site. The word "customer" came easily to Kirschner, a veteran of the worlds of both commerce and academe. "For educators to think of students as customers is seemingly painful, but there is nothing wrong with helping people realize the full value of what they pay for," she said. Moreover, Fathom made it easier for such venerable institutions as Columbia and the British Library not to bridle over calling students customers because the institutions were able to keep the for-profit aspect at arm's length and leave it to Fathom to handle the credit card transaction and deal with the "customer."

All of education could benefit from reorienting itself toward students as customers. Regarding students as customers need not and should not mean reducing all of higher education to a consumer transaction, which surely Fathom's parent, Columbia University, would find distasteful. Educational institutions, impelled by economic concerns, may start paying more attention to the way they treat students, whether enrolled in online courses or classroom-based courses.

This need not mean losing sight of larger purposes. There will always be a place in the greater constellation of higher education for the purposes that many Americans have come to value, even as e-learning adds to the diversity of the delivery system. Arthur E. Levine, the president of Teachers College, Columbia University, used his annual report on the college to comment on the purposes of the university in light of the new technologies, the information economy, and changing demographics.

Borrowing from Clark Kerr, the former president of the University of California, he described three central activities of the university—the preservation of eternal truths, the creation of new knowledge, and the improvement of service where truth and knowledge may serve the use of humanity.[4] While these tasks may seem somewhat remote from the ordinary needs of students and removed from the purview of some institutions, they do symbolize higher education at its ideal best. Online programs, especially those that are not university-based, tend to give short shrift to Kerr's three central activities, if they acknowledge them at all. Keeping such lofty ideals in sight may well be part of what will distinguish at least a portion of campus-based higher education in the era of virtual learning. Yet, education's larger purposes, however grandiloquent the language in which they are couched, should also make room for the mundane needs of students.

PURPOSES IN PUBLIC SCHOOLS

While the purposes of education, beyond the academics, may be less clear today in colleges and universities, the situation at the elementary and secondary levels is another matter. There still is widespread agreement, though the specifics may be a matter of dispute, that schools for younger pupils should play a role in character development, socialization, transmission of a common culture, and preparation for citizenship. Two of the main reasons why critics wonder about the appropriateness of online courses below the college level are because of these objectives and because of doubts about the suitability of e-learning for less mature students who may not so easily function on their own.

Character takes shape within the crucible of personal interaction. For example, young people learn sharing, honesty, and reliability in situations in which they witness the behavior of others and grow accustomed to conducting themselves in accord with certain mores and expectations. Socialization implies personal contact with others, not abstract skills learned and practiced in isolation. Online courses have interactive components that call on participants to deal with the thoughts and ideas of others by following tacit and explicit rules, but such virtual encounters hardly amount to the real thing with its nuances and visual cues. Aspects of culture can almost certainly be transmitted online, using both readings and electronic discussions. The question becomes, however, whether the transmission of culture from a distance, at a computer keyboard, amounts to more than an intellectual exercise. Perhaps passing along the culture requires more active, personal involvement and remains incomplete when conveyed only online. It may imperil cohesiveness when those who are supposed to participate have the option of remaining detached from the process, as they can online.

The role of schools in socialization gets taken for granted, but it is crucially important. Face-to-face interactions in both academic and nonacademic situations in schools teach children lessons in getting along with others. Personal confrontations force them to tolerate disagreement, to compromise, to reach consensus. While not all pupils benefit equally from these lessons, they nonetheless gain experiences that might not be part of the school day if they are schooled at home. They hone listening and speaking skills. They learn the give-and-take of conversation—though clearly not all students learn these skills with equal results. In other words, experiences at school teach children the rules of the game of life, which might not so readily come to them if they pursue their studies at home. There is a trade-off, to be sure. Home schoolers don't have to deal with bullies, and they don't run the risk of rejection and being left out of activities in favor of those who are more popular. These experiences constitute the dark side of public education, not so readily discussed but very much a part of socialization.

Karen Fulton, director of education policy for the Ohio Education Association, voiced reservations about online learning as she saw it carried out for children of elementary and secondary age in her state. "We are concerned about a lack of interaction with each other and with other adults," she said of cyber learners. "Education is more than just the content. It's about learning how to learn, about having assumptions tested." She continued: "There is a place for electronic learning; no one wants to stop progress. We don't want to block anything that will be quality education. Our concern is about the philosophy behind it. In Ohio, we've seen a philosophy [in electronic learning] that education is about content and that once you've learned that, you're educated, rather than acknowledging the myriad experiences that are part of education."

Some of the largest reservations about online learning for the youngest students have to do with the civic values that many citizens would like the public schools to help children develop. The flourishing and survival of a democratic society depend on young people's learning the responsibilities of citizenship. Lessons in books, no doubt, figure in this process, but probably are insufficient in and of themselves. Students can learn from readings and civics courses about the governmental system of checks and balances, the mechanics of voting, the history of the effort to create a democracy in North America, and the diversity represented by demographic statistics of the United States. But personal face-to-face contact may make the passion for democracy more palpable. The Center on Education Policy, a Washington, D.C. advocate for public education, identified what it called six fundamental purposes and principles of public schools:

1. effective preparation for life, work, and citizenship;
2. social cohesion and shared culture;
3. universal access and free cost;
4. equity and non-discrimination;
5. public accountability and responsiveness;
6. religious neutrality.[5]

The center proposed that people gauge the effects of education reforms by their effects on purposes and principles. Online learning, when laid out against these parameters, shows mixed, mostly questionable, implications. While the content of online courses might train a young person for work, one wonders about the preparation for life, citizenship, and a shared culture when a student's education occurs in isolation. This is less of an issue for the many high school students whose online courses are an addition to a schedule of classroom-based courses. An online course or two for a student who otherwise attends regular courses is unlikely to interfere with the larger purposes of education. But what of pupils whose entire schedules are online? Can they learn how to live a life as they must, eventually, in the presence of others, how to interact with others as a responsible citizen, and how to share a culture? Furthermore, online learning for youngsters below the college level raises questions about cost, equity, and accountability.

Therefore, it is not so clear that an entire schedule of online courses will prepare precollegiate students fully for the future. Borrowing from the statement on fundamentals and principles enunciated by the Center on Education Policy, one wonders, for instance, about whether youngsters who do not sit in classrooms with others will emerge with a cohesive sense of American society, its diversity, and its values. Similarly, what responsibility will they feel to a civil society if they are educated wholly in a classroom of one, not having to share and compromise—except perhaps in threaded electronic discussions—during their hours of instruction?

Some of these same issues arise in connection with home schooling, whether or not the children obtain their instruction from online sources. Children who remain at home for their education tend to have fewer encounters with peers, fewer occasions upon which they must consider life beyond the four walls of their houses. Admittedly, some parents structure lessons to get their children into the world, to expose them widely and to prod them to think about matters outside the home. They can arrange field trips and projects to get their children out of the house. Yet, this requires extra effort and probably many parents settle for lessons in and around the home. Now, in its short existence, online learning has opened a new window for families devoted to home schooling. Conceivably, online lessons could counteract some of the isolation of the students. But, on the other hand, controversies over home schooling are potentially multiplied by the ability of online learning to keep more children at home and away from classmates in whose presence they might better realize some of the purposes of schooling that extend beyond instruction.

NOT FOR EVERYONE

Art Institute, the chain of proprietary schools that offers prospective students the opportunity to attend courses in classrooms or online, took the view that e-learning was not intended as the perfect solution for everyone's education or training needs. In an interview, an official stated, "Some students desire or need to be involved in a traditional learning process. They may prefer a lecture format for learning and need to know a teacher is waiting for them in the classroom. They may need or want the facial expressions of approval from a teacher or the face-to-face socialization that occurs in hallways."

The suitability of online courses does not depend only on the learner. The way instructors approach their work also determines whether e-learning is right for students. "I'm not sure that any of us in the field are doing a good job dealing with the student's motivation and sense of responsibility," Kristi Smalley, principal of the University of Missouri High School, said of online educators. "If a student won't take the responsibility to get the work done, he will have lots of difficulties. It is difficult without a teacher standing over them. Students have problems prioritizing and scheduling their work." The University of Missouri High School sent reminders to students who were not submitting their work in timely fashion. Officials said they went so far as to "pester" students. They found that they could not count on parents to keep their youngsters on task in distance learning. But that should come as no surprise. Parents of many students attending brick-and-mortar high schools also seem unable or unwilling to monitor the progress of their children. Why should it be any different at a virtual high school?

The challenge presented by students who exhibit little academic initiative raises serious questions, of course, about the appropriateness of online learning for them. How will students take responsibility for learning in a classroom of one if they barely function in a classroom of 25, which at least has a teacher on duty? The easiest response to that question is that distance learning is not for everyone, that those who cannot work on their own are not candidates for this sort of education. The decision to learn from afar should be a product of one's desire. For K through 12 students, though, parents also figure in the equation. In Ohio, the Electronic Classroom of Tomorrow, a K through 12 virtual school, ran into problems with parents, especially at the high school level. Some parents were so unresponsive that school authorities thought the school might have been better off limiting enrollment to the elementary grades, which supplied the bulk of the enrollment anyway. Some high school students apparently sought to use their enrollment in online courses as a free pass to avoid schoolwork, trying to convert the school year into a holiday. Some parents seemed not to monitor these recalcitrant children and took it for granted that the virtual school would look after their children for them. The experience underscored the need for close communication between a virtual school and the families of students.

Yet, even strong and conscientious students may find online learning onerous. Morgan Arenson of New York City took online courses through the Center for Talented Youth of The Johns Hopkins University. She was a diligent student who got high marks in the private school she attended. This 17-year-old, in the process of applying to Michigan, Chicago, Princeton, MIT, and Harvard, was ultimately accepted by all of them and ended up at Harvard in the fall of 2002. She was an accomplished ballet dancer with the discipline to attend demanding lessons six days a week.

Prior to her raft of acceptances, Arenson was in search of greater academic challenge and a chance to pump up her transcript for her college application. Moreover, the courses in the school she attended were moving more slowly than she liked. She enrolled in online courses, first in precalculus and then in physics. Online learning of the sort made available through the Hopkins program proved to be as formidable an academic challenge as Arenson said she had ever encountered. Not only was the work tough—it was designed for America's highest achieving secondary school students—but she had to discipline herself to sit and work at the computer each day, even when she had assignments due the next day at her regular school. And her marks in the online courses were lower than those she was accustomed to attaining in the classroom. "It was very difficult," Arenson said.

Arenson's experience is not unique among high achievers. Online Advanced Placement courses have also confounded some other students who otherwise performed well in classroom-based courses. South Dakota, a sparsely populated state where some high schools cannot assemble a critical mass of students to offer Advanced Placement courses in face-to-face settings, welcomed online versions of AP courses. Teachers liked the idea of exposing their ablest students to the challenge of the courses. They found, though, that some students could not marshal the motivation and discipline to handle self-paced instruction regardless of their achievements in the classroom. Similarly, the work in online AP courses overwhelmed some high school students in California when it came on top of a regular schedule of classroom-based courses. That finding, in fact, might offer some insight into the circumstances under which students are most likely to succeed in e-learning. Perhaps online studies should be part of a regular schedule of courses and not an add-on that burdens students who carry a full load of classroom-based courses.

Arna Clark, old enough to be a mother to Arenson and the students in the online Advanced Placement courses, took her degree studies online through Western Governors University, but said that this approach might not suit students who need more structure and social contacts, students who do better in traditional classrooms with set hours and a circle of peers with whom to interact face-to-face. As a matter of fact, though she was successful, she said that if she had it to do over again she would opt for a program that contained more of a blend of online and real classroom settings.

The head of the Florida Virtual School proposed that secondary school students "self select" their way into online learning, where, according to her, success has more to do with personality than with previous grade-point average. Her suggestions to students making this choice were that they be able to manage time well, have self-motivation, and not need a teacher in the room in order to get their work done. Some experts use the phrase "self-regulated learning" to refer to the ability of students to take responsibility for their own education. Discipline undergirds self-regulation and, without it, people abandon exercise routines, go off diets, and, perhaps, stop doing their studies in online courses.

In a way, it is like the difference between exercising alone at home on one's own equipment and going to a gym to work out in the company others. Many say they need the fillip provided by being among fellow exercisers, even if most of the equipment could be duplicated (for a price) at home. Another impediment has to do with the fact that the home or the office is an alien place for formal learning. Home is a place to relax, to dine, to watch television, to sleep, maybe to do some plea-sure reading. The office is a place to work for income, not to pursue ed-ucation. Taking online courses in either setting may create dissonance, though the mental barrier is hardly insurmountable.

Despite the proliferation of online education at the elementary and secondary school levels, many observers wonder whether the approach is appropriate for these age groups. Usually, independent learning is as-sociated with adults, a logical step beyond the nontraditional, continu-ing education that colleges and universities have long served up for adults. Do younger students, especially those of elementary age, have the maturity to pursue studies on their own? Good lesson material may draw them in and good instructors may maintain contact with them. It remains to be seen, though, whether this paradigm is sufficient for very many younger students.

Similar questions reverberate, not quite so loudly, in higher educa-tion. The computer and the Internet have permeated academia, and be-fore long most classroom courses will have some online components. Putting entire courses online, however, is a separate matter and only time will tell which students are most suited for such courses. Conve-nience is a compelling factor, especially for part-time, commuting stu-dents. This is close to the profile of the students that the University of Phoenix seeks to enroll—working adults who, if they opt for online courses, can avoid the commuting part of their education. To try to en-sure the appropriateness of the program, Phoenix asks students to dis-cuss their plans with counselors over the phone before officially enrolling. The counseling process can consume up to three hours over more than a month. Those who enroll, in effect, self-select themselves.

Just as it is thought at this juncture that online learning is appropri-ate for only some students, some believe that online learning lends itself only to certain kinds of courses. Proponents of this view recognize that courses built around gaining a command of facts and procedures may be taught more easily online than other kinds of courses. Critics maintain that disciplines that seek to convey deep understanding of complex ideas do not lend themselves to instruction at a computer. They say such courses require face-to-face contact and a setting that allows for in-person dialogue. This ideal, however, does not always comport with the reality of the many classrooms in which courses fraught with complexities are taught by the lecture method to students who seldom engage in conversation with teachers or classmates. Surely, some students in online education are no worse off than some of their peers whose education takes place in such classrooms, regardless of subject matter.

On the other hand, online learning should try to be at least the equal of good classroom practice, not an emulation of the worst that the classroom has to offer. Courses over the Internet may not suit all students, but such courses have already shown that they can and do serve the needs of some students under certain circumstances. Any conversation about the purposes of education must take note of the need to make formal learning convenient for students. Online learning does this. One may safely conclude, even at this early juncture, that this new delivery system has already staked out a permanent place in education. Its role will be as lasting as that of the computer itself.

EPILOGUE

Realism and recognition have figured ever more prominently in online learning during the year and a half since I completed writing the hardcover edition of *A Classroom of One*. The hype continues to recede and people are more realistic about the strengths and weaknesses of learning online. At the same time, growing numbers of educators and lay people recognize that this form of education renders a unique contribution and acknowledge the Internet as an acceptable vehicle for learning.

It is clearer than ever, though, that online education will not displace the classroom. Face-to-face contact, with its immediacy and personalization, is the dominant form of education, as it will almost certainly remain during the lifetimes of those who read this book. Furthermore, stasis counts for a great deal in education and most teachers and students have difficulty imagining education occurring in a form other than that which has been the paradigm for centuries.

The grand promise of the late 1990s, when boosters of online learning projected its possibilities as boundless, has yielded to a more sober appraisal. In the wake of the dot-com collapse of the spring of 2000, the Internet has yet to recover its full allure as a venue for education. The lost illusions can be viewed through the prism of the now defunct Fathom on which Columbia University and several allied institutions had placed so many hopes. The description of Fathom on these pages still counts for a great deal in understanding how expectations for online learning did not comport with reality. It was a noble but flawed experiment, as has proved true, as well, of some other ventures into learning on the Internet.

What sustains online education, above all, is the desire to overcome obstacles of time and place, which still loom as major barriers to learning for some students. Education via the Internet remains the best way to bypass these obstructions and this fact alone bodes well for online learning. There are simply many students, especially working adults, who find it inconvenient to race back and forth between campus and life's other responsibilities.

The continued spectacular progress of the University of Phoenix Online demonstrates that, when tailored to the specific needs of learners, education online can grow and prosper. Moreover, individual courses at traditional colleges and universities increasingly are incorporating elements of online learning. I stand behind my prediction, offered in this book, that most courses in higher education by the end of this decade will in one way or another take advantage of the Internet. E-mail exchanges with students are steadily replacing office conferences for many faculty members. In addition, blended or hybrid courses that meet in classrooms twice a week and over the Internet once a week are growing ever more common.

Even the U. S. Open University, whose rise and fall is noted on these pages, has, since the publication of *A Classroom of One,* risen again, Lazarus-like, in new form as a partnership with the New School University, a New York City institution. This time, Britain's Open University, which spun off the late U. S. Open University as a stand-alone entity, regards the revamped effort as simply part of its worldwide outreach. Another of the enterprises described at length in this book, eArmyU, has proved increasingly popular with members of the military, for whom overcoming time and place is crucial. The institution has added 12 more institutions of higher education, offering 68 more degree programs online, to the programs from almost two dozen colleges and universities already available to soldiers.

Events of the last year and half underscore the appeal of online learning for future teachers and for those already teaching who want to upgrade their skills. An entity called "Teachers College" has been created by Western Governors University, one of the institutions described in this book. There is every indication that online education courses—for good or for bad—will become a staple for educators.

Also, some of the policy questions raised on these pages are starting to be addressed. Congress has amended copyright law to take cognizance of the needs of online instructors and federal student-aid restrictions on funds for students taking online courses face ever more scrutiny.

Activities involving online learning at the elementary and secondary level have been no less consequential during the past year and a half as course-taking by pre-collegiate students has increased. The creation of the North American Council for Online Learning gives promises of helping the entire sector. Florida Virtual School, one of the most responsible efforts at the pre-collegiate level, stands to benefit from a funding change approved by the state legislature to put the school on a more solid fiscal footing. Meanwhile, Michigan Virtual High School, also mentioned on these pages, has enjoyed great success, placing its enrollment second only to Florida Virtual School. More people are dropping their skepticism, coming to believe in what secondary students can gain from online learning.

When *A Classroom of One* was published, however, I noted that the elementary level was the most problematic area for education delivered online. That is even truer today. Home schooling has, as I predicted, seized on online learning—under the guise of cyber charter schools—to promote itself. Online lessons expand the ability of parents to provide education to their children. And so it makes sense that families dedicated to home schooling should exploit every advantage, though legislators and other officials have not fully weighed the implications of this trend.

Serious problems can arise if elementary-aged pupils are left to pursue education online without benefit of close supervision of parents or teachers. This is the great danger—a kind of watered-down home schooling without committed adults to ensure that the requisite controls are in place. Online learning, after all, requires focus and dedication, qualities that most youngsters of elementary-school age have yet to develop.

So, there you have it, a brief update of where online learning seems to be taking us. It remains one of the most exciting and controversial educational innovations of the last 50 years and surely a subject worthy of the interest of all Americans.

NOTES

CHAPTER 1

1. Futures Project, "Database of Institutions Offering Virtual Courses," 2001: www.futuresproject.org/publications/virtual_database.html
2. Judith Axler Turner, "'Distance Learning' Courses Get High Marks from Students and Enrollments Are Rising," *Chronicle of Higher Education,* 27 September 1989, 39.
3. Center for Education Reform, "Monthly Letter to Friends" (Washington, D.C.), September 2001, 5.
4. Gerald E. Sroufe, personal interview, 2002.
5. Ted Plafker, "Chinese Court Sentences a Leader of Tiananmen Protests," *Chronicle of Higher Education,* 1 May 1998, 42.
6. Dan Carnevale, "Distance Education Bill Receives Praise at Hearing," *Chronicle of Higher Education,* 6 July 2001, A31.
7. Jennifer 8. Lee, "Companies Compete to Provide Internet Veil for the Saudis," *New York Times,* 19 November 2001, C1.
8. Stanley N. Katz, "In Information Technology, Don't Mistake a Tool for a Goal," *Chronicle of Higher Education,* 15 June 2001, B7.
9. "Ten Public Policy Issues," Public Policy Paper Series No. 01–1 (Washington, D.C.: Association of Governing Boards), June 2001, 13.
10. Lowell C. Rose and Alec M. Gallup, "The 33rd Annual Phi Delta Kappa/Gallup Poll of the Public's Attitudes Toward the Public Schools," *Phi Delta Kappan,* September 2001, 46.
11. Michael Simonson, Sharon Smaldino, Michael Albright, and Susan Zvacek, *Teaching and Learning at a Distance: Foundations of Distance Education* (Upper Saddle River, N.J.: Prentice-Hall, 2000), iii-iv.

CHAPTER 2

1. Desmond Keegan and Greville Rumble, "Distance Teaching at University Level," in *The Distance Teaching Universities,* ed. Grenville Rumble and Keith Harry (London: Croom Helm, 1982), 15.

2. "Distance Education and Related Technologies Can Improve Both Teaching and Learning," *Chronicle of Higher Education,* Letters to the Editor, 5 May 2000, B3.

3. Nicholas C. Burbules and Thomas A. Callister, "Universities in Transition: The Promise and the Challenge of New Technologies," *Teachers College Record* 102, no. 2 (November 2000), 271–93.

4. "Professors Who Despise Their Students Should Take a Good Look at Their Teaching," *Chronicle of Higher Education,* Letters to the Editor, 7 September 2001, B4.

5. Charles E. Glassick, Mary Taylor Huber, and Gene I. Maeroff, *Scholarship Assessed: Evaluation of the Professoriate* (San Francisco: Jossey-Bass, 1997), 7.

6. San Diego State University. "Academic Policy and Planning Committee Distance Education Policy," April 2000: www.rohan.sdsu.edu/dept/senate/sendoc/distanceed.apr2000.html

7. American Federation of Teachers, Testimony to the Web-Based Education Commission, 18 August 2000: www.hpcnet.org/webcommission

8. Jeffrey R. Young, "Designer of Free Course-Management Software Asks, What Makes a Good Web Site?" *Chronicle of Higher Education,* 21 January 2002: www.chronicle.com/daily/2002

9. Donald A. Schon, *The Reflective Practitioner: How Professionals Think in Action* (New York: Basic Books, 1984).

CHAPTER 3

1. Lisa Guernsey, "Cyberspace Isn't So Lonely After All," *New York Times,* 26 July 2001, Science Times, 1.

2. Gayle B. Childs, "Problems of Teaching by Correspondence Study," in *The Changing World of Correspondence Study,* ed. Ossian Mackenzie and Edward L. Christensen (University Park: Pennsylvania University Press, 1971), 113.

3. Mary Hamm and Dennis Adams, "Collaborative Inquiry: Working Toward Shared Goals," *Kappa Delta Pi Record,* Spring 2002, 115–18.

4. Stanford Learning Lab, Stanford Learning Projects, Completed Projects, "Integration of Asynchronous Discussion in IHUM Courses" www.sll.stanford.edu/projects/

CHAPTER 4

1. William Pelz, "Course Information Document," undated: www.sln.suny.edu/courses/observ . . . fe05e852568d700712d71?Open Document.

2. World Campus, Pennsylvania State University, "WC Student Surveys: Outcome Survey—Spring 2001," unpublished.

3. Robert Kozma et al. "The Online Course Experience: Evaluation of the Virtual High School's Third Year of Implementation, 1999–2000," Hudson Public Schools, SRI Project 7289, November 2000, 30.

4. Ibid., 30.

5. Ibid., 31.

6. Martha A. Townsend, "Access to Faculty Out of the Classroom," unpublished survey (conducted in conjunction with presentation at the Seminar on Student Life in Higher Education, Hechinger Institute on Education and the Media, Teachers College, Columbia University, 21 October 2001).

7. "Retailers Struggled to Respond to Customers' Requests Online," season reports, Jupiter Media Metrix, online press release: www.jmm.com/xp/jmm/press/2002/pr_010302.xml, Jan. 3, 2002

8. Dan Carnevale, "Online Instructor Cautions Against Having Too Many Activities," *Chronicle of Higher Education,* 17 July 2001, online version: http://www.chronicle.com/daily/2001

9. Frank W. Connolly, "My Students Don't Know What They're Missing," *Chronicle of Higher Education,* 21 December 2001, B5.

10. Peter Navarro, "The Promise—and Potential Pitfalls—of Cyberlearning," in *Issues in Web-Based Pedagogy: A Critical Primer,* ed. Robert A. Cole (Westport, Conn.: Greenwood Press, 2000), 290–1.

11. Jeffrey R. Young, "Administrator Predicts that Handheld Computers Will Be Big on Campus," *Chronicle of Higher Education,* 5 July 2001, online version: www.chronicle.com/daily/2001

CHAPTER 5

1. Michael Simonson, Sharon Smaldino, Michael Albright, and Susan Zvacek, *Teaching and Learning at a Distance: Foundations of Distance Education* (Upper Saddle River, N.J.: Prentice-Hall, 2000), iii–iv.

2. Ibid., 64.

3. Byron W. Brown and Carl Liedholm, "Can Web Courses Replace the Classroom in Principles of Microeconomics?" (paper presented at meeting of the American Economics Association, January 2002), 4. Electronic version: www.msu.edu/%7Ebrownb/brown-liedholm%20aea%202002.pdf.

4. Ibid., 7–8.

5. Peter Shea et al., "Measures of Learning Effectiveness in the SUNY Learning Network," Web Center Learning Networks Effectiveness Research: www.alnresearch.org/JSP/db_entry.jsp?index=64. Eric Frederickson et.al., "Student Satisfaction and Perceived Learning with Online Courses," www.alnresearch.org/Data_Fi . . . /abstract/abs_frederickson00_1htm.

6. World Campus, Pennsylvania State University, unpublished survey.

7. Melody M. Thompson, "Faculty Satisfaction in Penn State's World Campus," unpublished.

8. Eric Fredericksen, Alexandra Pickett, and Peter Shea, "Factors Influencing Faculty Satisfaction with Asynchronous Teaching and Learning in the SUNY Learning Network," *JALN* 4, no. 3 (2000) (electronic version): www.alnresearch.org/Data_Fi ... Rticles/abstract/abs_hartman00.htm. R. Joel Hartman, Charles Dziuban, and Patsy Moski, "Faculty Satisfaction in ALNs: A Dependent or Independent Variable?" *JALN* 4, no. 3 (2000) (electronic version): www.alnresearch.org/Data_Fi ... Rticles/abstract/abs_hartman.htm. Mary Beth

Alameda and Kathleen Rose, "Instructor Satisfaction in University of California Extension's On-line Writing Curriculum," *JALN* 4, no. 3 (2000) (electronic version): www.alnresearch.org/Data_Files/articles/abstract/abs_almeda00.htm

9. Jane H. Leuthold, "Is Computer-Based Learning Right for Everyone?" Proceedings, 32nd Hawaii International Conference on Systems Sciences, IEEE Press Web Center: Learning Network Effectiveness Research (electronic version): www.alnresearch.org/Data_Fi ... Ticles/abstract/als_leuthold99.htm.

10. T. Mills Kelly, "Before Plugging In, Consider Your Options," *Chronicle of Higher Education,* 13 July 2001, 9.

11. Lenna Ojure and Tom Sherman, "Learning Styles: Why Teachers Love a Concept Research Has Yet to Embrace," *Education Week,* 28 November 2001, 33.

12. "The Third Shift: Women Learning Online," American Association of University Women (Washington, D.C.: 2001).

13. Gary Natriello, "Off the Record: Dropping Out of Distance Learning," *Teachers College Record,* 30 August 2001: www.tcrecord.org/Content.asp?ContentID

14. Campus Computing Project, "The 2001 National Survey of Information Technology in U.S. Higher Education," October 2001, 4: www.campuscomputing.net/summaries/2001/index.html.

CHAPTER 6

1. San Diego State University, "Do I Want to Learn at a Distance?" www.distance-educator.com/portals/quiz.html.

2. National Association of Secondary School Principals, *Breaking Ranks: Changing an American Institution* (Reston, Va.: National Association of Secondary School Principals, undated), 48–9.

3. Deborah Stipek, *Motivation to Learn: From Theory to Practice,* 3rd ed. (Boston: Allyn and Bacon, 1998), 177–81.

4. John W. Thomas, "Expectations and Effort: Course Demands, Students' Study Practices, and Academic Achievement" (paper presented at "Hard Work and Higher Expectations: A Conference on Student Achievement," sponsored by U.S. Department of Education, Washington, D.C., 8 November 1990.

5. Western Governors University, "Interpretation of Distance Learning Self-Assessment": www.wgu.edu/wgu/self_interpretation.asp.

6. Allison M. Ryan and Helen Patrick, "The Classroom Social Environment and Changes in Adolescents' Motivation and Engagement During Middle School," *American Educational Research Journal* 38, no. 2 (2001): 437–60.

7. Rena M. Palloff and Keith Pratt, *Lessons from the Cyber Space Classroom* (San Francisco: Jossey-Bass, 2001), 109.

8. John D. Brandsford, Ann L. Brown, and Rodney R. Cocking, eds., *How People Learn: Brain, Mind, Experience, and School* (Washington, D.C.: National Academy Press, 2000).

9. Glenn C. Altschuler, "The E-Learning Curve," *New York Times,* 5 August 2001, Education Life, 13.

10. Robert Kozma et al., "The Online Course Experience: Evaluation of the Virtual
     High School's Third Year of Implementation, 1999–2000," Hudson Public
     Schools, SRI Project 7728, November 2000, iv.
11. Ibid., 29.
12. Ibid., 30.

CHAPTER 7

1.   The Futures Project, "Institutions Offering Virtual Courses: Findings as of Feb-
     ruary 21, 2001": www.futuresproject.org/publications/virtual_database.html.
2.   Linda Cavalluzzo and Michael Higgins, "Who Should Fund Virtual Schools?"
     (Alexandria, Va.: Appalachian Technology in Education Consortium/CNA
     Corporation, December 2001).
3.   Anne Marie Borrego, "Stock Options Sweeten Packages for Executives in For-
     Profit Higher Education," *Chronicle of Higher Education,* 9 November 2001, A31.
4.   Mark Walsh, "Seed Money Drying Up for Education-Related Business." *Edu-
     cation Week,* 8 August 2001, 5.
5.   Robert Zemsky, "Gauging the Market for e-Learning: Report on the Weather-
     station Project," 2 April 2002 (unpublished).
6.   David Adamany, "Temple University President's Self-Study and Agenda," June
     2001.
7.   Ibid., 6.
8.   Kathleen F. Kelly, "Meeting Needs and Making Profits: The Rise of For-Profit
     Degree-Granting Institutions," Education Commission of the States, July 2001:
     www.ecs.org/clearinghouse/27/33/2733.htm.
9.   Peter Schmidt, "States Push Public Universities to Commercialize Research,"
     Chronicle of Higher Education, 29 March 2002, A26.
10. Benjamin Lowe, "Fathoming Where the Money Goes," *Columbia Daily Specta-
     tor,* 7 February 2001: www.columbiaspectator.com.

CHAPTER 8

1.   Katherine S. Mangan, "Expectations Evaporate for Online MBA Programs,"
     Chronicle of Higher Education, 5 October 2001, A31.
2.   Katherine S. Mangan, "Top Business Schools Seek to Ride a Bull Market in On-
     Line M.B.A.'s," *Chronicle of Higher Education,* 15 January 1999, 27.
3.   Allen Glenn, "AACTE and the Emergence of For-Profit, Education-Related
     Companies," prepared for the American Association of Colleges of Teacher Ed-
     ucation, Washington, D.C., 27 February 2001.
4.   "Successful Distance-Education Spinoffs," *Chronicle of Higher Education,* 11 Jan-
     uary 2002, B20.

CHAPTER 9

1.   John Merrow, "Double Click: Threat or Promise?" *Ed.,* Harvard Graduate
     School of Education, Spring 2001, 23.

2. Jeffrey R. Young, "The Cat-and-Mouse Game of Plagiarism Detection," *Chronicle of Higher Education*, 6 July 2001, A26.

3. Katie Hafner, "Lessons in the School of Cut and Paste," *New York Times*, 28 June 2001, G1.

4. Patrick M. Scanlon and David R. Neumann, *Journal of College Student Development*, May/June 2001.

5. Douglas Lederman, "NCAA Looks Into Academic Fraud," *Chronicle of Higher Education*, 29 June 1994, A31; Debra E. Blum, "Probe Raises Questions About Correspondence-Course Credits," *Chronicle of Higher Education*, 19 May 1995, A41; Debra E. Blum, "NCAA Rejects Bid to Ease Eligibility, Backs New Governance," *Chronicle of Higher Education*, 19 January 1996, A31.

6. Harold J. Noah and Max A. Eckstein. *Fraud and Education: The Worm in the Apple*, (Lanham, Md.: Rowan & Littlefield, 2001), xi.

7. Kathleen F. Kelly, "Meeting Needs and Making Profits: The Rise of For-Profit Degree-Granting Institutions," Education Commission of the States, July 2001, 15.

8. "Colloquium 2002: Technology and the Human Person," *Insight* (University of Virginia, Institute for Advanced Studies in Culture), Spring 2002, no. 6, 1.

CHAPTER 10

1. "Report to Congress on the Distance Education Demonstration Programs," U.S. Department of Education, Washington, D.C., January 2001, 17–18.

2. Judith S. Eaton, "Maintaining the Delicate Balance: Distance Learning, Higher Education, Accreditation, and the Politics of Self-Regulation," American Council on Education, Center for Policy Analysis, Washington, D.C., May 2002.

3. Ibid., 20.

4. "The Power of the Internet for Learning: Final report of the Web-Based Education Commission," December 2000: www.ed.gov/offices/AC/WBEC/Final-Report/WBECFinalReport.pdf.

5. Middle States Commission on Higher Education: www.msache.org/BEST.pdg.

6. Michael B. Goldstein, "Regulation of the Web: e-Learning in a Nation of States" (testimony in continuing legal education program at National Association of College and University Attorneys, Cyberspace 2000, Portland, Or., 4 March 2000), 7.

7. Southern Regional Education Board: www.electroniccampus.org/st . . .ecinfo/publications/principles.asp2000–2001.

8. U.S. Department of Education, National Center for Education Statistics, *Distance Education Instruction by Postsecondary Faculty and Staff: Fall 1998* (NCES 2002-155, by Ellen M. Bradburn, Washington, D.C., 2002), iv-v.

9. Ibid., vi-vii.

10. "Distance Education and Intellectual Property," *Academe*, May/June 1999, 43.

11. American Council on Education, "Developing a Distance Education Policy for 21st Century Learning": www.acenet.edu/washington/d . . .e_ed/2000/03march/distance_ed.html.

CHAPTER 11

1. Florence Olsen, "Sylvan Learning Systems Forms Division Focusing on Online Higher Education," *Chronicle of Higher Education*, 19 July 2001: www.chronicle.com/daily/2001/.

2. Kyo Yamashiro and Andrew Zucker, "An Expert Panel Review of the Quality of Virtual High School Courses: Final Report" (Arlington, Va.: SRI International, November 1999) viii.

3. "Measuring Up 2000" (San Jose, Calif.: National Center for Public Policy and Higher Education, 2000).

4. "Distance Education and Related Technologies Can Improve Both Teaching and Learning," *Chronicle of Higher Education*, Letters to the Editor, 5 May 2000, B3.

5. Excelsior College, "Outcomes Assessment Framework" (Albany, N.Y.: Excelsior College, 2001), 1.

6. Ibid., Appendix F., 31.

7. National Governors Association Center for Best Practices, "A Vision of E-Learning for America's Workforce," Commission on Technology and Adult Learning, 2001: www.nga.org/center/divisions/1,118,c_ISSUE_BRIEF^D_2128,00.html.

8. David C. Leonard, "The Web, the Millennium, and the Digital Evolution of Distance Education,." in *Issues in Web-Based Pedagogy: A Critical Primer*, ed. Robert A. Cole (Westport, Conn.: Greenwood Press, 2000), 23–34.

9. Washington State Higher Education Coordinating Board, "Distance Education Study" (HB 2952), January 2001.

10. American Federation of Teachers, "Virtual Revolution: Trends in the Expansion of Distance Education" (Washington, D.C. 2001), 4.

CHAPTER 12

1. David Rose and Anne Meyer, "The Future Is in the Margins: The Role of Technology and Disability in Educational Reform" www.air-dc.org/forum/AbRose_Meyer.htm.

2. Lawrence E. Gladieux and Watson Scott Swail, "The Virtual University & Educational Opportunity: Issues of Equity and Access for the Next Generation" (Washington, D.C.: College Board, April 1999), 23.

3. U.S. Dept. of Commerce, Bureau of the Census, press release, 6 September 2001: www.census.gov/Press-Release/www/2001/cboi-147.html.

4. "The Future of Children: Children and Computer Technology," report by David and Lucile Packard Foundation, 10, no. 2 (Fall/Winter 2000): 3.

5. "Gifford Delivers Inaugural Sussman Lecture," *Teachers College Today*, Summer/Fall 2001, 7.

6. "Teaching, Learning and Computing, 1998 National Survey," Center for Research on Information Technology and Organizations, University of California at Irvine.

7.   Jeffrey R. Young, "Does 'Digital Divide' Rhetoric Do More Harm Than Good?" *Chronicle of Higher Education,* 9 November 2001, A51.

8.   Michael Kirst and Andrea Venezia, "Bridging the Great Divide Between Secondary Schools and Postsecondary Education," *Phi Delta Kappan,* September 2001, 92.

9.   The Ford Foundation, "A Foundation Goes to School" (New York: The Ford Foundation, 1972), 35–6.

10.   Ibid., 43.

11.   "Raising Our Sights: No High School Senior Left Behind," National Commission on the High School Senior Year (Princeton: Woodrow Wilson National Fellowship Foundation, 2001), 23.

CHAPTER 13

1.   Vannevar Bush, "As We May Think," *Atlantic Monthly* 176, no. 1 (July 1945), 101–9: www.theatlantic.com/unbound/flashbks/computer/.

2.   Kevin Werbach, "Clicks and Mortar Meets Cap and Gown: Higher Education Goes Online," *Release 1.0,* September 2000, 1.

3.   Vartan Gregorian, "Higher Education's Accomplishments and Challenges" (lecture at University of Michigan Law School, 11 September 2001), 15.

4.   Nicholas C. Burbules and Thomas A. Callister, "Universities in Transition: The Promise and the Challenge of New Technologies, *Teachers College Record* 102, no. 2 (November 2000), 4.

5.   "Academic Freedom and Electronic Communications," *Academe,* American Association of University Professors, July-August 1997, 42.

6.   U.S. Department of Education, National Center for Education Statistics, *Distance Education Instruction by Postsecondary Faculty and Staff: Fall 1998.*

7.   Rena M. Palloff and Keith Pratt, *Lessons from the Cyberspace Classroom: The Realities of Online Teaching* (San Francisco: Jossey-Bass, 2001), 21.

8.   "Budget Shifts at One University," *Chronicle of Higher Education,* 16 November 2001, A35.

9.   "Students Log on to a Brave New World: Who Needs to Visit the Library When Salinger is Just a Click Away?" *Washington Post,* 16 March 2001, 66.

10.   Anthony Grafton, "Rare Book Collections in the Age of the Library without Walls," in *Collectors, Collections, and Scholarly Culture* (American Council of Learned Societies, ACLS Occasional Paper, No. 48, 2000), 10.

CHAPTER 14

1.   Frank Newman and Jamie Scurry, "Higher Education in the Digital Rapids" (Providence, R.I.: Brown University, The Futures Project: Policy for Higher Education in a Changing World, June 2001), 3–4.

2.   Chris Dede, testimony to the U.S. Congress, House of Representatives, Committee on Science, 10 May 2001, 4: www.house.gov/science/research/may10/dede.htm.

3. Ibid., 7.

4. National Center for Education Statistics: www.ed.gov/pubsearch/pubsinfo. asp?pudid=2001033

5. Sir John Daniel, "Lessons from the Open University: Low-Tech Learning Often Works Best," *Chronicle of Higher Education,* 7 September 2001, B24.

6. Audrey Bryan, unpublished survey, Teachers College, Columbia University, 2001.

7. Larry Cuban, Heather Kirkpatrick, and Craig Peck, "High Access and Low Use of Technologies in High School Classrooms: Explaining an Apparent Paradox," *American Educational Research Journal* 38, no. 4 (Winter 2001), 813–34.

8. National Association of State Boards of Education, "Any Time, Any Place, Any Path, Any Pace: Taking the Lead on E-Learning Policy" (Alexandria, Va.: National Association of State Boards of Education, 2001).

CHAPTER 15

1. Boston University, "The Changing Landscape of Higher Education. Report of the Task Force on a Changing Landscape": www.bu.edu/accreditation/chang-landscape.html.

2. Ibid.

3. Dan Carnevale, "Should Distance Students Pay for Campus-Based Services?" *Chronicle of Higher Education,* 14 September 2001, 35.

4. "Teachers College: The Soul of the University, 2000 Annual Report," Teachers College, Columbia University, 2001, 3–4.

5. Center on Education Policy, "Changing Schools, Enduring Principles" (Washington, D.C.: Center on Education Policy, undated broadside).

BIBLIOGRAPHY

"Academic Freedom and Electronic Communications." *Academe* (American Association of University Professors) 83, no. 4, July-August 1997: 42.

Adamany, D. "Temple University President's Self-Study and Agenda," June 2001.

Alameda, M. B., and K. Rose. "Instructor Satisfaction in University of California Extension's On-line Writing Curriculum." *JALN* (Journal of Asynchronous Learning Networks) 4, no. 3 (2000): www.alnresearch.org/Data_Files/articles/abstract/abs_almeda00.htm.

Altschuler, G. C."The E-Learning Curve," *New York Times,* 5 August 2001, Education Life, 13.

American Council on Education, "Developing a Distance Education Policy for 21st Century Learning": www.acenet.edu/washington/d . . .e_ed/2000/03march/distance_ed.html

American Federation of Teachers. Testimony to the Web-Based Education Commission, 18 August 2000: www.hpcnet.org/webcommission.

———. "Virtual Revolution: Trends in the Expansion of Distance Education" (Washington, D.C., 2001), 4.

Axler, J. T., "'Distance Learning' Courses Get High Marks from Students and Enrollments Are Rising." *Chronicle of Higher Education,* 27 September 1989, 39.

Blum, D. E. "NCAA Rejects Bid to Ease Eligibility, Backs New Governance." *Chronicle of Higher Education,* 19 January 1996, A31.

———. "Probe Raises Questions About Correspondence-Course Credits," *Chronicle of Higher Education,* 19 May 1995, A41.

Borrego, A. M. "Stock Options Sweeten Packages for Executives in For-Profit Higher Education." *Chronicle of Higher Education,* 9 November 2001, A31.

Boston University. "The Changing Landscape of Higher Education. Report of the Task Force on a Changing Landscape": www.bu.edu/accreditation/changlandscape.html.

Brandsford, J. D., A. L. Brown, and R. R. Cocking, eds. *How People Learn: Brain, Mind, Experience, and School* (Washington, D.C.: National Academy Press, 2000).

Brown, B. W., and C. Liedholm. "Can Web Courses Replace the Classroom in Principles of Microeconomics?" Paper presented at meeting of the American Economics Association, Atlanta, January 2002, 4: www.msu.edu/%7Ebrownb/brown-liedholm%20aea%202002.pdf.

Bryan, A. Unpublished survey for Office of Institutional Studies, Teachers College, Columbia University, 2001.

"Budget Shifts at One University," *Chronicle of Higher Education*, 16 November 2001, A35.

Burbules, N. C., and T. A. Callister. "Universities in Transition: The Promise and the Challenge of New Technologies." *Teachers College Record* 102, no. 2 (November 2000): 271–93.

Bush, V. "As We May Think." *Atlantic Monthly* 176, no. 1 (July 1945), 101–9: www.theatlantic.com/unbound/flashbks/computer/

Campus Computing Project. "The 2001 National Survey of Information Technology in U.S. Higher Education," October 2001, 4: http://www.campuscomputing.net/summaries/2001/index.html.

Carnevale, Dan. "Distance Education Bill Receives Praise at Hearing." *Chronicle of Higher Education,* 6 July 2001, A31.

———. "Online Instructor Cautions against Having Too Many Activities." *Chronicle of Higher Education,* 17 July 2001: online version: www.chronicle.com/daily/2001

———. "Should Distance Students Pay for Campus-Based Services?" *Chronicle of Higher Education,* 14 September 2001, 35.

Cavalluzzo, L., and M. Higgins. "Who Should Fund Virtual Schools?" (Alexandria, Va.: Appalachian Technology in Education Consortium/CNA Corporation, December 2001).

Center for Education Reform. "Monthly Letter to Friends." Washington, D.C., September 2001, 5.

Center on Education Policy. "Changing Schools, Enduring Principles" Washington, D.C.: undated broadside.

Childs, G. B. "Problems of Teaching by Correspondence Study." In *The Changing World of Corrrespondence Study,* ed. Ossian Mackenzie and Edward L. Christensen (University Park: Pennsylvania University Press, 1971), 113.

"Colloquium 2002: Technology and the Human Person." *Insight.* (University of Virginia, Institute for Advanced Studies in Culture) 1, no. 6 (Spring 2002): 1.

Connolly, F. W. "My Students Don't Know What They're Missing." *Chronicle of Higher Education,* 21 December 2001, B5.

Cuban, L., H. Kirkpatrick, and C. Peck. "High Access and Low Use of Technologies in High School Classrooms: Explaining an Apparent Paradox," *American Educational Research Journal* 38, no. 4 (Winter 2001): 813–34.

Daniel, Sir J. "Lessons from the Open University: Low-Tech Learning Often Works Best." *Chronicle of Higher Education,* 7 September 2001, B24.

Dede, C. Testimony to the U.S. Congress, House of Representatives, Committee on Science, 10 May 2001, 4: www.house.gov/science/research/may10/dede.htm

"Distance Education and Intellectual Property." *Academe* 85, no. 3 (May/June 1999): 43.

"Distance Education and Related Technologies Can Improve Both Teaching and Learning." *Chronicle of Higher Education,* Letters to the Editor, 5 May 2000, B3.

Eaton, J. S. "Maintaining the Delicate Balance: Distance Learning, Higher Education, Accreditation, and the Politics of Self-Regulation." American Council on Education, Center for Policy Analysis, Washington, D.C., May 2002.

Excelsior College. "Outcomes Assessment Framework." (Albany, N.Y.: Excelsior College, 2001), Appendix F, 31.

The Ford Foundation. "A Foundation Goes to School." (New York: The Ford Foundation, 1972), 35–6.

Fredericksen, E., A. Pickett, and P. Shea. "Factors Influencing Faculty Satisfaction with Asynchronous Teaching and Learning in the SUNY Learning Network." *JALN* 4, no. 3 (2000): http://www.alnresearch.org/Data_Fi . . . Rticles/abstract/abs_hartman00.htm.

Fredericksen, E. A., et al. "Student Satisfaction and Perceived Learning with Online Courses." www.alnresearch.org/Data_Fi . . . /abstract/abs_frederickson00_1htm.

"The Future of Children: Children and Computer Technology." David and Lucile Packard Foundation, 10, no. 2 (Fall/Winter 2000): 3.

Futures Project, "Database of Institutions Offering Virtual Courses," 2001: www.futuresproject.org/publications/virtual_database.html.

———. "Institutions Offering Virtual Courses: Findings as of February 21, 2001." www.futuresproject.org/publications/virtual_database.html.

"Gifford Delivers Inaugural Sussman Lecture." *Teachers College Today*, Summer/Fall 2001, 7.

Gladieux, L. E., and W. S. Swail. "The Virtual University & Educational Opportunity: Issues of Equity and Access for the Next Generation." (Washington, D.C.: College Board, April 1999), 23.

Glassick, C. E., M. T. Huber, and G. I. Maeroff. *Scholarship Assessed: Evaluation of the Professoriate* (San Francisco: Jossey-Bass, 1997), 7.

Glenn, A. "AACTE and the Emergence of For-Profit, Education-Related Companies." Prepared for the American Association of Colleges of Teacher Education, Washington, D.C., 27 February 2001.

Goldstein, M. B. "Regulation of the Web: e-Learning in a Nation of States." Testimony in continuing legal education program at National Association of College and University Attorneys, Cyberspace 2000, Portland, Or., 4 March 2000, 7.

Grafton, A. "Rare Book Collections in the Age of the Library Without Walls, in *Collectors, Collections, and Scholarly Culture*." American Council of Learned Societies (ACLS) Occasional Paper, no. 48 (2000), 10.

Gregorian, V. "Higher Education's Accomplishments and Challenges." Lecture at University of Michigan Law School, 11 September 2001, 15.

Guernsey, L. "Cyberspace Isn't So Lonely After All." *New York Times*, 26 July 2001, Science Times, 1.

Hafner, K. "Lessons in the School of Cut and Paste." *New York Times*, 28 June 2001, G1.

Hamm, M., and D. Adams. "Collaborative Inquiry: Working toward Shared Goals." *Kappa Delta Pi Record* 38, no. 3 (Spring 2002): 115–18.

Hartman, R. J., C. Dziuban, and P. Moski. "Faculty Satisfaction in ALNs: A Dependent or Independent Variable?" *JALN* 4, no. 3 (2000): www.alnresearch.org/Data_Fi . . . Rticles/abstract/abs_hartman.htm.

Katz, S. N. "In Information Technology, Don't Mistake a Tool for a Goal." *Chronicle of Higher Education*, 15 June 2001, B7.

Keegan, D., and G. Rumble. "Distance Teaching at University Level." In *The Distance Teaching Universities*, ed. Grenville Rumble and Keith Harry (London: Croom Helm, 1982), 15.

Kelly, Kathleen F. "Meeting Needs and Making Profits: The Rise of For-Profit Degree-Granting Institutions." Education Commission of the States, July 2001: www.ecs.org/clearinghouse/27/33/2733.htm.

Kelly, T. M. "Before Plugging In, Consider Your Options." *Chronicle of Higher Education,* 13 July 2001, 9.

Kirst, M., and A. Venezia. "Bridging the Great Divide Between Secondary Schools and Postsecondary Education." *Phi Delta Kappan,* September 2001, 92.

Kozma, R. et al. "The Online Course Experience: Evaluation of the Virtual High School's Third Year of Implementation, 1999–2000." Hudson Public Schools, SRI Project 7289, November 2000, 30.

———, "The Online Course Experience: Evaluation of the Virtual High School's Third Year of Implementation, 1999–2000." Hudson Public Schools, SRI Project 7728, November 2000, iv.

Lederman, D. "NCAA Looks Into Academic Fraud." *Chronicle of Higher Education,* 29 June 1994, A31.

Lee, Jennifer 8. "Companies Compete to Provide Internet Veil for the Saudis." *New York Times,* 19 November 2001, C1.

Leonard, D. C. "The Web, the Millennium, and the Digital Evolution of Distance Education." In *Issues in Web-Based Pedagogy: A Critical Primer,* Ed. Robert A. Cole (Westport, Conn.: Greenwood Press, 2000), 23–34.

Leuthold, J. H. "Is Computer-Based Learning Right for Everyone?" Proceedings, 32nd Hawaii International Conference on Systems Sciences, IEEE Press Web Center: Learning Network Effectiveness Research: www.alnresearch.org/Data_Fi . . . Ticles/abstract/als_leuthold99.htm.

Lowe, B. "Fathoming Where the Money Goes." *Columbia Daily Spectator,* 7 February 2001: www.columbiaspectator.com

Mangan, Katherine S. "Top Business Schools Seek to Ride a Bull Market in On-Line M.B.A.'s," *Chronicle of Higher Education,* 15 January 1999, 27.

———. "Expectations Evaporate for Online MBA Programs." *Chronicle of Higher Education,* 5 October 2001, A31.

"Measuring Up 2000." (San Jose, Calif.: National Center for Public Policy and Higher Education, 2000).

Merrow, J. "Double Click: Threat or Promise?" *Ed.* (Harvard Graduate School of Education) (Spring 2001): 23.

Middle States Commission on Higher Education: www.msache.org/BEST.pdg.

National Association of Secondary School Principals, *Breaking Ranks: Changing an American Institution.* (Reston, Va.: National Association of Secondary School Principals, undated), 48–9.

National Association of State Boards of Education. "Any Time, Any Place, Any Path, Any Pace: Taking the Lead on E-Learning Policy." (Alexandria, Va.: National Association of State Boards of Education, 2001).

National Center for Education Statistics: www.ed.gov/pubsearch/pubsinfo.asp?pudid=2001033.

National Commission on the High School Senior Year. "Report to Congress on the Distance Education Demonstration Programs." U.S. Department of Education, Washington, D.C.: (January 2001), 17–18.

National Governors Association Center for Best Practices. "A Vision of E-Learning for America's Workforce." Commission on Technology and Adult Learning, 2001: www.nga.org/center/divisions/1,118,c_ISSUE_BRIEF^D_2128,00.html.

Natriello, G. "Off the Record: Dropping Out of Distance Learning." *Teachers College Record,* 30 August 2001: www.tcrecord.org/Content.asp?ContentID.

Navarro, P. "The Promise—and Potential Pitfalls—of Cyberlearning." In *Issues in Web-Based Pedagogy: A Critical Primer,.* Ed. Robert A. Cole (Westport, Conn.: Greenwood Press, 2000), 290–1.

Newman, F. and J. Scurry. "Higher Education in the Digital Rapids." (Providence, R.I.: Brown University, The Futures Project: Policy for Higher Education in a Changing World, June 2001), 3–4.

Noah, H. J. and M. A. Eckstein. *Fraud and Education: The Worm in the Apple.* (Lanham, Md.: Rowan & Littlefield, 2001), xi.

Ojure, L., and T. Sherman. "Learning Styles: Why Teachers Love a Concept Research Has Yet to Embrace." *Education Week,* 28 November 2001, 33.

Olsen, F. Sylvan Learning Systems Forms Division Focusing on Online Higher Education." *Chronicle of Higher Education,* 19 July 2001: www.chronicle.com/daily/2001/

Palloff, R. M., and K. Pratt. *Lessons from the Cyberspace Classroom: The Realities of Online Teaching.* (San Francisco: Jossey-Bass, 2001).

Pelz, W. "Course Information Document," undated: www.sln.suny.edu/courses/observ . . . fe05e852568d700712d71?Open Document.

Plafker, T. "Chinese Court Sentences a Leader of Tiananmen Protests." *Chronicle of Higher Education,* 1 May 1998, 42.

"The Power of the Internet for Learning: Final Report of the Wed-Based Education Commission." December 2000, 91: www.ed.gov/offices/AC/WBEC/FinalReport/WBECFinalReport.pdf.

"Professors Who Despise Their Students Should Take a Good Look at Their Teaching." *Chronicle of Higher Education,* Letters to the Editor, 7 September 2001, B4.

"Raising Our Sights: No High School Senior Left Behind." (Princeton: Woodrow Wilson National Fellowship Foundation, 2001), 23.

"Retailers Struggled to Respond to Customers' Requests Online." Season reports, Jupiter Media Metrix. Online press release: www.jmm.com/xp/jmm/press/2002/pr_010302.xml, Jan. 3, 2002.

Rose, D., and A. Meyer. "The Future Is in the Margins: The Role of Technology and Disability in Educational Reform.": www.air-dc.org/forum/AbRose_Meyer.htm.

Rose, L. C., and A. M. Gallup. "The 33rd Annual Phi Delta Kappa/Gallup Poll of the Public's Attitudes toward the Public Schools." *Phi Delta Kappan,* September 2001, 46.

Ryan, A. M., and H. Patrick. "The Classroom Social Environment and Changes in Adolescents' Motivation and Engagement During Middle School." *American Educational Research Journal* 38, no. 2 (2001): 437–60.

San Diego State University. "Academic Policy and Planning Committee Distance Education Policy," April 2000: www.rohan.sdsu.edu/dept/senate/sendoc/distanceed.apr2000.html

———. "Do I Want to Learn at a Distance?": www.distance-educator.com/portals/quiz.html

Scanlon, P. M., and D. R. Neumann. "Internet Plagiarism Among College Students." *Journal of College Student Development.* (May/June 2001).

Schmidt, P. "States Push Public Universities to Commercialize Research." *Chronicle of Higher Education,* 29 March 2002, A26.

Schon, D. A. The Reflective Practitioner: How Professionals Think in Action (New York: Basic Books, 1984).

Shea, P. et al., "Measures of Learning Effectiveness in the SUNY Learning Network," Web Center Learning Networks Effectiveness Research: www.alnresearch.org/JSP/db_entry.jsp?index=64.

Simonson, M., S. Smaldino, M. Albright, and S. Zvacek. *Teaching and Learning at a Distance: Foundations of Distance Education.* (Upper Saddle River, N.J.: Prentice-Hall, 2000), iii–iv.

Southern Regional Education Board: www.electroniccampus.org/st . . .ecinfo/publications/principles.asp2000–2001.

Stanford Learning Lab, Stanford Learning Projects, Completed Projects, "Integration of Asynchronous Discussion in IHUM Courses": www.sll.stanford.edu/projects/.

Stipek, D. *Motivation to Learn: From Theory to Practice,* 3rd ed. (Boston: Allyn and Bacon, 1998), 177–81.

"Students Log on to a Brave New World: Who Needs to Visit the Library When Salinger is Just a Click Away?" *Washington Post,* 16 March 2001, 66.

"Successful Distance-Education Spinoffs." *Chronicle of Higher Education,* 11 January 2002, B20.

"Teachers College: The Soul of the University, 2000 Annual Report." Teachers College, Columbia University, 2001, 3–4.

"Teaching, Learning and Computing, 1998 National Survey." Center for Research on Information Technology and Organizations, University of California at Irvine.

"Ten Public Policy Issues." Public Policy Paper Series No. 01–1 (Washington, D.C.: Association of Governing Boards, June 2001) 13.

"The Third Shift: Women Learning Online." (Washington, D.C.: American Association of University Women 2001).

Thomas, J. W. "Expectations and Effort: Course Demands, Students' Study Practices, and Academic Achievement." Paper presented at Hard Work and Higher Expectations: A Conference on Student Achievement, sponsored by U.S. Department of Education, Washington, D.C., 8 November 1990.

Thompson, M. M. "Faculty Satisfaction in Penn State's World Campus," unpublished.

Townsend, M. A. "Access to Faculty out of the Classroom." Unpublished survey conducted in conjunction with presentation at the Seminar on Student Life in Higher Education. Hechinger Institute on Education and the Media, Teachers College, Columbia University, 21 October 2001.

U.S. Department of Commerce, Bureau of the Census. Press release, 6 September 2001: www.census.gov/Press-Release/www/2001/cboi–147.html.

U.S. Department of Education, National Center for Education Statistics. *Distance Education Instruction by Postsecondary Faculty and Staff: Fall 1998* (NCES 2002–155, by Ellen M. Bradburn. Washington, D.C., 2002), iv–v.

Walsh, M. "Seed Money Drying up for Education-Related Business." *Education Week,* 8 August 2001, 5.

Washington State Higher Education Coordinating Board. "Distance Education Study." HB 2952, January 2001.

Werbach, K. "Clicks and Mortar Meets Cap and Gown: Higher Education Goes Online." *Release 1.0* (September 2000), 1.

Western Governors University, "Interpretation of Distance Learning Self-Assessment: www.wgu.edu/wgu/self_interpretation.asp

World Campus, Pennsylvania State University. "WC Student Surveys: Outcome Survey—Spring 2001," unpublished.

Yamashiro, K., and A. Zucker. "An Expert Panel Review of the Quality of Virtual High School Courses: Final Report" (Arlington, Va.: SRI International, November 1999), viii.

Young, Jeffrey R. "Administrator Predicts that Handheld Computers Will Be Big on Campus." *Chronicle of Higher Education*, 5 July 2001. Online version: www.chronicle.com/daily/2001.

———. "The Cat-and-Mouse Game of Plagiarism Detection." *Chronicle of Higher Education*, 6 July 2001, A26.

———. "Designer of Free Course-Management Software Asks, What Makes a Good Web Site?" *Chronicle of Higher Education*, 21 January 2002: www.chronicle.com/daily/2002.

———. "Does 'Digital Divide' Rhetoric Do More Harm Than Good?" *Chronicle of Higher Education*, 9 November 2001, A51.

Zemsky, R. "Gauging the Market for e-Learning: Report on the Weatherstation Project." 2 April 2002 (unpublished).

INDEX